"Among evangelical Christians today, the doctrine o
least preached doctrine, and therefore the least unders
this are many: it is not a pleasant doctrine to contemp...... ...... a uocuiie likely to win the
approval of the unbelieving world; it is not a doctrine amenable to the man-centered, man-pleasing
gospel that is prevalent in most evangelical churches today. For these reasons, Peter Sammons's
book is needed and should be read and studied by many. Dr. Sammons's work on this neglected
doctrine is thorough, eminently biblical, and rigorously logical. There may be those who disagree
with the conclusions and arguments of this book, but because Dr. Sammons's work is so thorough
and so well done, they will not be able to simply dismiss those conclusions and arguments. For
those who have never studied the doctrine of reprobation, this book will be an eye-opener and
hopefully an encouragement to preach this truth compassionately and confidently."
—Kevin D. Zuber, Professor of Theology, The Master's Seminary

"The doctrine of reprobation is always under attack from those who would limit God's sovereignty
by humanity's liberty. Reprobation is a difficult teaching, to be sure, but to reject it ultimately
unravels the whole fabric of salvation by grace alone. Peter Sammons employs faithful biblical
exegesis (especially of Romans 9), tried and true explanations of systematic theology, and careful
logic to show that God is absolutely sovereign over salvation and damnation, yet people remain
responsible for their moral choices. Though the arguments are deep, the aim is simple: from heaven
to earth and even in hell itself, know that God is God, God is good, and all glory belongs to him."
—Joel R. Beeke, President, Puritan Reformed Theological Seminary,
Author of *Debated Issues in Sovereign Predestination*

"Election is selection and implies rejection. I often make this statement to my students when
studying God's decrees. Peter Sammons here makes an important and detailed contribution
to the conversation surrounding the frequently misunderstood doctrine of reprobation.
Reprobation and God's Sovereignty is certainly worth your time. Especially important is his
clear, wonderful, and important distancing of reprobation and hyper-Calvinism: 'Reprobation, when properly understood in the Reformed tradition, should not be associated with
hyper-Calvinism. There are five aspects associated with reprobation that are distinct from
hyper-Calvinism: 1) Reprobation does not hinder the free offer of the gospel to all men,
since we do not know who the elect are. 2) Reprobation does not hinder the assurance of
believers, since assurance is not based on understanding eternal decrees. 3) Reprobation is
not symmetrical to election. 4) Reprobation does not teach that God has no benevolence
toward the reprobate. 5) Reprobation does not deny common grace.'"
—Sam Waldron, President, Covenant Baptist Theological Seminary

"God's intention in damnation is one of the darkest and yet most telling parts of Christian
theology. In this sweeping introduction to the biblical and theological discussions surrounding
God's eternal decree of reprobation, Peter Sammons organizes, analyzes, and argues a thoughtful,
traditional Reformed reading. The book itself is an invaluable resource as a compilation of historical
interpretations of the doctrine. I commend this faithful study to the thoughtful reader's attention."
—Mark Dever, President of 9Marks.org and
Senior Pastor of Capitol Hill Baptist Church, Washington, DC

"Peter Sammons faithfully explains what the Bible teaches about reprobation. He is tethered
to Scripture, and he is historically informed."
—Andy Naselli, Associate Professor of Systematic Theology and New Testament,
Bethlehem College & Seminary

"Peter Sammons shines the light of Scripture on the doctrine of reprobation to clear away misunderstanding and confusion. He carefully explores numerous passages of Scripture and brings clear thinking to plumb the depths of this awe-inspiring biblical doctrine so that we can better understand what the Bible means when it says, 'Jacob I have loved, but Esau I hated.' Anyone who wants a better understanding of these brief but powerful words would do well to read this book."

—J. V. Fesko, Professor of Systematic and Historical Theology, Reformed Theological Seminary

"With a keen theological mind, Peter Sammons is able to analyze difficult doctrines and teach them with both clarity and confidence. This is precisely what he has done with the challenging truth of reprobation. In this book, this gifted author provides us with a comprehensive overview and detailed exposition of this highly charged subject. You would do well to carefully read his arguments and honestly weigh your own position."

—Steven J. Lawson, President, OnePassion Ministries

"This is undoubtedly the most thorough examination of the thorny and controversial doctrine of reprobation that exists. Sammons nearly exhausts the exegetical and theological arguments for and against this doctrine. He presents a cogent argument for the classic Reformed position on reprobation spanning from Augustine to Calvin, Edwards, and Sproul. He leaves no stone unturned, answering common objections to the doctrine and showing how it affirms the meticulous sovereignty of God while exonerating him from moral culpability for the evil men do. Sammons demonstrates a mastery of the sources, both old and new, for the questions that arise, and writes in an accessible manner. He shows the implications the doctrine of reprobation has for the problem of evil. What is especially useful is Sammons's thorough treatment of the causes, both primary and secondary, that stand behind the execution of God's decree of reprobation. He takes the sting out of the unfortunate mischaracterizations of the doctrine and shows them to be unfounded. This is a must-read for anyone who would delve into the deep waters of this important doctrine."

—Scott Christensen, Associate Pastor, Kerrville Bible Church, Kerrville, TX, author of *What about Free Will?*

"Dr. Sammons's timely book on reprobation weds pastoral care and theological insight to provide an excellent resource for the church today. Many prefer to remain silent on this issue, but Scripture does not. Accordingly, Dr. Sammons does not. I applaud Dr. Sammons for speaking where Scripture speaks—for not shrinking back from the beautiful truths of God's Word. He handles this sensitive topic with skill, precision, and grace."

—Whitney Gamble-Smith, Director of Interdisciplinary Studies, The Master's University

"A real contribution! That is what Peter Sammons has provided for us in *Reprobation and God's Sovereignty*. His helpful book is a biblical, theological, and historical exploration of one of the most challenging doctrines that the church has ever wrestled with: the doctrine of reprobation. Sammons takes up this issue with pastoral sensitivity and a keen desire to be faithful to the teaching of the Bible. If you are a Christian who is interested in studying the questions related to God's sovereignty and predestination in more detail, look no further than this book. If you are a pastor or are preparing for pastoral ministry, then this book is a must-read."

—Guy M. Richard, President and Associate Professor of Systematic Theology, Reformed Theological Seminary

REPROBATION AND GOD'S SOVEREIGNTY

Recovering a Biblical Doctrine

Peter Sammons

KREGEL
ACADEMIC

Reprobation and God's Sovereignty: Recovering a Biblical Doctrine

© 2022 by Peter Sammons

Published by Kregel Academic, an imprint of Kregel Publications, 2450 Oak Industrial Dr. NE, Grand Rapids, MI 49505-6020.

The Hebrew font, NewJerusalemU, and the Greek font, GraecaU, are available from www.linguistsoftware.com/lgku.htm, +1-425-775-1130.

ISBN 978-0-8254-4743-3

Printed in the United States of America

22 23 24 25 26 / 5 4 3 2 1

To my faithful wife, Gabrielle

*For following me as I strive to see sound, orthodox,
and soul-searching ministry promoted in the church*

*For bringing up our children in the
knowledge and admonition of the Lord*

*For modeling a love for our Covenant King Jesus Christ
that helps remind me of our earthly pilgrimage*

CONTENTS

FOREWORD

There is profound pain in the contemplation of eternal conscious suffering. This truth, admittedly, is deeply disturbing. At the same time, however, it is designed by God into his eternal plan as cause for worship. The complex and wrenching realities of eternal punishment are resolved in one distinct and all-pervasive truth—the eternal God is absolutely sovereign and does what he wills for his own glory (Dan. 4:35).

This doctrine is the most emotionally difficult truth to believe. On the other hand, the absolute sovereign will and purpose of God is the basis of all saving faith. It is his total control over everything that encompasses eternal salvation and eternal reprobation. His glory is manifest in both and we can only worship him fully when we acknowledge the reality of both.

So, eternal punishment is not unacceptable nor unjust. It is acceptable and justified in God's eternal holy perfection. To worship him as the one true sovereign God is to worship him for his glory revealed in heaven and his glory revealed in hell.

Peter Sammons has provided for us what is undoubtedly the most thorough explanation and defense of the doctrine of predestination and reprobation, and I strongly commend it to you.

—John MacArthur
Grace Community Church

ACKNOWLEDGMENTS

*T*his book is essentially the fruit of my doctoral work. It was a difficult but nevertheless gratifying endeavor. The process of transforming my doctoral thesis into an accessible, lay-level treatment was not done in a vacuum; making this work accessible to a broader audience was achieved with the help of many others. I could not have completed this task without the sacrifice of a number of people who aided me in this endeavor. If you benefit at all from this book, you owe it to Josh Niemi, who labored to read through the manuscript multiple times, spell-checking, formatting, and providing critical feedback for it (any errors you find are mine alone!). I must also thank Carissa Arend for her exquisite work in editing this volume down to a more digestible format. I am indebted to Jacob Trotter for the exhaustive work of indexing.

I am grateful for the men who stood with me through thick and thin, encouraging me when I needed encouragement, challenging me when I needed correction, and guiding me based on their faithfulness to Jesus Christ: Don Green, Phil Johnson, Dennis Helton and Pete Coeler for all they have done to help me succeed—their reward in heaven will be great. I am also thankful for my blessed friendship with Mike Riccardi, the kind of guy who sticks closer than a brother (Prov. 18:24), of whom I am not worthy to have in my life, but with whom I am wonderfully blessed to labor in the vineyard of the Lord.

I am beyond thankful for the oversight, opportunity, and prayers of my pastor and friend John MacArthur. I am not only indebted to

him for the kind foreword he wrote for me, but also for the fact that
he believed in me—a poor kid from Jefferson City, Missouri—when
few others did. He has been a constant model for me of consistency
and conviction, a man who will stand for truth no matter the cost,
and an example I can only hope to emulate until the day I die. In the
same vein, I must thank Mark Dever for investing and encouraging
me when things seemed most uncertain in my life. I count it a true
privilege to consider Mark a counselor and friend.

I must also thank my family: my father, for providing an open
atmosphere in the home to discuss spiritual things, and Cynthia Hay-
ter, David Besenger, and Jennifer Boyce, who were all kind blessings
of providence from the Lord in my youthful years to take care of me
in many ways.

I will be forever indebted to my lovely and gracious wife, Gabrielle
Sammons. She knew it would be a difficult road when she first met me
and agreed to be my wife. The greatest treasure of my earthly life has
been the comfort of the Lord through her. She has a harder job than
anyone could imagine in being married to a man who is seemingly
always at war with the world. I could have imagined no one better.
Thank you, my love!

Last, but not least, I want to thank my covenant head, my high
priest, my Lord and Savior Jesus Christ. It is by his sovereign will and
work alone that I am what I am. *Soli Deo gloria.*

INTRODUCTION

Predestination is a difficult word, in that many in the church use it, but rarely do they mean the same thing. Discussions about the doctrine of predestination often result in a great deal of emotion and passion. In fact, debates between theologians concerning predestination and free will can be traced through virtually every century of the church. For example, it was this doctrine that led to the initial divide between Calvinism and Arminianism.[1]

The debate centers on the issue of theodicy, often referred to as "the problem of evil." Theodicy is concerned with one of the greatest paradoxes in all of theology and philosophy: *How does an omnibenevolent and omnipotent God exist and interact with sin in the world?* It is vital to answer that question, not merely in reconciling theological and philosophical concerns, but in answering life's all-important question: "Who is God?"

The approaches to theodicy are many. Biblical commentators and theologians rarely object to God's ordaining of good things (cf. Rom. 8:28 or 11:36), but when Scripture alludes to the divine ordination of men unto damnation, a wide variety of objections and alternative

---

1 Episcopius, delegated to represent the Remonstrance position at the Synod of Dort, believed that reprobation was the easiest to dismantle of the Calvinist doctrines and that to refute it would mean the demise of the entire system. See Fredrick Calder, *Memoirs of Simon Episcopius, The Celebrated Pupil of Arminus* (London: Simpkin & Marshall, 1835).

explanations are offered.[2] The spectrum of interpretations ranges from Open Theism to hyper-Calvinism, with many divergent viewpoints in between.

In surveying the various arguments brought against Calvinistic predestination, the primary objection raised by non-Calvinistic critics relates to the doctrine of reprobation. In investigating this doctrine carefully, several questions need to be answered. What is the doctrine of reprobation? Can it be defended from Scripture? If so, what importance does it have for a proper understanding of God's Word?

A wide variety of opinions concerning reprobation can be found among commentaries and systematic theologies. It is a doctrine often either assumed or rejected outright. Accordingly, reprobation has received little attention in scholarly literature, even though it has divided the church since the fourth century. In fact, the lack of literature on this subject is primarily due to the topic's perceived divisiveness, which leaves many to conclude that it is best left to the mysteries of God (Deut. 29:29).[3]

The Reformed position maintains that God's eternal decree of reprobation does not require him to implant sin into men to guarantee his desired outcome. Rather, God preserves both the volition of the creature and his own holiness by secondary causes. "Secondary causality" (with respect to reprobation) refers to the various means God uses to bring about his decree concerning the eternal destiny of

---

2   One such serious objection is raised by Roger Olson: "Taken to their logical conclusion, that even hell and all who suffer there eternally are foreordained by God, God is thereby rendered morally ambiguous at best and a moral monster at worst. I have gone so far as to say that this kind of Calvinism, which attributes everything to God's will and control, makes it difficult (at least for me) to see the difference between God and the devil. Some of my Calvinist friends have expressed offense at that, but I continue to believe it is a valid question worth pursuing. What I mean is that if I were a Calvinist and believed what these people teach, I would have difficulty telling the difference between God and Satan." Roger Olson, *Against Calvinism* (Grand Rapids: Zondervan, 2011), 23.

3   To see the history of this debate see R. C. Sproul, *Willing to Believe: The Controversy over Free Will* (Grand Rapids: Baker Books, 1997); Erwin Lutzer, *The Doctrine That Divides: A Fresh Look at the Historic Doctrines That Separate Christians* (Grand Rapids: Kregel, 1998).

the non-elect.[4] The intention of this book is to help faithful Christians understand reprobation properly and to help them recognize and establish the role of secondary causes. This process helps clarify a vast number of Scripture passages that are often neglected, avoided, or distorted by many in the church. A clear understanding of secondary causes preserves God's holy sovereignty and man's accountability with respect to reprobation.

The purpose of this book is twofold: to properly define reprobation and explore God's use of secondary causes in this doctrine. Since the Synod of Dort in 1618, many in Christendom have been speaking past one another when it comes to this doctrine, simply because adequate care has not been given to defining it biblically. It is the aim of this book to articulate biblical and theological categories for the different means (or secondary causes) that God uses to accomplish his work of reprobation. These secondary causes are instrumental in rightly defining the doctrine of reprobation while simultaneously preserving God's holiness and man's culpability.

This book will then seek to define, clarify, and explain a biblical view of reprobation against misunderstandings of it by retrieving a proper definition from Scripture and history. It will then examine the necessary categories for properly understanding God's use of secondary causes as he executes the decree of reprobation.

It is not within the scope of this book to address every issue related to predestination (i.e., providence, election, or the order of the divine decrees).[5] By focusing specifically on the doctrine of reprobation, this

---

4   There are a variety of views related to "secondary causality," Jos Salins claims that "[o]ne of the strategies used by Calvinists to get God off the hook, so as to say, as the author of sin and evil, is to appeal to secondary causes." *Satan's Big Lie: The Doctrine of Predestination* (Grand Rapids: Xlibris, 2013), 68. On the opposite end of the spectrum is Paul Helm, who notes, "God ordains evil but does not intend evil as evil, as the human agent intends it. In God's case there is some other description of the morally evil action which he intends the evil action to fill. There are other ends or purposes which God has in view." *The Providence of God* (Downers Grove, IL: InterVarsity Press, 1994), 190.

5   With respect to the order of the divine decrees, four major positions stand out: Arminianism, Amyraldism, Infralapsarianism, and Supralapsarianism. The Infra- and Supra- positions are strongly associated with the doctrine of reprobation, which is rejected by the two former positions. For more discussion on Supralapsarianism and Infralapsarianism see Joel R. Beeke, "Did Beza's Suprelapsarianism Spoil Calvin's

study seeks both to define the doctrine historically and biblically, and to provide theological categories for understanding God's use of secondary means to accomplish his sovereign purposes. By articulating these categories (related to secondary causality), this project will make a helpful contribution to theological studies, especially in soteriology. This book will limit itself to those biblical texts most frequently addressed throughout history and texts related to secondary causality in part four of the book.

Furthermore, this book does not seek to exhaustively deal with every opposing view against the doctrine of reprobation. Opposing views are limited to arguments which directly display a misunderstanding of reprobation or secondary causality. Other opposing views will be addressed briefly throughout in footnotes.

ASSUMPTIONS AND PRESUPPOSITIONS

While attempting to be objective, this study assumes several key presuppositions. First, it presupposes that God's Word is not silent

---

Theology?," *RTJ* 13 (Nov. 1997): 58–60; Joel. R. Beeke, "Theodore Beza's Supralapsarian Predestination," *RRJ* 12, no. 2 (Spring 2003): 69–84; William Hastie, *The Theology of the Reformed Church* (Edinburgh: T&T Clark, 1904); Heinrich Heppe, *Reformed Dogmatics*, trans. G. T. Thomson (London: Allen & Unwin, 1950), 147–48.

Both Infra- and Supra- camps have argued using various lines in the *Institutes* that Calvin held to their position. However, the debate was in its infant state when he was alive. See William Cunningham, *The Reformers and the Theology of the Reformation* (Edinburgh: T&T Clark, 1862), 364; Richard A. Muller, *Dictionary of Latin and Greek Theological Terms: Drawn Principally from Protestant Scholastic Theology* (Grand Rapids: Baker, 1986), 292. John Fesko claims that the Westminster Confession confirmed Infralapsarianism as the official Reformed position. See John Fesko, "The Westminster Confession and Lapsarianism: Calvin and the Divines," in *The Westminster Confession into the 21st Century, Volume 2: Essays in Remembrance of the 350th Anniversary of the Westminster Assembly*, ed. J. Ligon Duncan (2004; repr., Fern, Scotland: Mentor, 2005), 2:497–501.

However, this is not conclusive. The Westminster divines were split on the subject; for example William Twisse, the proctor of the Westminster Assembly, and William Perkins were both adamant Supralapsarians, therefore, the Westminster Standards were left ambiguous on the issue. John Murray states, "The confession is non-committal on the debate between the Supralapsarians and the Infralapsarians and intentionally so, as both the terms of the section and the debate in the Assembly clearly show." Iain H. Murray, ed., *Collected Writings of John Murray* (Edinburgh: Banner of Truth, 1977), 4:209.

concerning the topic. As William Perkins noted, "If there be an eternal decree of God, whereby he chooseth some men, then there must needs be another whereby he doth pass by others and refuse them."[6] Such a statement is not merely a logical deduction. Rather, it is based on passages of Scripture where God is said to "create" or "prepare" "vessels of wrath prepared for destruction" (Rom. 9:22), appoint men to destruction (1 Peter 2:8), and mark them "out for . . . condemnation" (Jude 4).

Second, God's Word—not history, emotions, logic, or philosophy—is the ultimate authority on this subject. God's Word is not contrary to the history of God's church. It is not detached from human emotion, nor independent of the rules of logic and philosophy. However, these are not the chief contributors to the following conclusions. Scripture alone is the final authority for any doctrine's establishment. The author affirms and embraces the verbal, plenary inspiration and inerrancy of Scripture.

Third, God is recognized as impeccably holy. God is the only inherently holy being. He is so holy that holiness is equated with his name (Isa. 6:3; Rev. 4:8). Not only is he holy, but he cannot be the direct agent or cause of any form of sin or temptation (James 1:13, 17; 1 John 1:5).

Fourth, God is acknowledged to be meticulously sovereign.[7] God rules over everything, including calamity (Lam. 3:38), disaster (Amos 3:6), the casting of lots (Prov. 16:33), the hearts of kings (Prov. 21:1), and even the crucifixion (Acts 2:23).

---

6   William Perkins, "Creed of the Apostles," in *The Workes of that Famous and Worthy Minister of Christ in the Universitie of Cambridge, Mr. William Perkins*, ed. John Legatt (London: John Legatt, 1626), 1:287. Hereafter *Works*.

7   A. W. Pink summarizes the Puritan/Reformed definition of God's sovereignty well: "The Sovereignty of the God of Scripture is absolute, irresistible, infinite. When we say that God is Sovereign we affirm His right to govern the universe which He has made for His own glory, just as He pleases. We affirm that His right is the right of the Potter over the clay, i.e., that He may mold that clay into whatsoever form He chooses, fashioning out of the same lump one vessel unto honor and another unto dishonor." A. W. Pink, *The Sovereignty of God* (1930; repr., Grand Rapids: Baker Books, 1984), 21. There is an edition of *The Sovereignty of God* published by Banner of Truth (2009), however, it has omitted important sections related to reprobation (particularly chapter 5), and therefore I could not recommend it over the Baker edition.

Fifth, humans are responsible for every act they commit. In their hearts, humans love sin (John 3:20) and hate God (Rom. 8:7). Thus, we commit iniquity in accordance with our nature (Luke 6:45; John 8:44). The degree of our culpability in sin aligns with our knowledge (Rom. 1:19). These final two presuppositions lead to a compatibilist understanding of the human will.[8] All these presuppositions are highlighted in the Westminster Confession when it states: "God from all eternity did, by the most wise and holy counsel of his own will, freely and unchangeably ordain whatsoever comes to pass; yet so as thereby neither is God the author of sin, nor is violence offered to the will of the creatures, nor is the liberty or contingency of second causes taken away, but rather established."[9]

While these convictions may not be held by all readers, the author is concerned with presenting the information objectively and faithfully. Acknowledging these theological presuppositions at the forefront allows the book to focus on the primary issue at hand: how defining God's use of secondary causes clarifies the doctrine of reprobation, while simultaneously preserving God's holiness and man's responsibility.

---

8   As opposed to a libertarian understanding of the human will, supported by those of the Arminian persuasion. For those who hold to a compatibilist view of the will see Martin Luther, *The Bondage of the Will*, trans. J. I. Packer and O. R. Johnston (Grand Rapids: Fleming H. Revell, 1990); John Calvin, *The Bondage and Liberation of the Will: A Defense of the Orthodox Doctrine of Human Choice against Pighius*, ed. A. N. S. Lane, trans. G. I. Davies (Grand Rapids: Baker Books, 1996); Jonathan Edwards, *The Freedom of the Will*, vol. 1, *The Works of Jonathan Edwards*, ed. Paul Ramsey (1834; repr., Edinburgh: Banner of Truth, 1995).
         For those of the opposing view, libertarian free will, see Roger E. Olson, *Arminian Theology: Myths and Realities* (Downers Grove, IL: InterVarsity Press, 2006); William Lane Craig, *The Only Wise God: The Compatibility of Divine Foreknowledge and Human Freedom* (Eugene, OR: Wipf & Stock, 1999); Norman L. Geisler, *Chosen but Free: A Balanced View of God's Sovereignty and Free Will* (Grand Rapids: Baker Books, 2010).

9   Philip Schaff, *Creeds of Christendom, Volume III: The Creeds of the Evangelical Protestant Churches* (1877; repr., Grand Rapids: Baker Book House, 1977), 3:609.

CHAPTER 1

GOD IS LORD OVER ALL

*T*he lordship of God is a very muddy issue for a lot of believers. For most people terms like "decree," "sovereignty," "omnipotence," "providence," and "predestination" are all sort of catch-all terms that really are saying the same thing. And in the end people assume that if you believe any set of these truths than you must be some super-Christian, a doctrine freak, or even worse, a Calvinist. However, these truths are not something that is reserved for the spiritual elite; they are intended for the comfort and reassurance of all Christians.[1] These doctrines are certainly high mysteries that need to be handled with precision, special prudence, and extreme care.

Therefore, our goal in embarking on studying these lofty doctrines is not to gain some sort of spiritual edge in an argument, but rather that the believer may have a greater admiration for God that elicits higher praise, reverence, and trust in who the Bible reveals God to be. Now, before we jump into the deep end theologically, it is important to start by establishing some distinctions and definitions necessary for the believer to more accurately embark on the study of predestination.

---

1   B. B. Warfield once wrote, "A firm faith in the universal providence of God is the solution of all earthly troubles." *Selected Shorter Writings of Benjamin B. Warfield*, ed. John E. Meeter (Phillipsburg, NJ: P&R, 1970), 1:110.

DECREE

The term *decree* refers to the determination of God's will concerning everything that would ever take place in time. "God, from all eternity, did, by the most wise and holy counsel of his own will, freely, and unchangeably ordain whatsoever come to pass."[2] The decree of God encompasses the doctrine of predestination but is ultimately a broader category. While predestination is God's decree concerning the eternal destinies of all men (in election and reprobation, the major subject of the remainder of this book), the decree of God is much broader than merely predestination.

God's decree is ultimately the execution of his will to plan all things before they come to pass. You've heard the saying, "It is the will of God." It's so easy to say those words as a sort of catchphrase to explain things that to us sometimes seem inexplicable. However, they are much easier said than understood. As a result few concepts in theology generate more confusion than the will of God.

One problem we face is the etymological and lexical use of the terms for the will of God in Scripture. The Bible uses the phrase "will of God" in numerous ways. There are ten unique terms used for "will" in the Hebrew Old Testament, and two in the Greek New Testament.[3] They encompass a number of rich concepts, such as God's council, disposition, attitude, and plan, among others. And there is roughly two thousand years of church history involving how to classify the will of God.

Issues like this make distinctions necessary—sometimes fine distinctions, even technical distinctions—with respect to will of God. Now by these distinctions we are not saying that there is more than one will in God. So let me say that clearly at the outset. Metaphysically there is only one will in God. Will is according to nature, not according to person, yet we can see multiple aspects of the solitary will of God refracted in his Word. The main category we need to concern ourselves with is what is known as the will of God's decree.[4]

---

2   Westminster Confession of Faith 3.1 (hereafter WCF).

3   William Wilson, *Wilson's Old Testament Word Studies* (McLean, VA: Kregel, 1978), 482. NT *boulē* and thēlema.

4   The other main category we will not discuss is known as "The will of God's command." This will is often called the perceptive will or the revealed will of God. Brakel

This is often referred to as the will of God's pleasure, God's secret will, or his sovereign will. The will of God's decree is, "God's purpose and good pleasure which He will bring to pass, either by Himself directly or by the agency of others."[5]

Scriptural basis for this is seen in texts like the following:

- Daniel 4:35: "All the inhabitants of the earth are accounted as nothing, but He does according to His will in the host of heaven and among the inhabitants of earth; and no one can ward off His hand or say to Him, 'What have You done?'"
- Ephesians 1:5, 11: "He predestined us to adoption as sons through Jesus Christ to Himself, according to the kind intention of His will . . . also we have obtained an inheritance, having been predestined according to His purpose who works all things after the counsel of His will."
- Psalm 115:3: "But our God is in the heavens; He does whatever He pleases."

Now we should add some qualifications to this category. When we talk about God's will of decree we are saying, as Brakel explains, "This refers to the ultimate out coming of all things which will be according to God's decree which He either has not revealed at all to man or which He reveals only after a period of time."[6] It is important to remember that the majority of the time this will, from the human perspective, is only perceived in retrospect.

God's decrees are dependent on his desire, his will, his good pleasure. He does not act spontaneously as a result of some whim or

---

said, "This will has reference to the regulative principle of life as well as to the laws which God has made known and prescribed to man in order that his walk might be regulated accordingly" (Wilhelmus à Brakel, *Christian's Reasonable Service* (Grand Rapids: Reformation Heritage, 2012), 1:113). In as much as God has determined it fitting to reveal His hidden will to men, then the revealed will and decreed will intersect. However, the will of God's command is mostly descriptive of man's duty to God as His creatures and image bearers.

5 Brakel, 1:113.
6 Brakel, 1:113.

sudden impulse. He does not act under compulsion, forced to change a previous course of action in response to some external factor. And so his decrees are unconditional in the fact that they are dependent on God's will alone. God's decrees are according to his will.

So that brings us to the necessary question, What are the decrees of God? The Westminster Shorter Catechism explains it briefly: "A: His eternal purpose according to the counsel of His own will, whereby for His own glory He has foreordained whatever comes to pass."[7]

First, Scripture testifies that God's plan for creation existed in his mind apart from and prior to creation. Matthew 25:34 says, "Then the King will say to those on His right, 'Come, you who are blessed of My Father, inherit the kingdom prepared for you from the foundation of the world.'" 1 Peter 1:20 explains, "For He was foreknown before the foundation of the world, but has appeared in these last times for the sake of you." God's plan is not time-based (a reaction in time) but is before time since it was established in eternity. It is called an "eternal" purpose or decree. This eternal nature of God's decrees negates the notion that God constructed or conformed his "plan" according to the decisions of other moral agents—angelic or human.

One example of God's decree is seen in how God determines both natural and moral calamities to be a part of his larger plan. One such example is found in the narrative of Joseph. Joseph himself, the one who suffered so much through these events, recognized that God was the determiner of it all. He suffered natural calamity during his time in Egypt. For example, Egypt experienced a great famine that impacted everyone who lived there. Joseph would have been (in some measure) impacted by this natural calamity, however, this calamity was prophesied to have been an act of God (Gen. 41:32; 47:13–27). However, Joseph also experienced moral calamity at the hands of his brothers, which he likewise attributed to God (Gen. 50:20).

---

7   Joel R. Beeke and Sinclair B. Ferguson, "Westminster Shorter Catechism," *Reformed Confessions Harmonized* (Grand Rapids: Baker Books, 2000), 29.

So God's decree is all encompassing; he decreed before time everything that would ever happen in history, from general natural calamity down to very specific moral calamity.

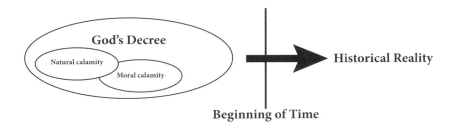

Figure 1.1

In this generic figure we can see the decree of God is all encompassing. Everything we read in Scripture or every bad thing that happens in our lives can fit within one of those categories and is ultimately under the divine will. It is an exercise of the solitary will of God whereby he determines every event that transpires in history, before time ever begins. This decree is unconditional and dependent upon nothing but the will of God.

OMNIPOTENCE

God has infinite, eternal, and unchangeable power. By that we mean that he is able to do all that is not contrary to his nature. In other words, his power is limited only to his own essence and not to anything external. This power is seen in numerous ways; two that stand out are the creation event and the miracles recorded in Scripture. There's no question when someone reads the Bible that they see it clearly teaches that God is all-powerful.

God is all-powerful and is able to do whatever he, in his perfect wisdom, has decreed to do. Now we should not take that to mean God can do anything without distinction. God is purposeful. He does what he decreed to do. So God's power is largely related to his will. God has every power that is logically possible for him to have. Feinberg simply says, "God is able to do everything Scripture shows him doing."[8]

The attribute of God's power is essential to his nature because all of his actions in human history depend on his ability to perform those acts. Therefore, God's mercy and justice depend on God's power to be carried out; it is one thing to want to be merciful and quiet and another thing to have the ability to carry it out.[9] Thomas Goodwin explains that while God is omnipotent, "yet He is not omnivolent (willing to do all things); thought he can do all things infinitely more than he hath done, yet He doth not will to do all things that He is able, for His power is limited by His will."[10]

That God is all-powerful means that God is never hindered by any external force in the exercise of his power. There is no personal being (such as Satan), impersonal law (such as the principle of "free will"), or force (such as evil) that is able to challenge or frustrate God's efforts. What God wills, he does. And because his power is infinite, he never gets tired or exhausts his power when he uses it.

All of God's attributes exist and function in harmony with each other—and God's omnipotence is no exception. Because God is immutable (unchanging), God's power neither waxes nor wanes. Because God is holy and righteous, his power is never used to do evil. Because God is all-wise, his power is never used foolishly. Because God is self-sufficient, his power depends only on himself and never on external supplies. Because God is sovereign, the exercise of his power can never be resisted. As Frame states, "God's power is everything that he is; all his attributes manifest his power."[11]

---

8   John S. Feinberg, *No One Like Him: The Doctrine of God* (Wheaton, IL: Crossway, 2006), 289.

9   Because of the divine attribute of Simplicity (God is not made up of parts), God's power cannot be limited, which explains why power is used as a name for God (Mark 14:62). As God's power relates to the rest of His attributes (Simplicity) Beeke points out, "God's knowledge pertains to things possible; God's wisdom speaks of the fitness of how things are done; God's will resolves that things should be done; and God's power enables Him to do them" Beeke, 74.

10   Thomas Goodwin, "Exposition of Ephesians," in *The Works of Thomas Goodwin* (Grand Rapids: Reformation Heritage, 2006), 1:216–17

11   John M. Frame, *The Doctrine of God* (Phillipsburg, NJ: P&R, 2002),522.

Omnipotence does not mean God can do anything. Certainly, with God, all things are possible. But Scripture does not allow us to leave "all things" undefined. Scripture affirms that there are particular things which God cannot do: God cannot lie or repent: "God is not a man, that He should lie, nor a son of man, that He should repent; has He said, and will He not do it? Or has He spoken, and will He not make it good?" (Num. 23:19). And most memorably, God cannot change: "For I, the LORD, do not change; therefore you, O sons of Jacob, are not consumed" (Mal. 3:6).

So can we say that God can do anything? No. God's omnipotence is always exercised in ways that are consistent with his essence. His power is never at odds with his holiness, faithfulness, wisdom, immutability, or any other attribute. In other words, his power is never self-refuting.

In fact, the term "inability"—to say God is unable to do something—is not necessarily negative at all. True, we typically think that to be "unable" or "incapable" of doing something implies a defect or imperfection. That is our experience as creatures—especially as fallen ones. But with God, being "unable" to do certain things is the very opposite. His "inability" to do certain things is actually the mark of perfection.

Thus, hypothetical propositions—like creating a stone too big to lift, or calling into being a circular triangle, or telling a lie, or growing old and changing—would require God to deny his own perfection. This would be no "ability" at all. This can be likened to the batter who hits 1.000 in baseball, or the hockey goaltender with a save percentage of 1.000. To say that the batter is defective because he is "incapable of striking out," or that the goaltender is defective because he is "incapable of allowing a goal," would be ludicrous![12]

PROVIDENCE

Providence is the teaching that God is involved in everything that happens on earth. He upholds all things (Heb. 1:3). His providence

---

12 Charles Hodge said, "When, therefore, it is said that God is omnipotent because He can do whatever He wills, it is to be remembered that His will is determined by His nature." Charles Hodge, *Systematic Theology* (Peabody, MA: Hendrickson, 2008), 1:409

is exercised in such a way that nothing happens without his involvement. Now that does not mean God forces everything that happens, thereby violating natural law, or the will of creatures, or exercising some universal meticulous dominion where the properties of creation are upended. Rather, providence is God's working with the properties of creation directing them to act as they do. As the Westminster Confession of Faith says, "Yet so, as thereby neither is God the author of sin, nor is violence offered to the will of the creatures; nor is the liberty or contingency of second causes taken away, but rather established."[13]

Furthermore, the issues related to providence are how God operates in a world full of sin. In this sin-cursed world, how does a holy God operate and yet not become a sinner himself? This is commonly related to the issue of theodicy, but providence is broader than merely God's working in a world full of sin. Providence has to do with God's working with all creation in a natural way to sustain and energize all things. The orbit of the moon, the circulation of the air on the earth, the tides of the ocean, the rains from the skies all the way down to the division of cells on the chromosome level in every human body. Without God's providence, none of these things would operate the way they do.

SOVEREIGNTY

The final term is the sovereignty of God. The sovereignty of God is not his power, his determination to do something, or how he operates in the world; rather sovereignty is concerned with God's right, God's authority. What right does God have to exercise his power, according to his decree, in the manner in which he does? His right comes from his authority over all things. So what right does God have? God is the highest authority; he is higher in authority than the celestial bodies, any human court, any nation, and any ecclesiological organization. There is no one who has more authority than God. Strictly speaking, sovereignty is dependent upon power. Sovereignty exists when power is effectively exercised. Sovereignty is absent when the one

---

13   Joel R. Beeke and Sinclair B. Ferguson, "Westminster Confession of Faith 1647," in
      Reformed Confessions Harmonized (Grand Rapids: Baker Books, 2000), 29. WCF 3.1.

with power chooses not to use it. While omnipotence describes how much power God has, providence refers to how he uses that power; it is sovereignty that describes God's right to use that power. So how should a believer go about understanding God's authority? Scripture speaks plenty about the nature of God's sovereignty in a number of helpful categories.[14]

First, God's sovereignty is exclusive. The biblical writers emphasize that God is not only sovereign but that he is incomparably so. There is no exercise of authority that can remotely compare with or challenge his. "Who would not fear You, O King of the nations? Indeed it is Your due! For among all the wise men of the nations and in all their kingdoms, there is none like You" (Jer. 10:7; cf. Deut. 4:39, 32:39; Ps. 95:3–5).

Second, God's sovereignty is unhindered. God never experiences frustration or failure in his exercise of power in the governance of his creation and the achievement of his purposes. Whatever he pleases, he does. "Why should the nations say, 'Where, now, is their God?' But our God is in the heavens; He does whatever He pleases" (Ps. 115:2–3; cf. Ps. 103:19; 135:5–6; Prov. 21:1).[15]

Third, we could say God's authority is all-inclusive. Scripture testifies that God is sovereign not only over the big issues of history but also the minute details of an individual's life. God governs all realms and all details. He rules meticulously.

In her prayer of thanksgiving Hannah confesses,

> The LORD kills and makes alive; He brings down to Sheol and raises up. The LORD makes poor and rich; He brings

---

14   These helpful categories are loosely borrowed from Louis Berkhof.
15   Charles Hodge said, "We can do very little. God can do whatever He wills. We, beyond very narrow limits, must use means to accomplish our ends. With God means are unnecessary. He wills, and it is done. He said, Let there be light; and there was light. He, by a volition created the heavens and the earth. At the volition of Christ, the winds ceased, and there was a great calm. By an act of the will He healed the sick, opened the eyes of the blind, and raised the dead. This simple idea of the omnipotence of God, that He can do without effort, and by a volition, whatever He wills, is the highest conceivable idea of power, and is that which is clearly presented in the Scriptures." Hodge, *Systematic Theology*, 1:407.

low, He also exalts. He raises the poor from the dust, He lifts the needy from the ash heap to make them sit with nobles, and inherit a seat of honor; for the pillars of the earth are the LORD's, and He set the world on them. He keeps the feet of His godly ones, but the wicked ones are silenced in darkness; for not by might shall a man prevail. Those who contend with the LORD will be shattered; against them He will thunder in the heavens, the LORD will judge the ends of the earth; and He will give strength to His king, and will exalt the horn of His anointed." (1 Sam. 2:6–10; cf. Job 1:20–21; 2:9–20; Ps. 22; 103:19)

And to summarize this point, Abraham Kuyper famously said, "There is not a square inch in the whole domain of our human existence over which Christ, who is Sovereign over all, does not cry: 'Mine!'"[16]

Fourth, we should say God's sovereignty is immutable. You see, God never has to "fight" for more sovereignty, nor are there times when his sovereignty waxes or wanes. It is constant, established, and permanent. It is as real and comprehensive today as it will be in eternity future. "The LORD reigns, He is clothed with majesty; the LORD has clothed and girded Himself with strength; indeed, the world is firmly established, it will not be moved. Your throne is established from of old; you are from everlasting" (Ps. 93:1–2; cf. Eccl. 3:14; Isa. 14:24; Eph. 3:11).

In addition to testifying about the *nature* of God's sovereignty, Scripture also emphasizes particular realms where God displays this sovereignty. First, God's sovereignty is demonstrated in his creation and ownership of the material universe. This is where we see the authority of God over the natural world. There is nothing that does not belong to him, and therefore, nothing which is not rightfully under his authority and control:

---

16   James D. Bratt, ed., *Abraham Kuyper: A Centennial Reader* (Grand Rapids: Eerdmans, 1998), 488. R. C. Sproul likewise exclaims, "If there is one single molecule in this universe running around loose, totally free of God's sovereignty, then we have no guarantee that a single promise of God will ever be fulfilled." *Chosen by God* (Wheaton, IL: Tyndale, 1986), 26–27.

By the word of the LORD the heavens were made, and by the breath of His mouth all their host. He gathers the waters of the sea together as a heap; He lays up the deeps in storehouses. Let all the earth fear the LORD; let all the inhabitants of the world stand in awe of Him. For He spoke, and it was done; He commanded, and it stood fast." (Ps. 33:6–9; cf. Ps. 50:10–12; Matt. 10:29)

God's sovereignty extends to his rule over the "laws" of nature. Everything is held together by virtue of his authority, and if for a moment he would fail, creation would explode into chaos. This extent of God's authority is frequently found in Christian hymns, motivational cards, and artwork, among other things. Isaac Watts famously penned, "There's not a plant or flower below but makes your glories known; and clouds arise and tempests blow by order from your throne."[17]

The extent of God's sovereignty isn't limited to the weather, inanimate objects, or the beasts of the field. Scripture routinely shows God is sovereign over all the nations: "The LORD nullifies the counsel of the nations; He frustrates the plans of the peoples. The counsel of the LORD stands forever, the plans of His heart from generation to generation" (Ps. 33:10–11); "He rules by His might forever, His eyes keep watch on the nations; let not the rebellious exalt themselves" (Ps. 66:7; cf. Ps. 2; Prov. 21:1; Isa. 40:15). There's no escaping the fact that the highest level of earthly authorities—whether it be kings, princes, czars, dictators, or pharaohs—are all accountable to God and are ultimately lesser authorities under the authority of God.

However, more than just being over the affairs of the realms of men, God is also sovereign over the authorities in the spiritual realm. Even though those caught in the spiritual warfare movement fret about the power of Satan, Scripture is clear that God is infinitely more powerful than Satan and all his hosts. In fact, Satan has power only to the extent that God allows it (Job 1–2; Matt. 4:10–11; 6:28–34; Col. 1:15–17).

---

17 Isaac Watts, "I Sing the Mighty Power of God," *Trinity Hymnal* (Philadelphia: Great Commission, 1990), #106.

One other arena of God's authority extends to the salvation of sinners. One of the most difficult concepts for us to accept is God's sovereignty in salvation. But Scripture testifies unequivocally to this:

> Jesus answered, "Truly, truly, I say to you, unless one is born of water and the Spirit he cannot enter into the kingdom of God. That which is born of the flesh is flesh, and that which is born of the Spirit is spirit. Do not be amazed that I said to you, 'You must be born again.' The wind blows where it wishes and you hear the sound of it, but do not know where it comes from and where it is going; so is everyone who is born of the Spirit." (John 3:5–8; cf. John 17:1–2; Rom. 9:15–16; Eph. 1:11–12; James 1:18)

And while we will discuss this matter more in the following chapters, it must be clearly affirmed that to acknowledge God's sovereignty in salvation is *not* to affirm fatalism, that some blind force determines all things. In God's wise governance, we are still completely responsible for our decisions and actions. However, to reject fatalism does not automatically mean one is only left with Arminianism. And we will come back to this shortly.

ATTITUDE OF THE BELIEVER

The real issue believers need to concern themselves with is what our attitude should be when embarking on studying the difficult doctrine of predestination. While we can see these truths on every page of Scripture, we aren't supposed to accept them in some cold calculated manner; much less are we to wield them as a heartless sword against interlopers who dare to disagree with our presentation of the matter. Rather, believers throughout history who adore the doctrine of election and are sobered by the matter concerning the non-elect have genuinely had the same approach: reverence, humility, gratitude, and compassion are often the consequences of studying the doctrine of predestination.

Something in the reality of humanity's hopelessness, God's sovereignty, and the fact that there are individuals who will spend eternity in hell always seems to produce in true believers a reverent humility that is nothing short of a divine work in their hearts. It's the fact that our own works contributed nothing but rested on the good will of God that produces in believers a readiness to forgive others (even if they aren't believers), an eagerness to share the gospel, and a passion to worship God. Their prayer lives are richer, their study of God's Word more humbling, and their quickness to love others heightened, and what's most telling is how these doctrines sober them and prepare them for death. Spurgeon summarizes it well:

> There is no attribute more comforting to His children than that of God's sovereignty. Under the most adverse circumstances, in the most severe trials, they believe that sovereignty has ordained their afflictions, that sovereignty overrules them, and that sovereignty will sanctify them all. There is nothing for which the children ought more earnestly to contend than the doctrine of their Master over all creation—the kingship of God over all the works of His own hands—the throne of God and His right to sit upon that throne.[18]

---

18   Charles H. Spurgeon, "Divine Sovereignty," Sermon #77, *The New Park Street Pulpit* (London: Passmore & Alabaster, 1856), 185.

CHAPTER 2

GOD IS LORD OVER CONDEMNATION

*Y*ou often hear people make dismissive comments about judgment in order to justify their behavior. Phrases like "no one can judge me," or the misappropriation of "judge not lest ye be judged" fly from the lips of people with a sort of flippancy. Most seem to believe justice is a standard they hold others to while blithely ignoring that they themselves will one day stand before the judge of all.

However, something that both Calvinists and Arminians can agree on is that at the end of the age God has an authoritative right to judge every person based on the life they have lived. God has the authority to judge life. While there are numerous reasons for this, there are two chief themes in Scripture: humanity's responsibility (or better, accountability) and God's justice.

HUMANITY'S ACCOUNTABILITY TO GOD'S AUTHORITY

Humanity's accountability to God does not begin with our broken relationship with God; it precedes that. All are naturally accountable to God as his image bearers. This is demonstrated in the fact that God's law is written on the heart of every individual to the point that they are left without excuse (Rom. 1:20; 2:14). Genesis 1:27 explains to us, "God created man in His own image, in the image of God He created him; male and female He created them." What this means is that humanity was responsible to represent, mirror, and reflect God's communicable attributes to the rest of creation. R. C. Sproul said, "We are icons of God, creatures made with a unique capacity to mirror and reflect the character of God."[1] Ultimately this means that humanity is God-related and in a covenant relationship with the Creator. Theologically this has been spoken of as the covenant of works.[2]

The early church fathers were in agreement that the image of God in humanity consisted primarily in man's rational and moral characteristics. We see this in how humanity is created with a rational will and moral soul. God is Spirit, and the human soul is spirit. The essential attributes of a spirit are reason, conscience, and will. So when God made humanity in his own image, he endowed them with moral attributes that reflect his own.

We see this in numerous cases throughout Scripture. One clear text is Romans 2:15, which says, "In that they show the work of the Law written in their hearts, their conscience bearing witness and their thoughts alternately accusing or else defending them." Concurring with this conclusion, James Montgomery Boice rightly stated:

> An element in being created in the image of God is morality. Morality includes the two further elements of freedom and responsibility. To be sure, the freedom which men and women possess is not absolute. Even in the beginning the first man, Adam, and the first woman, Eve, were not autonomous. They were creatures and were responsible for acknowledging their status by their obedience.[3]

---

1   R. C. Sproul, *Essential Truths of the Christian Faith* (Wheaton, IL: Tyndale House, 1998), 131.

2   The covenant of works is often used as a shorthand to refer to a whole host of Christian doctrine. People made in the image of God naturally owe God obedience as their creator. See: Francis Turretin, *Institutes of Elenctic Theology*, trans. George Musgrave Giger (Phillipsburg, NJ: P&R, 1992), 1:575, 577–78. Thomas Boston, "A View of the Covenant of Works," in *The Complete Works of Thomas Boston* (Lafayette, IN: Sovereign Grace, 2001), 11:260. Geerhardus Vos, *Reformed Dogmatics*, eds. Richard B. Gaffin and Richard de Witt, trans. Annemie Godbehere, et al. (Bellingham, WA: Lexham, 2013).

3   James Montgomery Boice, *Foundations of the Christian Faith: A Comprehensive and Readable Overview of Christian Beliefs* (Downers Grove, IL: InterVarsity Press, 1986),

In fact, any text that speaks of transgression or sin shows how humanity is morally accountable to God. God has the intrinsic authority as Lord of creation to set the standard by which we are to live. First Peter 1:16 says, "Because it is written, 'YOU SHALL BE HOLY, FOR I AM HOLY.'" Because God sets the standard, he then has the right to hold us accountable to keeping that standard.

Our moral accountability before God is built into our very existence, and this is the basis by which God condemned the world before Moses in the flood of Noah. They had no recorded moral standard, but God's moral standard had been stamped on their very hearts. Thereby his right to judge them was written on the very fabric of their existence.

HUMANITY'S LEGAL ACCOUNTABILITY TO THE JUDGE

Scripture frequently portrays humanity's accountability and relationship to God in legal terms. This naturally brings up another important question to consider: "What is law?" Law appears five different ways in Scripture. It is used as the whole of God's revelation (Ps. 1:2), the OT as a whole (John 15:25), the Pentateuch (Luke 24:44), the Ten Commandments (Matt. 22:36–40), and even the ruling power of human nature (Rom. 7:23).[4]

No matter what the context is, where the term "law" is found, it always appears as a standard. It is natural that "God governs by teaching partly in making law and partly in establishing it. A law is made by commanding or forbidding. A law is established by promising or threatening."[5]

There are a few key elements to law: command, prohibition, and consequences. A command is an imperative demand to do something. We see this in Genesis 42:18, "Do this and live"; and Leviticus 18:5,

---

150–151. Simply as R.L. Dabney said, "The dominion bestowed upon man is the appropriate result of his moral likeness to his Maker" Robert Lewis Dabney, *Systematic Theology* (Edinburgh: Banner of Truth Trust, 1985), 294.

4   "The word "law" (הַתּוֹרָה, νόμος) is employed in the Scripture with certain latitude of meaning, but always carrying the force of meaning contained in the general idea of a regulative principle" (Dabney, *Systematic Theology*, 351).

5   William Ames, *Marrow of Theology*, 111.

"So you must keep My statutes and My judgments, by which a man may live if he does them; I am the LORD."

A prohibition is an imperative demand to not do something. We see this in Genesis 2:17, "but from the tree of the knowledge of good and evil you shall not eat, for in the day that you eat from it you will surely die," and again in Genesis 3:3, "but from the fruit of the tree which is in the middle of the garden, God has said, 'You shall not eat from it or touch it, or you will die.'"

Consequences are rewards of blessing or cursing based on obedience or disobedience. The fact that humanity owes obedience is often referred to as the natural demands of the law. As we see frequently in Scripture, natural demands of the law always have attached to it a reward, and penal demands always have attached a punishment.

This truth about the law is very telling about the character of God. God's generosity and benevolence are expressed in his desire to bless obedience (Lev. 26:3–4; Deut. 11:13–14), and his holiness and justice are displayed in his need to punish disobedience (Gen. 2:17; 3:3). J. I. Packer helpfully explains, "Man was not created autonomous, that is, free to be a law to himself, but theonomous, that is, bound to keep the law of his Maker."[6] Moral obligations require a standard by which to measure those moral obligations, so if the law is violated or unfulfilled, there is intrinsically a need for legal justification.

The next legal relationship to God is as a criminal under the penal demands of the law. When it comes to penal consequences, it is important to understand that this has to do with consequences of actions. The penal demands of the law are only applicable to fallen creatures.

Penal demands are only required by law violators. Therefore, it applied to Adam only after the fall; before the fall he wasn't under a penalty, but after the fall he was, and all his posterity are under the demands of penal law. This penal relationship is founded in his judicial right as God. In this category stand all reprobate men or angels. Charles Hodge helpfully explains,

---

6   J. I. Packer, *Concise Theology: A Guide to Historic Christian Beliefs* (Wheaton, IL: Tyndale House, 1993), 91.

> As the Scriptures everywhere present God as a judge or moral ruler, it follows of necessity from that representation, that His rational creatures will be dealt with according to the principles of justice. If there be no transgression, there will be no punishment. And those who continue holy thereby continue in the favor and fellowship of Him whose favor is life, and whose loving-kindness if better than life.[7]

And so on account of man's moral responsibilities to God, it is necessary that the nature of the judge be considered. This demand (God's vindicatory justice, his retributive justice, and the penal demands of the law) was what made atonement necessary but also what makes hell necessary.

GOD'S JUSTICE

The righteousness and justice of God refer to his moral perfection. God is the source and standard of absolute moral perfection, and as such, all that he determines, all that he speaks, all that he requires from his creatures, and all that he does in his creation conforms to this perfection.

This emphasis focuses on God's relationship to evil and sin—on God's *moral separation* from all that is *immoral* and represents what is *antithetical* to God and his character. As Pink states, "As God's power is the opposite of the native weakness of the creature, as His wisdom is in complete contrast from the least defect of understanding or folly, so His holiness is the very antithesis of all moral blemish or defilement."[8] To describe it another way, there is no trace of moral impurity in God himself, nor is there the slightest tinge of any impurity in any of God's dealings with his creation. It is impossible for him to think or act in a way contrary to this inherent and impeccable righteousness.

God is righteous in his character. We see this throughout Scripture. "The Rock! His work is perfect, for all His ways are just; a God

---

7   Hodge, *Systematic Theology*, 2:118.
8   Pink, *The Attributes of God*, 51.

of faithfulness and without injustice, righteous and upright is He"
(Deut. 32:4; cf. Deut. 10:17; 2 Chron. 12:6; 19:6–7; Ezra 9:15; Ps.
11:7, 25:8). Everything he does (*ad extra*) is perfect to the infinite
degree. We must also remember that because of the doctrine of divine
simplicity,[9] God's righteousness is equal to God's justice, and this is
even seen in his works in the economy of redemption.

It is important to stress that God's conformity to righteousness is
not a conformity to an external standard. If there existed an external,
higher standard of righteousness, then God's righteousness would be
a *derivative righteousness*—a righteousness that was derived from and
defined by that external standard.

That external standard would then serve as the ultimate authority
on all matters pertaining to what is right; it would judge and justify
God. Rather, God's conformity to righteousness is a conformity to
his own essence. Righteousness isn't something he has created; it is
who he is eternally. He does not simply *possess* righteousness; he *is*
righteousness. And because he *is* the very essence of moral perfection,
all that he says and does will be consistent with that same standard.

God reveals his righteousness to humans through commands, laws,
and statutes. These laws are never arbitrary or hollow. What they require
always in some way reflects the absolute moral purity of God. More-
over, God metes out his judgment on humanity not in some random,
prejudicial manner, but according to the laws he has established for
them in the covenant of works. As a result, one of the most frequent
depictions of God in the Bible is that of lawgiver and judge.

Because God is righteous, he must always condemn and punish
that which contradicts and rebels against his righteous character. Each
deviation from his law must be punished because it challenges absolute
moral purity. He cannot ignore sin or "sweep it under the rug" as if

---

9   Divine Simplicity does not mean God is slow or dim-witted, nor do we mean that
     God is easy to understand. Simple as a divine attribute, is the opposite of compound.
     The simplicity of God means is not made up of his attributes. He does not consist of a
     little bit of goodness, a little bit of mercy, a little bit of power, and a little bit of justice.
     Simplicity teaches that God is goodness, mercy, justice, and power. Every attribute of
     God is identical with His essence. Meaning, one cannot be removed, diminished, or
     augmented, without the very essence of God being impacted.

it never existed. If God ceased to condemn and punish sin, even in the smallest forms, he would no longer be the source and standard of absolute moral purity.

Instead, he would be complicit with sin and unjust in his upholding of righteousness. Consequently, God will never treat people worse than they deserve but will always act with absolute justice and equity in his dealings with humanity. Thus, God's wrath upon sinners is never unjust or exaggerated. Consequently, the ultimate determination of what is "right" or "just" is found in whether something conforms to the character of God. Our understanding of righteousness is finite at best and certainly impacted by our fallenness as well. As a result, our version of righteousness—when it is based on our own intuition—is skewed and partial.

When we talk about distributive justice, we are saying God does not have a "one size fits all" approach with respect to punishment or reward. Rather, God metes out justice exactly and fairly according to the crime committed and distributes rewards exactly and fairly according to the obedience rendered. "He who justifies the wicked and he who condemns the righteous, Both of them alike are an abomination to the Lord" (Prov. 17:15).

The notion that God gives punishment and reward to the same degree to everyone is called "egalitarian justice." As Feinberg states, "It is significant that nowhere does Scripture even vaguely suggest that God operates on principles of egalitarian justice."[10] The prophet Jeremiah states, "I, the Lord, search the heart, I test the mind, even to give to each man according to his ways, according to the results of his deeds" (Jer. 17:10). Thus, those who are punished by God receive exactly what they deserve. As Daniel confesses with respect to Israel's disobedience to the covenant, "Therefore the Lord has kept the calamity in store and brought it on us; for the Lord our God is righteous with respect to all His deeds which He has done, but we have not obeyed His voice" (Dan. 9:14).

By justice we mean, as Thomas Watson explained, "'Justice is to give everyone his due.' God's justice is the rectitude of His nature,

---

10   Feinberg, *No One Like Him*, 347

whereby He is carried to the doing of that which is righteous."[11] For us, righteousness refers to a conformity to the standard of God, and God's justice is the measuring rod.

While holiness is why God takes offense to sin, it is his justice that demands and decides how retribution is to be carried out. So, when souls suffer in hell it is because they have offended an infinitely holy God, and the just punishment to an infinite offence is an infinite judgment. John Owen said, "But this is that universal perfection of God, which, when He exercises [it] in punishment the transgressions of His creatures, is called vindicatory justice."[12]

God's moral purity requires him to hate sin and not leave it unpunished. He can never look with neutrality on that which is antithetical to his moral perfection. If he did, he would deny himself and permit sin to reign in victory. God's retributive justice is extended through his penal demands on sinners. So those go together: retributive justice and penal demands of the law. It is summarized in the threats of the law. In the day you disobey, you will die.

WHO IS IN CONTROL OF HELL?

In many modern TV shows, cartoons, and movies, hell is depicted as a place in the center of the earth where the devil runs around in a red suit with a pitchfork. It is thought of as a place where bad people go and are tortured by the devil. This concept, however, is far from the biblical notion of the actual judge of hell. That idea borrows more from the pagan fiction of the Greek pantheon of gods, one of which rules the underworld whose name is *Hades*, or in other cultures, Mephisto, Hela, or Loki. However, these concepts are nothing less than a perversion of the truth and most certainly a denial of it.

According to Scripture, Satan will not be the chief of hell but its chief captive. "Satan has never been in Hell and does not control

---

11   Thomas Watson, *A Body of Divinity: Contained in Sermons upon the Westminster Assembly's Catechism* (Edinburgh: Banner of Truth Trust, 2000), 87.

12   John Owen, "Divine Justice," *Works of John Owen*, ed. William H. Goold (London: Banner of Truth Trust, 1968), 10:513.

Hell."[13] Because God is the one offended, because God alone is holy and perfectly just, only he is qualified to punish the wicked in hell. "That it is the cause, source, and rule of all punishments to be inflicted; for this is the right of God, 'that those who commit sin are worthy of death.' From this right of God it follows that 'the wages of' every 'sin is death.'"[14]

God's judgments, however, are just in that they require evidence; that is why he weighs the heart and renders justice according to works (Prov. 24:12). There is no secret sin, or no offense that can be hidden, buried, or destroyed from his eyes. "For God will bring every act to judgment, everything which is hidden, whether it is good or evil" (Eccl. 12:14). While the human justice system may be bribed, swayed, or even tampered with based on the presentation of evidence or lack thereof, the divine justice system cannot be. The human justice system can only judge, even if it does so rightly, the external evidence. Human justice cannot judge the most crucial or revealing testimony: the human heart.

God knows the hearts and thoughts of men. "God is just in punishing the wicked, because He never punishes them but upon full proof of evidence."[15] Therefore, there must be a day of judgment, and the just penalty for that judgment is eternal hell. "For He is coming to judge the earth. He will judge the world in righteousness" (Ps. 96:13). Anyone outside of Christ who does not have a substitute will be judged on their own accord. They will not be able to have another take their place on that day, but each will take his or her own place before the divine tribunal.

And because there is no one who has been perfect apart from the God-man Jesus Christ, all outside of him will reap their just reward. "Therefore, for vindicating the justice of God, there must be a day wherein there shall be a righteous distribution of punishments and rewards to men, according to their actions."[16]

---

13   James Montgomery Boice, *Foundations of the Christian Faith: A Comprehensive and Readable Theology* (Downers Grove, IL: InterVarsity Press, 1981), 173.

14   Owen, "Divine Justice," 10:515.

15   Watson, *Body of Divinity*, 89.

16   Watson, *Body of Divinity*, 311.

It is common to refer to this judgment as punishment, and it could be called thus rightly so, however this punishment must not be confused with the punishment or chastisement that comes as a result of being disobedient children. This is not a disciplinary action for their correction, but a judgment for his vindication. John Owen has a very precise way of referring to God's justice executed on those in hell: "But this is that universal perfection of God, which, when He exercises [it] in punishment the transgressions of His creatures, is called vindicatory justice."[17] Vindicatory justice is a correct way of referring to hell in relation to the attributes of God. His justice vindicates and clears the holiness of God for the patience with which he allowed sinners to disdain his name throughout their lives here on earth.

So it is right to note that the wrath of God is in hell, however, it may also be observed that each member of the Trinity, in his own personal way, is involved in this judgment.[18] The Spirit is involved indirectly, in that while in this life, he restrained the wicked, convicted them of sin, and caused them to withhold from being utterly depraved. The reason why no one has been as bad as they could have been is because of the restraining power of the Holy Spirit; in hell this will not be the case. His involvement can be seen in the parable of Jesus in Luke 16:25: "But Abraham said, 'Child, remember that during your life you received your good things, and likewise Lazarus bad things; but now he is being comforted here, and you are in agony.'"

One thing that can be gleaned from this parable is that the wicked will remember things here on this earth while they are in hell. They will forever remember how things were. Yet it will be of no comfort to them. This recollecting in the mind of the good things they took

---

17   Owen, "Divine Justice," 10:513.

18   Because God is Pure Act and Simple, the doctrine of Inseparable Operations is a vital conclusion to combat Social Trinitarianism. Inseparable Operations simplified means that when one member of the Trinity acts all three persons are also acting, since there is only one God. However, in the economy of God's work (*ad extra*) we are able to appropriate specific work to each person. For a great treatment of this very important topic see Adonis Vidu, *The Same God Who Works All Things: Inseparable Operations in Trinitarian Theology* (Grand Rapids: Eerdmans, 2021).

for granted heightens their torment. This recollection will be a supernatural work of the Holy Spirit.

The Father can be said to be the one who determines the verdict
of hell. He determined who would go there before the foundations of
the world. However, he is not the one who gives out the judgment,
for he is not the judge of hell. The Father's role then will be in the
outpouring of wrath. The Scripture does not tell us the source of the
wrath upon the wicked other than it is God's. His wrath was what was
poured out on Christ, and his wrath will be what is poured out on the
defiant sinner in hell.

The clearest judge of hell given in Scripture is Jesus Christ. This right
is given to him by the Father. "For not even the Father judges anyone,
but He has given all judgment to the Son" (John 5:22). He is the one
who will judge the living and the dead (2 Tim. 4:1; Acts 10:42). Acts
17:31 seems to indicate a that the agency through which the Father
judges is the Son "because He has fixed a day in which He will judge
the world in righteousness through a Man whom He has appointed,
having furnished proof to all men by raising Him from the dead."
John 5:26–27 speaks this same truth: "This right to act as judge over
the whole universe is something that the Father has given the Son."[19]

It has been prophesied from long ago that he would execute
judgment. Daniel 7:10 has him as the one reading the books and
sentencing judgment. "It is a great honor put upon Christ; He who
was Himself judged, shall be Judge: He who once hung upon the
cross, shall sit upon the throne of judgment."[20] When men go to jail,
or when they stand before a firing squad, they are always terrified.
Men in ages past were frightened to speak to a king lest they be put
to death. The demons shuddered, shrieked, and feared when Christ
arrived because they knew he was their future judge. In Acts 24:25
Felix was frightened when Paul spoke of the "judgment to come";
how much more so will the wicked collapse under despair before
Christ on that great day!

---

19   Wayne Grudem, *Systematic Theology* (Grand Rapids: Zondervan, 2000), 1142.
20   Watson, *Body of Divinity*, 311.

John Murray explains, "The exaltation bestowed upon Him is the highest exaltation conceivable and this exaltation will be verified and consummated in the judgment of the whole world."[21] Revelation 6:16–17 describes, "and they said to the mountains and to the rocks, 'Fall on us and hide us from the presence of Him who sits on the throne, and from the wrath of the Lamb; for the great day of their wrath has come, and who is able to stand?'"

In Christ's first coming he came meek and lowly, he was a humble servant, but in his second coming he will be a righteous judge. "The Lamb of God will then be turned into a lion, the sight of whom will strike terror into sinners."[22] He will be blameless when he judges the world concerning sin (Job 21:14; Ps. 51:4; Matt. 25:41; Eph. 1:20–21; Phil. 2:10–11; Heb. 1:3; 1 Peter 3:22; Rev. 1:17–18; 6:16–17; 20:12).

THE OBJECTS OF HELL

The objects of hell are twofold: reprobate humans and angels. All reprobate, young and old—those who have sinned against God and rejected him—will be judged. The wicked are not limited by age, ethnicity, gender, or location. People from all over the world will one day be in hell. It does not matter if they have heard the gospel or not, for there is only one name under heaven given to men to be saved (John 14:6; Acts 4:12).

In modern times parents neglect gospel teaching to their children. They assume that their child is innocent, harmless, and therefore undeserving of divine judgment. But parents ought to be warned this sort of thinking could be very dangerous because the Bible does not give a clear-cut age of accountability. This is not to say that all infants go to hell, but it ought to be a warning that if a child is old enough to be saved than they are most certainly old enough to be damned.

There are many children who are saved at the ages of five, seven, or eleven, and therefore it is safe to say that if these same children had

---

21   John Murray, "The Last Things," in *Collected Writings of John Murray* (1967; repr., Edinburgh: Banner of Truth, 2009), 2:415–16.
22   Watson, *Body of Divinity*, 312.

not been saved than they would have been damned because all have sinned and fallen short of the glory of God (Rom. 3:23).

Therefore, all those outside of Christ will experience the wrath of God. John Gerstner makes this astonishing warning: "God will not excuse children nor does He forget their sins and the aggravation that they have sinned away the best time for their conversion."[23] There will be men, women, and children in hell, for "it is clear that all unbelievers will stand before Christ for judgment, for this judgment includes 'the dead, great and small (Rev. 20:12).'"[24]

God has not only made hell for the wicked who know not Christ but for the devil and his angels, as Christ says in Matthew 25:41: hell "has been prepared for the devil and his angels." Second Peter 2:4 says, "God did not spare angels when they sinned, but cast them into Hell and committed them to pits of darkness, reserved for judgment." As was mentioned before, Satan will be the chief captive of hell. "The Bible tells us that God has created Hell, preparing it in part for the devil and his angels, and that Satan will one day end up there." Satan and the reprobate angels, who are not currently in hell (unlike those in Jude 6), will one day be cast there.

WHY DO PEOPLE REJECT PREDESTINATION?

The doctrine of God's justice in hell is intended in Scripture to warn the unbelieving to repent and believe (Rom. 2:4); to be a hope for the oppressed that one day justice will be perfectly meted out (Job 5:15–16; Ps. 9:9; 10:17–18, 103:6); and to display true justice that will come at the hands not of imperfect men, social reform, or military might but from the very hand of God (Deut. 32:35; Rom. 12:19). More shockingly in Scripture, hell is something that God's people will actually worship him for. And when the world is full of all sorts of injustices, it's not a surprise that people willing accept the Bible's teaching on condemnation and God's justice.

---

23   John H. Gerstner, *The Rational Biblical Theology of Jonathan Edwards* (Orlando, FL: Ligonier Ministries, 1993), 3:513

24   Grudem, *Systematic Theology*, 1142.

However, what people seem to struggle with the most is the idea that God has determined who will be instruments of justice before the foundation of the world, that God has decreed who will be vessels of justice prepared for justice before they are ever born, before they commit any evil acts. What right does God have to assign someone to the standard of justice without taking any actions they will ever commit? This is frightening to most, and yet it is what faithful Christians have taught to one degree or another since the early church up to modern days.[25] What authority does God have to determine the destinies of the non-elect unconditionally before time began? Where do we even begin to find answers to these questions? Romans 9 has the answers, and that is precisely where we must go next.

---

25 For more on this see Peter Sammons, *Reprobation: From Augustine to the Synod of Dort: The Historical Development of the Reformed Doctrine of Reprobation*, Reformed Historical Theology 63 (Göttingen: Vandenhoeck & Ruprecht, 2020).

THE PLACE OF ROMANS 9 AND REPROBATION

*R*eprobation is defined as the eternal, unconditional decree of God for the non-elect. In this decree, he chooses to exclude the non-elect from his electing purposes of mercy and to hold them accountable to the strict standards of justice to display the glory of his righteous wrath. This doctrine is founded on biblical passages that describe sinners as "vessels of wrath prepared for destruction" (Rom. 9:22), appointed to "doom" (1 Peter 2:8), and "long beforehand marked out for this condemnation" (Jude 4). The case for reprobation also incorporates biblical evidence demonstrating God's rule over everything, including calamity (Lam. 3:38), disaster (Amos 3:6), the hearts of kings (Prov. 21:1), and even the most heinous crime ever committed—the crucifixion (Acts 2:23). If God is sovereign over evil, including the wicked deeds of sinners, his sovereignty necessarily extends to the eternal destinies of all people, including those in hell.

Romans 9 contains the longest and possibly most detailed biblical account the nature of reprobation.[1] As a result, it is a controversial

---

1   John Frame observes this when he says, "The passage deals with both historical and eternal reprobation, and that fact has confused some readers." John Frame, *Systematic Theology: An Introduction to Christian Belief* (Phillipsburg, NJ: P&R, 2013), 222.

passage. Norman Geisler said, "This is a favorite passage of extreme Calvinists, especially those who believe in double predestination. For it appears to say that God not only loves just the elect, but also He even hates the non-elect. . . . [F]ew Scriptural texts are more misused by extreme Calvinists than this one."[2] Romans 9:6–23 has historically been at the center of the debate related to reprobation and is critical to understanding the nature of this truth.

Unlike other New Testament books, Paul's epistle to the Romans was not prompted by a specific dispute among believers. While some of Paul's writings are letters written in response to specific questions and problems, Romans addresses the broad issue of corporate solidarity among Jews and Gentiles in the church (cf. Rom. 1:16; 15:7–9). That general theme allows Paul to address foundational issues such as human depravity, justification by faith alone, and union with Christ. Additionally, Paul answers the following questions: "Why has national Israel rejected salvation? How can national Israel receive salvation? When will national Israel come to salvation?" These three questions become the specific impetus for Paul's words in Romans 9–11. In these chapters, he outlines the redemptive work of God in eternity past (Rom. 9), present (Rom. 10), and future (Rom. 11).

THE PLACE OF ROMANS 9 IN THE CONTEXT OF THE EPISTLE

To understand what Romans 9 teaches about reprobation, it is first necessary to determine its place within the context of Paul's overall argument. Some scholars assert that chapters 9–11 are independent from chapters 1–8, believing that after chapter 8, Paul inserted an old sermon, thereby breaking up the letter's continuity.[3] Others recognize the essential place of these chapters in Paul's argument, even seeing them as the climax of the letter.[4]

---

2   Norman Geisler, *Chosen but Free: A Balanced View of God's Sovereignty and Free Will*, 2nd ed. (Minneapolis: Bethany House, 2010), 82.

3   C. H. Dodd, *The Epistle of Paul to the Romans* (1932; repr., London: Hodder & Stoughton, 1947), 161–63; Archibald M. Hunter, *Introducing the New Testament*, 3rd rev. ed. (Philadelphia: Westminster, 1972), 96.

4   Joseph A. Fitzmyer, *Romans: A New Translation with Introduction and Commentary*, AB 33 (New York: Doubleday, 1993), 541. A few commentators see a contradiction

In their immediate context, chapters 9–11 show significant continuity with the earlier chapters of this epistle. As Paul has outlined various aspects of salvation in chapters 1–7, Romans 8 is likewise redemptive in nature, having often been referred to as "the Golden Chain of Redemption." In Romans 8:30 the word ἐκάλεσεν ("called") is used, which also appears throughout Romans 9 (in vv. 7, 11, 24–26). The "call" in Romans 8 is tied to personal salvation, since it is immediately followed by justification (Rom. 8:30).

The next occurrence of the form of καλέω ("call") is Romans 9:7: "THROUGH ISAAC YOUR DESCENDANTS WILL BE NAMED." The word translated "named" is κληθήσεταί. The term appears again in verse 11, which establishes Jacob and Esau as objects of God's sovereign call. The text does not signal that Paul is using the term in a different way. Therefore, the calling which appears in verse 11 (καλοῦντος) is the calling of God, inseparably leading to justification and salvation. A form of the verb (ἐκάλεσεν) appears again in verse 24 in the context of God's choice of instruments for glory: "even us, whom He also called, not from among Jews only, but also from among Gentiles." The climactic promise of salvation in Romans 8 receives a natural rebuttal in Romans 9:6. Gutbrod explains: "Can the new community trust God's Word when it seems to have failed the Jews?"[5]

Verse 33 connects the election of God to eternal destinies: "Who will bring a charge against God's elect?" Paul connects that charge to "condemnation" (κατακρινῶν) in 8:34. This picks up his theme from 8:1, in which he says, "Therefore there is now no condemnation (κατάκριμα) for those who are in Christ Jesus." Paul understands

---

within Romans 9–11. See Erich Dinkler, "The Historical and the Eschatological Israel in Romans Chapters 9–11: A Contribution to the Problem of Pre-Destination and Individual Responsibility," *JR* 36, no. 2 (1956): 115.

5   Walter Gutbrod, "Ἰουδαῖος, Ἰσραήλ, Ἑβραῖος in the New Testament," *Theological Dictionary of the New Testament*, ed. Gerhard Kittel (Grand Rapids: Eerdmans, 1983), 3:386. Many have recognized that Israel not obtaining salvation is the foundation of Paul's expression of love for them in 9:1–5 and the rhetorical statement, "It is not as though the word of God has failed" (9:6). Johannes Munck states, "If God has not fulfilled his promises made to Israel, then what basis has the Jewish-Gentile church for believing that the promises will be fulfilled for them?" Johannes Munck, *Christ and Israel: An Interpretation of Romans 9–11* (Minneapolis: Fortress, 1967), 35.

election primarily in light of the eternal destinies of individuals, not the temporal destinies of national heritage.

Paul uses similar language at the beginning of chapter 10 when he says, "Brethren, my heart's desire and my prayer to God for them is for their salvation" (Rom. 10:1). Paul once again stresses his desire to see Jews saved. The word σωτηρίαν "salvation" is pivotal to the context of the entire section. By bracketing his words between two chapters concerned with eternal destinies, it is clear that Paul's concern in chapter 9 also regards the salvation of individuals. Paul's emphasis in Romans 8 is salvation, and Romans 10 begins with his concern for the salvation of Israel (not merely their restoration); so it makes sense that Romans 9 also discusses salvation.

Chapter 9 addresses the promise of salvation through Israel's Messiah. But the fact that national Israel does not believe in him calls into question the validity and veracity of God's promise. Anticipating this concern, Paul unfolds the reason why they do not believe. He begins in Romans 9:1–3 by expressing pain over the predicament of his people. In verses 4–5, he then lists the privileges which national Israel is presently not receiving, in spite of the promises given to them, due to their unbelief. He then begins to explain the reason why God's promises have not come to fruition in ethnic Israel as a whole (9:6). John Piper explains, "In Paul's view, the theme of Rom 9–11 assumes that Rom 9:6a (God's word has not fallen) is the main point which Rom 9–11 was written to prove, in view of Israel's unbelief and rejection."[6]

RECOGNITION OF GOD'S SOVEREIGNTY (ROMANS 9:1–5)
In Romans 9:1–5, Paul writes,

> I am telling the truth in Christ, I am not lying, my con-science testifies with me in the Holy Spirit, that I have great sorrow and unceasing grief in my heart. For I could

---

6   John Piper, *The Justification of God: An Exegetical and Theological Study of Romans 9:1–23* (Grand Rapids: Baker, 1993), 19.

wish that I myself were accursed, separated from Christ for the sake of my brethren, my kinsmen according to the flesh, who are Israelites, to whom belongs the adoption as sons, and the glory and the covenants and the giving of the Law and the temple service and the promises, whose are the fathers, and from whom is the Christ according to the flesh, who is over all, God blessed forever. Amen.

Paul opens with the clause Ἀλήθειαν λέγω ("I tell the truth"), similar to the one he employs in 2 Corinthians 12:6 (ἀλήθειαν γὰρ ἐρῶ), in order to establish the authenticity of his claims. Here, however, he claims the source of his validity is ἐν Χριστῷ ("in Christ"). By doing this, he places Jesus as the witness and authenticator of his gospel.[7] This gives the highest level of credibility to Paul's claims, so to deny Paul would be to call Jesus a liar.[8] Paul makes a second affirmation of his trustworthiness when he says οὐ ψεύδομαι ("I am not lying"). By insisting that he is "not lying," Paul shows his commitment to the truth of the gospel, despite the fact that so many of the Jewish people rejected Jesus.[9] Paul then uses a third statement to reinforce his truthfulness, by bringing his conscience in the Holy Spirit to witness. This threefold witness would be expected from a Jewish author (cf. Deut. 17:6; 19:17). These phrases are connected back to Romans 8,[10] highlighting that Paul still sees God's faithfulness in salvation in spite of Israel's apostasy.

Paul indicates the empathy he feels for his kinsmen in verse 2 by using two phrases to describe his disappointment in the Israelite

---

7   John Murray, *The Epistle to the Romans: The English Text with Introduction, Exposition and Notes*, NICNT (1965; repr., Grand Rapids: Eerdmans, 1968), 2:1; Fitzmyer, *Romans*, 543; Robert Jewett, *Romans: A Commentary*, ed. Eldon Jay Epp, Hermeneia (Minneapolis: Fortress, 2007), 557.

8   Jewett, *Romans*, 557.

9   It is not necessarily true that defending the Gospel is devoid of empathy toward Israel. The one does not negate the other. See Jewett, *Romans*, 558.

10 C. E. B. Cranfield, *A Critical and Exegetical Commentary on the Epistle to the Romans*, ICC (Edinburgh: T&T Clark, 1983), 2:452.

people.[11] First he says, λύπη μεγάλη ("my grief is great"); this grief is a pain of the heart.[12] Paul experiences an affliction of the mind and spirit.[13] This affliction (λύπη) is modified with an adjective (μεγάλη) ("great") to indicate that it is profoundly deep and intense.[14] Paul stresses his strong desire to see his fellow Israelites saved in light of what he previously wrote in chapters 1–8.

The second phrase is ἀδιάλειπτος ὀδύνη ("unceasing emotional distress") which describes Paul's emotional dissatisfaction with the Jews' response to the coming of the Messiah.[15] Jewett traces Paul's tone by saying, "Although heartsick and profoundly sorrowful, Paul does not yet specify why, which renders the emotional shift from the glorious, joyous certainty of 8:37–39 all the more stark."[16] Paul is distressed, because the Jewish people have rejected what was promised to them in the Messiah, forfeiting all the glorious realities Paul had just recounted.[17] While this is disappointing to Paul on a human level, he knows it is according to God's plan. He elaborates on this through the rest of chapter 9 and through to chapter 11.

The next proof of Paul's compassion for his people is an extension of the emotional agony he feels over their spiritual condition. This is illustrated by his desire to be cut off from God for their sake. The

---

11   Interpreters know this is referring to ethnic Jews because Paul describes them as "kinsmen according to the flesh" (συγγενῶν μου κατὰ σάρκα). See Wilhelm Michaelis, "συγγενής, συγγένεια," *TDNT* 7:741; Walter Bauer, *A Greek-English Lexicon of the New Testament and Other Early Christian Literature*, 3rd. ed., ed. Wlliam Danker (Chicago: University of Chicago Press, 2001), 950, hereafter, *BDAG*.

12   Rudolf Bultmann, "λύπη, λυπέω, ἄλυπος, περίλυπος, συλλυπέομαι," *TDNT* 4:320; Murray, *The Epistle to the Romans,* 2:2–3, states, "In a word Paul's sorrow is the reflection of the gravity pertaining to Israel's unbelief. The intensity of the apostle's sorrow . . . is marked by its greatness, its continuance, and its depth." See also Jewett, *Romans*, 559.

13   "λύπη," *BDAG*, 204.

14   Otto Bets, "μέγας," *Theological Dictionary of the New Testament*, ed. Gerhard Kittel (Grand Rapids: Eerdmans, 1983), 2:400.

15   Douglas J. Moo, *The Epistle to the Romans*, NICNT (Grand Rapids: Eerdmans, 1996), 557.

16   Jewett, *Romans*, 560.

17   Murray, *The Epistle to the Romans*, 2:3; Leon Morris, *The Epistle to the Romans*, PNTC (Grand Rapids: Eerdmans, 1988), 346; Moo, *The Epistle to the Romans*, 557; Cranfield, *Epistle to the Romans*, 2:453–54.

word translated "wish" is ηὐχόμην, a word commonly used for prayer. However, Paul realizes that the answer to this prayer is unattainable, as indicated by his use of the imperfect tense (indicating a past action never to be completed).[18]

As Paul continues to pray for his people, he expresses a desire to be their substitute. Stating it as being "cut off," Paul employs the term ἀνάθεμα, which is used in reference to eternal destruction and judgment. Paul used this same term to describe how false teachers were to be excommunicated out of the church (Gal. 1:8–9) and condemned for preaching a false gospel. Despite his noble desire to take judgment upon himself, Paul knew it was an impossibility, in view of the reality that there is only one substitute for sinners (1 Tim. 2:5). Furthermore, he knew it was impossible for any believer to be separated from Christ (Rom. 8:39).

Paul's primary concern is to see people saved. He does not say here, "I wish the nation were restored" but "I wish my brothers were saved!" For the nation to be restored to the land without the members being saved would ultimately be pointless. They would still remain under the judgment of God.

As he continues, Paul identifies his people as Ἰσραηλῖται ("Israelites"). This title is not just an observation of their ethnic identity but serves as their honorary identity as the people of God. Fitzmyer states, "Instead of the common ethnic or political title Ioudaioi, "Jews" (see 3:28–29; cf. Mark 15:2, 9, 12, 26) Paul readily makes use of the honorific title 'Israelites' bestowed of old by Yahweh himself on a patriarch of his people."[19] The promises are not to be confined to Israel in the past. All the promises continue to apply to Paul's present-day kinsmen, as individuals, and those yet to be born. Throughout Romans 9, Paul is concerned with individual salvation, and not merely national restoration.

---

18 Cranfield, *Epistle to the Romans*, 2:455; Jewett, *Romans*, 560.
19 Fitzmyer, *Romans*, 545. Furthermore, Dunn comments, "Ἰσραηλίτης is therefore deliberately chosen by Paul to evoke his people's sense of being God's elect, the covenant people of the one God." Dunn, *Romans 9–16*, 526.

THE PRIVILEGES OF ISRAEL

Paul describes these people who he longs to see saved with a series of ten adjectives. These adjectives outline specific blessings promised to and expected by Israel on a national scale. The first attribute is ἡ υἱοθεσία, "adoption as sons." This term has left many scholars in bewilderment because it is a word never used in the LXX and only once in other early Jewish literature.[20] However, this concept is present in Paul's previous comments about the relationship between God and the elect. Romans 8:15 and 8:23 state,

> For you have not received a spirit of slavery leading to fear again, but you have received a spirit of adoption as sons by which we cry out, "Abba! Father!" . . . And not only this, but also we ourselves, having the first fruits of the Spirit, even we ourselves groan within ourselves, waiting eagerly for our adoption as sons, the redemption of our body.

The concept of sonship was nothing new to Israelites, but the idea of adoption provides a new perspective for this familiar concept.

Next, Paul reaffirms Israel's δόξα ("glory"). This glory belongs to anyone who believes in Christ, being promised first to Israel. Due to their unbelief, the Israelites are missing out on the glory they were promised as God's chosen people. This is similar to the next characteristic, καὶ αἱ διαθῆκαι ("and the covenants"). These covenants would include all the biblical covenants promised in the Old Testament. Related to the covenants is the giving of the Law (ἡ νομοθεσία). The term νομοθεσία only appears here in the NT and is associated with the following phrase: καὶ ἡ λατρεία ("and the temple service").[21]

---

20   Eduard Schweizer, "υἱοθεσία," *TDNT* 8:399; Jewett, *Romans*, 562.
21   Heinrich August Wilhelm Meyer, *Critical and Exegetical Handbook to the Epistle to the Romans*, trans. John C. More, Edwin Johnson, William P. Dickson, and Frederick Crombie (London: T&T Clark, 1873), 2:116; W. Sanday and Arthur C. Headlam, *A Critical and Exegetical Commentary on the Epistle to the Romans* (New York: Scribner, 1913), 231; Morris, *The Epistle to the Romans*, 349.

Sixth, Paul explains that Israel is the nation to which belongs αἱ ἐπαγγελίαι "the promises." The promise of salvation, first given in Genesis 3:15, is likely the most prominent in Paul's mind. But the promises are not strictly limited to salvation. Throughout Romans, the use of ἐπαγγελία almost exclusively refers to the Abrahamic promises (land, seed, and blessing; not to the neglect of salvation, but on the basis of salvation). The promises Paul has in mind in Romans 9 are further specified by being modified with ὧν οἱ πατέρες "to whom are the fathers," which would include Isaac, Jacob, David, as well as the other patriarchs.[22]

Two more clauses are used in verse 5 to describe Israel. First, Paul describes his kinsmen as the ones from whom Christ came (ἐξ ὧν ὁ Χριστὸς). The Messiah was expected to come from Israel and came as promised. Jesus was not merely their promised Messiah, but he came from Israel in the flesh (τὸ κατὰ σάρκα), a reminder that he is their "kinsman" just as Paul is (cf. Rom. 9:3). The height of Israel's audacious refusal of Jesus is found here. They were the original recipients of God's honored promises and to them belonged the glory of being God's people. They had the covenants, the Law, and prescribed worship. These were all to prepare them to receive the promise of the coming Messiah. He came from their midst and yet they rejected him.

SUMMARY REMARKS

This section of Romans 9 introduces the dilemma that Paul will not bring to full resolution until Romans 11:25–32. The great doctrines of human depravity (Rom. 3), justification (4–5), sanctification (6–7), and the whole of salvation (8), provide the context for the apostle's words in Romans 9–11.

This section deals with God's plans for Jews and Gentiles from eternity past. The power of the Gospel is put forth by Paul at the

---

22 Cranfield states, "Compare 11:28. Paul no doubt means specifically Abraham (cf. e.g., 4:12, 16; Luke 1:73; 3:8; John 8:29, 56), Isaac (cf. 9:10), Jacob (cf. John 4:12), and the twelve patriarchs, the sons of Jacob (cf. Acts 7:12, 15)—possibly also other outstanding figures of OT history such as David (cf. Mk 11:10: in Acts 2:29 he is called ὁ πατριάρχης)." Cranfield, *Epistle to the Romans*, 2:464.

front of the epistle in Romans 1:16: "for it is the power of God for salvation to everyone who believes, to the Jew first and also to the Greek." Yet, this promise of salvation appears to have failed in light of the fact that the nation of Israel had rejected its Messiah (which is why Paul asserts in 9:6, "it is not as though the word of God has failed"). That is the tension Paul seeks to resolve.

Chapters 9 through 11 explain God's redemptive plan for both Jews and Gentiles. While it appears that the Jews have been cut off, since it is primarily Gentiles who are being saved in the church age, Paul explains the true purpose this serves. He begins in Romans 9:6 to reveal the plan of God in Israel's rejection by establishing a principle of individual salvation and reprobation to explain the future salvation and restoration of the nation (Rom. 11:26). Paul wants his readers to understand the supremacy of election in God's plan, which supersedes ethnic heritage.

CHAPTER 4

THE PURPOSE OF ELECTION

*T*he opening verses of Romans 9 not only establish the dilemma of Israel's rejection of Christ but also cement the reality that no one was better prepared to receive the Messiah than the Israelites. From a human perspective, they had more knowledge and a society built upon God's special revelation to receive the Messiah, yet they reject him. The whole purpose of such a stunning rejection is the electing and reprobating purposes of God. The apostle continues in verses 6–13 with these words:

> But it is not as if the Word of God has failed. For not all who are from Israel are Israel; nor is it that they are all his children who are Abraham's descendants, but: "Through Isaac will your descendants be called." That is, those who are the children of the flesh are not necessarily the children of God, but the children of promise are considered as descendants. For the Word of promise is this: "At that time I will return, and Sarah will have a son." Not only this, but also Rebekah, having intercourse with one man, Isaac our father; for when they were not yet born and had done nothing good or bad, in order that God's selective purpose would stand, not from works but because Him who calls, it was said to her, "The older will

serve the younger." Just as it is written, "Jacob I loved, but Esau I hated."[1]

EXEGESIS OF ROMANS 9:6–13

Paul starts the section by highlighting the truth that in spite of his personal grief, God's Word has not failed.[2] On the contrary, this was God's plan all along. Paul does not make the statement, "But it is not as though the word of God has failed," to discuss whether or not God has the ability to succeed in his plans. Instead, he corrects anyone who would misunderstand his emotional response to Israel's unbelief as believing God had failed.[3] Paul's response to the idea that God's Word failed is simply, "For they are not all Israel who are descended from Israel." Paul picks up on a theme he already established in Romans 4:13–16:

> For the promise to Abraham or to his descendants that he would be heir of the world was not through the law, but through the righteousness of faith. For if those who are of the law are heirs, faith is made void and the promise is nullified; for the law brings about wrath, but where there is no law, there also is no violation. For this reason it is by faith, in order that it may be in accordance with grace, so that the promise will be guaranteed to all the descendants, not only to those who are of the Law, but also to those who are of the faith of Abraham, who is the father of us all.

---

1 Translation mine.

2 "God's word" means God's promises, previously mentioned. See Piper, *Justification of God*, 49; John Calvin, *The Epistle to the Romans*, vol. 19, *Calvin's Commentaries*, trans. John Owen (Grand Rapids: Baker, 2005), 197; Charles Hodge, *Commentary on the Epistle to the Romans* (1950; repr., Grand Rapids: Eerdmans, 1994), 305; Murray, *The Epistle to the Romans*, 2:9; C. K. Barrett, *The Epistle to Romans*, BNTC (1957; repr., Peabody, MA: Hendrickson, 1991), 180.

3 Cranfield, *Epistle to the Romans*, 2:471, states, "In support of his categorical statement in v. 6a to the effect that what he has just said about his grief (vv. 1–5) does not imply that the revealed purpose of God, His purpose in election, has failed." Piper explains, "In Rom 9:11c Paul says that God elected Jacob and not Esau 'in order that the purpose of God according to election might remain.' The *remaining* of God's *electing purpose* is the opposite of the *falling* of God's *word*." Piper, *The Justification of God*, 49. Also see Meyer, *Epistle to the Romans*, 2:132, and Murray, *The Epistle to the Romans*, 2:14.

Paul's point—demonstrating that God has not failed despite the unbelief of ethnic Israel—is that not all of Israel are children of promise. There is an elect Israel within Israel, and Paul uses such a distinction to spring into the doctrine of election. By discussing election and saying that "not all Israel is Israel," he does not intend to convey that there is no future for ethnic Israel in God's redemptive plan. He picks up on the theme of a restored national Israel in Romans 11, culminating in verse 26: "and so all Israel will be saved." The meaning of "Israel" in Paul's vocabulary should be interpreted according to the context of 9:4. Paul is not claiming the church has replaced Israel in 9:6; rather, Paul's distinction is between believing Israel (the elect) and merely physical Israel.[4]

Verse 7 continues Paul's argument: "nor are they all children because they are Abraham's descendants, but: 'through Isaac your descendants will be named.'"[5] Paul explains that not everyone who has descended from Abraham is an heir to the promises given to Abraham. This is the same reasoning Paul will pick up in verse 9 and following. Jewett recognizes this when he states, "The distinction between the broader category 'children' and the restricted term 'seed' thus corresponds exactly to that between all Israel and the true Israel in v. 6b."[6] Paul's argument is just further proof elaborating the same idea found in verse 6. Here, the promised seed is divinely separate from the natural seed.[7]

God has made a divine distinction unto salvation for the children of promise, who are "true Israel," while simultaneously rejecting those who are not the children of promise. In his proof, Paul cites Genesis

---

4   Fitzmyer, *Romans,* 560. Cranfield is mistaken and misunderstands what most commentators recognize. He appears to try so hard to remove the idea of replacement theology that he says, "The point Paul is making is that not all who are included in the comprehensive Israel are included also in the selective, special Israel. But this does not mean what it has so often been taken to mean—that only part of the Jewish people is the elect people of God." Cranfield, *Epistle to the Romans,* 2:473. Cranfield goes on to explain the elect people within the elect nation in very Barthian terms and cites Barth as validation. Karl Barth, *Church Dogmatics,* vol. 2, part 2, *The Doctrine of God,* trans. T. H. L. Parker and J. L. M. Haire (Edinburgh: T&T Clark, 1957), 214.

5   Both Meyer, *Epistle to the Romans,* 2:125, and Jewett, *Romans,* 575, recognize the grammatical pattern connecting this denial to the previous one in verse 6.

6   Jewett, *Romans,* 575.

7   Siegfried Schulz and Gottfried Quell, "σπέρμα," *TDNT* 7:545.

21:12 to point out how the patriarchs have always observed distinctions between children.

However, it was God's choice that Isaac, not Ishmael, would receive the blessing, because Isaac was the child of promise. Paul returns to the theme of salvation by using the word κληθήσεταί ("call") as the distinguishing factor between the descendants of Abraham. Many English translations take this to mean "will be named." Although "named" is within the semantic range of καλέω (which last appeared in Romans 8:30), out of the 148 uses in the NT it is only rendered as "name" in three places by English translations. In this context, God's effectual calling is in view as the basis for the inheritance of God's promises.[8]

Paul's conclusion in verses 6 and 7 culminates with an example from Genesis 21:12 to distinguish the children of promise from the children of natural descent. To drive home his point, Paul says, "That is, it is not the children of the flesh who are children of God, but the children of the promise are regarded as descendants" (v. 8).

Paul removes a misconception that was prevalent in the Jewish community at that time—namely, that being a natural descendent of Abraham automatically entitled one to spiritual blessing. After addressing that misunderstanding, Paul naturally mourns the spiritual loss of Jewish people who have rejected Christ (9:1–3).[9]

After emphasizing God's sovereign choice, Paul provides an example of God's faithfulness to his promise. The apostle picks up the major theme of the previous verse and explains the substance of God's promises. Quoting from Genesis 18:10 and 18:14, he provides the example of Sarah: "I will surely return to you at this time next year; and behold, Sarah your wife will have a son. . . . At the appointed time I will return to you, at this time next year, and Sarah will have

---

8   Piper, *Justification of God*, 66–70; Murray, *The Epistle to the Romans*, 2:10–11; Colin G. Kruse states, "In chapter 9 Paul's concern is for the salvation of Israel. He explains the rejection of the gospel by many of them as the result of God's choice. Only the believing Israelites are chosen for salvation; only believing Israelites are Abraham's true children, not ethnic Israel as a whole." Colin Kruse, *Paul's Letter to the Romans*, PNTC (Grand Rapids: Eerdmans, 2012), 376.

9   Dunn, *Romans 9–16*, 548.

a son."[10] Paul accomplishes two objectives by using Scripture as the source of his theology. First, his citation of Genesis 18 proves that God's choice in election is not based upon natural descent but on God's promises. Second, Paul proves that God's Word does not fail (9:6); he always fulfills his promises.

Verse 10 starts a four-verse explanation of Paul's argument introduced in verse 9.[11] To further establish God's sovereign choice over man's ethnically based entitlement, Paul provides the example of Rebekah. Paul connects the example of Rebekah with that of Sarah (v. 9). The adjunctive use of καὶ indicates these two examples are to be understood as teaching the same concept.

Here, Paul establishes God's sovereign choice by giving the example of the conception of twins, born of the same mother and father, and conceived at the same time.[12] The phrase used to express this in verse 10 means "having conceived by one man," which puts the twins on the same familial standing.

Paul emphasizes there was nothing that distinguished the boys from one another. It is not that one was born from the legitimate mother and the other from an illegitimate mother, because both were conceived at the same time by the same parents. At this point in his argument, Paul is not concerned with discussing the national descent of Israel. Rather, he is focusing on Israel's unbelief in the Messiah. In the same way that the divine will alone distinguished between natural-born Jacob and Esau, so God is sovereign over those who believe and those who do not.

---

10   Paul's citation of Genesis delineates God's coming with the promise from his previous encounters. He captures the essence of Genesis 18:10. Some have noted that Paul use of the verb ἐλεύσομαι is different than the LXX, but they believe it is to avoid some form of functionless reference. See Jewett, *Romans*, 577.

11   It has been observed that Paul's argument here from 9:10–13 is a unit, however, it is an incomplete sentence. Fitzmyer explains, "The grammar is at fault here. Paul fails to use a finite verb, expressing his idea only by a participial phrase *koitēn echouse*, 'having a pregnancy,' which is followed in v 11 by a gen. absol., in which the pl. subject, 'children,' is not expressed, but understood." Fitzmyer, *Romans*, 561–62. Therefore the finite verb is taken from the previous verse, which all the more connects the ideas of Paul's argument. See Jewett, *Romans*, 577.

12   Cranfield, *Epistle to the Romans*, 2:476–77.

ELECTION OF NATIONS OR INDIVIDUALS?

Is Paul referring to the election of nations or individuals? The answer to that question sets a trajectory for how to interpret the rest of Paul's argument. Some believe Romans 9:10–23 contains elements of both national (corporate) election as well as individual (personal) election; believing that 9:6–13 refers to national election but verse 14 and following refer to personal election.[13] Others believe it is solely teaching corporate election. Representing this position, Sanday and Headlam state, "The absolute election of Jacob—the 'loving' of Jacob and the 'hating' of Esau—has reference simply to the election of one to higher privileges as head of the chosen race, than the other. It has nothing to do with their eternal salvation. In the original to which St. Paul is referring, Esau is simply a synonym for Edom."[14] N. T. Wright argues,

> Paul is not, then, producing an abstract essay on the way in which God always works with individuals, or for that matter with nations and races. This is specifically the story of Israel, the chosen people; it is the unique story of how the creator has worked with the covenant people, to bring about the purpose for which the covenant was made in the first place.[15]

Norman Geisler has similarly asserted, "The reference here is not to individual election but to the corporate election of a nation—the chosen nation of Israel."[16]

---

13   Archibald Thomas Robertson, *Word Pictures in the New Testament*, vol. 4, *The Epistles of Paul* (New York: Harper & Brothers, 1931), 383. Ernst Käsemann similarly states, "Paul is no longer concerned with two peoples and their fate but rather in a permanent way with the election and rejection of two persons [Jacob and Esau] who have been raised to the level of types," Ernst Käsemann, *Commentary on Romans*, trans. and ed. Geoffrey W. Bromiley (Grand Rapids: Eerdmans, 1980), 264. Piper explains that the flaw in this line of reasoning is that it fails to show the connection in Paul's argument as a whole, in particular, why Paul switches from nations to individuals as types without explaining this. See Piper, *Justification of God*, 64.

14   Sanday and Headlam, *The Epistle to the Romans*, 245.

15   N. T. Wright, "The Letter to the Romans," in *Acts to First Corinthians*, NIB 10 (Nashville: Abingdon, 2002), 634.

16   Geisler, *Chosen but Free*, 82. Also see Sanday and Headlam, *The Epistle to the Romans*, 245, where they state, "the absolute election of Jacob . . . has reference simply to the

However, these conclusions are largely driven by theological pre-suppositions rather than a careful exposition of the text. Historically, this text has been maintained to teach predestination. Alford states,

> It is most true that the immediate subject is the national rejection of the Jews: but we must consent to hold our reason in abeyance if we do not recognize the inference that the sovereign power and free election here proved to belong to God extend to every exercise of his mercy . . . whether national or individual.[17]

Romans 9:6–13 sets a course for how to approach the subsequent discourse. It is interesting to trace the popularity of the corporate election view of Romans 9, particularly since it was not a position originated by Arminius.[18] Arminius believed Romans 9 was merely teaching conditional election (ultimately, a form of the prescient view). He states, "Ishmael and Isaac, Esau and Jacob, are to be considered not in themselves, but as types, in those passages which he cites. The other, that they are to be considered as types of 'the children of the flesh' and 'of the promise.' For the Apostle proves neither, but assumes both; and not without reason."[19] Furthermore he adds, "Isaac is reckoned in the seed: Isaac is the type of all the children of

---

election of one to a higher privileges as head of the chosen race, than the other. It has nothing to do with their eternal salvation."

17   Henry Alford, "Romans," in *The Greek Testament Critical Exegetical Commentary*, 5th ed. (London: Gilbert & Rivington, 1863), 2:408.

18   The corporate election view is presented by Sanday and Headlam, *The Epistle to the Romans*, 246–47. Piper's explanation is exceptional when he asks, "How else could Paul have argued from the OT for the principle of God's freedom in election, since the eternal salvation of the individual as Paul teaches it is almost never the subject of discussion in the OT? Therefore Paul's selection of texts may reflect the limited scope of his sources rather than a desire on his part to guard against the implication of predestination unto individual salvation." Piper, *Justification of God*, 64.

19   Jacobus Arminius, *The Works of James Arminius*, ed. W. R. Bagnall (1853; repr., Grand Rapids: Baker, 1977), 3:490. For a modern source which interacts with Romans 9 more thoroughly than Arminius did, and develops the classical Arminian view of conditional election, see chapter 5 of F. Leroy Forlines, *Classical Arminianism: A Theology of Salvation*, ed. J. Matthew Pinson (Nashville: Randall House, 2011).

the promise: Therefore all the children of the promise are reckoned in the seed."[20] Arminius also claims that whatever can be said of Isaac is true of Ishmael (and Jacob to Esau as well).[21] Therefore, he continues, "Ishmael is not reckoned in the seed: Ishmael is the type of all the children of the flesh: Therefore none of the children of the flesh are reckoned in the seed."[22] He asserts that election is based on God's foresight of faith.[23]

By the time of John Wesley, it was a popular to interpret Romans 9 as teaching national election. Wesley proposes the national election view when commenting on Romans 9:12–13, stating,

> It is undeniably plain, that both these scriptures relate, not to the persons of Jacob and Esau but to their descendants; the Israelites sprung from Jacob, and the Edomites sprung from Esau. In this sense only did "the elder" (Esau) "serve the younger"; not in his person (for Esau never served Jacob) but in his posterity. This posterity of the elder brother served the posterity of the younger.[24]

Despite these claims, Wesley makes no lexical, syntactical, or even logical arguments. His own words indicate a predetermined position when he states: "Whatever that Scripture proves, it can never prove this. Whatever its true meaning be, this cannot be its true meaning. . . . No Scripture can prove predestination."[25] He calls unconditional

---

20 Arminius, *Works*, 3:491.
21 Arminius, *Works*, 3:491.
22 Arminius, *Works*, 3:491.
23 Arminius, *Works*, 3:494. He even makes a distinction between what role works plays into election and reprobation. For election works play no role, only faith does, but for reprobation they are the decisive factor in God's choice to reject them from being children of promise. Arminius states, "[B]y the Apostle according to their own specialty—that the former [the children of the flesh] are 'of works,' but the latter [the children of the promise] of the faith by which obedience is rendered to the call of God." Arminius, *Works*, 3:493–94.
24 John Wesley, "Predestination Calmly Considered," in *The Works of the Rev. John Wesley: In Ten Volumes* (New York: Harper, 1827), 10:237. Hereafter *Works*.
25 Wesley, "Free Grace," in *Works*, 3:556.

predestination "a doctrine full of blasphemy . . . such as makes the ears of a Christian tingle . . . worse than the devil, as both more false, and more cruel and more unjust."[26]

The influence of corporate election on many modern commentators is not merely a product of Wesleyan theology, but also due to the theological influence of the neo-orthodox theologian Karl Barth.[27] The strongest arguments (for corporate election) from a theological standpoint originated with Barth.[28]

For Barth, predestination is identical with being elect in Jesus Christ. Predestination is when God chooses to be in loving relationship with humans through Jesus Christ. In Barth's scheme, Jesus Christ is the archetypical elect one, and everyone is either elect or reprobate based on their union with him. Barth redefined the discussion, saying, "It is grounded in the knowledge of Jesus Christ because He is both the electing God and elected man in One."[29] Karl Barth's deliberate attempt to reinterpret the Bible to make election less offensive has had a pervasive influence on commentators after his time.[30]

EVALUATING THE CORPORATE/NATIONAL ELECTION VIEW

Can the position of national or corporate election be defended from the text of Romans 9:13? A number of considerations show that

---

26 Wesley, "Free Grace," in *Works*, 3:554–55.

27 According to Barth Jesus is both elect and reprobate, and represents all humanity in both aspects. The neo-Orthodox tradition is a separate strand that is not within the scope of the book. Barth will be dealt with throughout the footnotes where it is appropriate.

28 B. L. McCormack, "Grace and Being: The Role of God's Gracious Election in Karl Barth's Theological Ontology," in *The Cambridge Companion to Karl Barth*, ed. J. Webster (Cambridge: Cambridge University Press, 2000), 92.

29 Barth, *The Doctrine of God*, vol. 2, pt. 2, *Church Dogmatics*, 3. For more on the influence and teaching of Barth on election and predestination, see Michael O'Neil, "Karl Barth's Doctrine of Election," *EvQ* 76, no. 4 (2004): 311–26.

30 Most scholars have recognized Barth's numerous "contributions" as reconfigurations. For example, with respect to reprobation, as O'Neil observes, "In accord with the Reformed tradition Barth posits a double predestination, albeit one which has been radically reconfigured. . . . [H]e rejects the absolute decree which divided humanity into those elect and those rejected, and insists, rather, in the primal decree God elected Himself for rejection, and in Jesus Christ bore that rejection in time, so that humanity could be elect in Him." O'Neil, "Karl Barth's Doctrine of Election," 316.

corporate election to the exclusion of individual election is unable to be well-supported. While the rejection of individual election in favor of corporate election is intended to harmonize God's discriminating choice with his love and kindness, it accomplishes no such thing.

Grammatical Considerations

The grammatical evidence for unconditional, individual election and reprobation in Romans 9 is abundant. Thomas Schreiner has demonstrated that Paul's use of the singular throughout Romans 9 requires an understanding of individual election and not national election.[31] Romans 9:15, in particular, emphasizes unconditional election of individuals. Paul uses the pronoun ὅν ("whom"), which is masculine singular. If Paul had intended to stress nations, he would have used the plural form.

Romans 9:16 uses two terms: θέλοντος ("desiring") and τρέχοντος ("running"), both masculine singular participles. Because these participles refer to the singular pronouns from the preceding verse, most translations have translated these as "the man who desires" and "the man who runs" rather than "those who desire" and "those who run."[32] It is difficult to see corporate or national implications in this text based on the grammar. Paul is stressing an individual's desires or works in relation to the choice of God.

Another use of the singular occurs in Romans 9:18: "So then He has mercy on whom He desires, and He hardens whom He desires." Paul once again uses masculine singular pronouns to describe the hardening of Pharaoh. If Paul intends to convey national election, this summary statement would change from the singular (Pharaoh) to the plural (nations). With Paul's use of the singular in Romans 9:18 and 9:19, he demonstrates the individual nature of these particular verses. The proximity of Romans 9:16 also employs singular pronouns, confirming that Paul's scope of thought has remained consistently focused on the individual.

---

31 Thomas R. Schreiner, "Does Romans 9 Teach Individual Election unto Salvation? Some Exegetical and Theological Reflection," *JETS* 36, no. 1 (1993): 25–40.

32 One translation that purposefully makes this text ambiguous is the ESV. It reads, "So then it depends not on *human* will or exertion."

Lexical Evidence

Paul has demonstrated the ability to distinguish between national entities and individual entities throughout the epistle. While it is true that Jacob and Esau can have national implications in Scripture, those nations nevertheless began as individuals. At the very least, those two were representatives of their progeny and their offspring were either in the covenant or outside the covenant based on God's choice of their parent, either Jacob or Esau.

Paul's decision to use Ἰακώβ ("Jacob") and not Ἰσραήλ ("Israel") in Romans 9:13 only stresses the fact that he intends to discuss individual election rather than national election. In Romans 9:6 it is evident that Paul is making a distinction between the individual entity and the elect within that national entity. He says, "For they are not all Israel who are descended from Israel." It would be illogical for Paul to be saying, "Not all national Israel is national Israel"; that is a contradiction. Rather, Paul is expressing the election of some individuals within Israel as opposed to the entire nation. Additionally, if Paul had intended to speak of national Israel when referring to Jacob, his readers would have hardly been able to follow his argument from 9:6.

Paul's choice of terms in each of his subsequent arguments makes it even more difficult to maintain national election. The apostle does not use Μωϋσῆς ("Moses"), Φαραώ ("Pharaoh"), πηλός ("clay"), φύραμα ("lump"), σκεῦος εἰς τιμὴν ("vessel of honor"), and σκεύη ὀργῆς ("vessels of wrath") to describe national entities. If he was doing so here, it would be the only time he does so. It would seem inconsistent for Paul to use Jacob and Esau in a corporate sense, when these other examples all refer to individuals.

The Immediate Context

The immediate context demonstrates that national election cannot be offered as a viable option. It ignores the context and problem raised in Romans 9:1–5. If Paul is discussing the problem that Israel has been rejecting Jesus, yet is simply saying that national Israel ("Jacob") is being saved, the dilemma seems to be nonexistent. As was previously mentioned, it is unreasonable to believe Paul is talking about national election in light of his argument in 9:6, that "not all Israel is Israel." The context following that passage, concerning Moses and Pharaoh and lumps of clay (9:14–23), simply will not fit with a national interpretation.

The Broader Context

The notion of national election cannot be reconciled with the broader context of Romans 9. It does little to explain Romans 9:6, because this would necessitate a nation within a nation. If Israel is included in chapter 9 as Jacob then the question arises, "Why would Paul say it again in chapter 11, but change the manner in which it is represented?"

The corporate election view undermines the lesser-to-the-greater argument. Paul is establishing that if God can save individuals in the midst of unbelieving national entities (Jew and Gentile) than surely he can save all of Israel (Rom. 11:26). Paul had just told the Roman Christians that nothing could separate them from the love of God (Rom. 8:31–39). However, the natural objection that is raised is presented in chapters 9–11, summarized as follows: "How do we (Roman Gentile Christians) know that these promises from God are secure, considering the current unbelief and judgment of Israel? They were given promises, yet individual Jews don't appear to be very secure." Referring to corporate election would be of no benefit to the natural question raised. Instead, by saying that it is only the elect individuals within Israel that are secure (true Israel), and that all elect individuals have always been secure, Paul adequately addressed the natural concern.

Paul returns to the theme of election in Romans 11. There he illustrates the elect individuals within the Israelite nation by referencing Elijah, who believed he was the only one still following the Lord. God's response to Elijah's lamentation is given in Romans 11:4: "I HAVE KEPT for Myself SEVEN THOUSAND MEN WHO HAVE NOT BOWED THE KNEE TO BAAL." This verse indicates that God preserved elect individuals within the nation, not merely nations as a whole. This characterization was intended to apply to individuals of Paul's current day. If Romans 9 were about national election, appealing to individuals in Romans 11 would be illogical.

Paul's Use of the Old Testament
An additional argument against the national election interpretation of Romans 9 is based on the hermeneutical principles Paul uses in his citation of Old Testament texts. Paul is very careful when he cites a text, so as not to distort the meaning of the precise words he quotes. The best example of this is Paul's use of Malachi 1:2, as found in Romans 9:13.[33] The controversial text reads, "Jacob I loved, but Esau I hated." In Malachi, the oracle switches from the singular and present in 1:1–3 to the plural and future in verses 4–5. Malachi 1:1–3 reads,

> The oracle of the word of the LORD to Israel through Malachi. "I have loved you," says the LORD. But you say, "How hast Thou loved us?" "Was not Esau Jacob's brother?" declares the LORD. "Yet I have loved Jacob; but I have hated Esau, and I have made his mountains a desolation, and appointed his inheritance for the jackals of the wilderness."

The switch to the plural and future is found in verses 4–5 which read,

> Though Edom says, "We have been beaten down, but we will return and build up the ruins"; thus says the LORD of hosts, "They may build, but I will tear down; and men will call them the wicked territory, and the people toward whom the LORD is indignant forever." And your eyes will see this and you will say, "The LORD be magnified beyond the border of Israel!"

Malachi's change from the singular and the present tense in verses 1–3 to the plural and future tense in verses 4–5 signifies the change

---

33   While one could also look at Paul's use of Genesis 25:23, this has been briefly touched on at this point. Paul, in similar fashion to his use of Malachi 1:2, he does not cite the portion which speaks of nations in Genesis 25:23; and this is because his argument is with respect to individuals, so citing the portion which spoke to nations would either require further explanation or it would require him to distort its meaning, neither of which Paul does here.

in scope from individuals (vv. 1–3) to nations addressed by God (v. 4). Paul is careful to only cite as his example the portion relating to the individuals and not the sections referring to nations. In fact, within the context of Malachi it is apparent that God intends to refer to Jacob and Esau as individuals because he is defending his love to a grumbling nation.

God's point in rebuking the questioning Israelites in Malachi 1:2 is to teach unmerited favor and unconditional election. God did not elect Israel based on foreseen merit, otherwise this would make God's choice prejudicial and biased. God rebukes Israel by pointing out that he appointed Esau and his descendants to destruction because he has the sovereign right to do so. Both the national view of election and the prescient view of election topple under these exegetical details.

CHAPTER 5

UNCONDITIONAL DOUBLE PREDESTINATION?

THE CASE FOR UNCONDITIONAL ELECTION AND REPROBATION FROM ROMANS 9:11–13

*R*omans 9:11–13 are only one sentence in the Greek, so they represent a solitary unit. This passage stresses the unconditional choice of God regardless of the actions of individuals. The absolute liberty of God is stressed in verse 11. The stage is set by describing the condition of the twins. The two participles in the verse, γεννηθέντων and πραξάντων ("having been born" and "having done," respectively), serve to indicate the inactivity of Jacob and Esau. Both of these participles are dependent on the clause in the very next verse: ἐρρέθη αὐτῇ ("it was said to her").[1] This stresses that the promise (and its intended recipient) was determined before the twins were born. It removes any potential preference given to one or the other based on birth order, inheritance, or hierarchy in the home as well as any works performed by either of them. These are not considerations in God's mind when he makes his electing choice.

In verse 11 the promise is said to be made before either twin had any mental or physical capability to earn God's favor; God's choice was

---

1   Cranfield, *Epistle to the Romans*, 2:477; Jewett, *Romans*, 578.

made before they did anything good or bad (ἀγαθὸν, φαῦλον). The two negatives (μήπω, μηδὲ) indicate that nothing the twins did served as conditions for their election in God's eternal plan. The divine choice to bless the younger Jacob and not the eldest Esau was made before they were born—a point which Paul makes in order to emphasize the freedom of God's will and the unconditionality of this choice.[2]

The final phrase of verse 11 uses a *hina* clause to give the purpose for God's discrimination: ἵνα ἡ κατ᾽ ἐκλογὴν πρόθεσις τοῦ θεοῦ μένῃ ("in order that God's elective purposes might continue"). The purpose clause, introduced with ἵνα, signals that Paul is about to provide the reason why God chose one brother over the other. A form of the phrase κατ᾽ ἐκλογὴν πρόθεσις ("the purpose of election") was previously used by Paul in Romans 8:28, κατὰ πρόθεσιν κλητοῖς ("the purpose of His calling"). Once again, the divine purpose is shown to be uninfluenced, unconditionally determining what will become of man. This further links the concept of salvation between Romans 8:28 and 9:11. John Piper summarizes the importance of these points when he states,

> So far then we may say that the prediction of Rom 9:12c ("the older will serve the younger") is an expression of God's predetermination of (at least some aspect of) the destinies of Jacob and Esau. Moreover this predetermination is not based on any actual or foreknown distinctives of the brothers. It is based solely on God who calls. . . . In short God's purpose is to be free from all human influences in the election he performs.[3]

The purpose (πρόθεσις) of God is a key theological concept for Paul. The "purpose" of God is meticulous; it overlooks nothing and is concerned with everything. God's Word does not fail, even when one is rejected and another selected. In fact, rejection and selection are the

---

2   James Denney, "Romans" in *The Expositor's Greek Testament*, ed. William Robertson Nicoll (Grand Rapids: Eerdmans, 1956), 2:661.

3   Piper, *Justification of God*, 53.

very establishments of his purposes. Jewett comments, "That 'God's selective purpose' should continue, that is, be carried through in the destinies of Jacob and Esau, directly answers the issue in v. 6."[4] Both are according to God's choice. Both are according to his plan. The use of μένη (the only occurrence in Romans) stresses God's immutability in the decision.[5] Linguist Fredrich Hauck explains,

> In the OT the abiding of God and things and persons relating to God is of religious and theological significance. As distinct from the mutability and transitoriness of everything earthly and human, God is characterized by the fact that he endures. . . . In the NT, too, μένειν is used 1. of the immutability of God and the things of God, e.g., His counsel, which cannot be changed, R. 9:11, His Word, which remains as compared with what is human and corruptible, 1 Pt. 1:23, 25.[6]

The use of the word καλοῦντος ("Him who calls") hearkens back to the internal call unto salvation demonstrated in Romans 8:29–30.[7] Once again, this could not be referring to anything non-salvific because Paul has salvation in mind and brings it up once again by using this word. Paul is stressing the distinction between divine election and human effort. While some Jews mistakenly believed that obedience to the Mosaic law was necessary to maintain election, Paul turns that idea on its head.[8] Likewise, this nullifies the Arminian doctrine of simple

---

4 Jewett, *Romans*, 578. Most commentators recognize the relationship between μένη in 9:11, "to remain/stand" and ἐκπέπτωκεν 9:6, "to fall/fail" form a contrast. See Cranfield, *Epistle to the Romans*, 2:478; Murray, *The Epistle to the Romans*, 2:14.

5 Murray, *The Epistle to the Romans*, 2:14–15, states, "In verse 11 he is asserting the security and immovability of the electing purpose in eloquent contrast to the supposition that the word of God could be invalidated."

6 Fredrich Hauck, "μένω," *TDNT*, 4:575.

7 Theologians often distinguish between the internal call and the external call. The external call cannot be in mind in Romans 8, and subsequently Romans 9, because in Romans 8 it says, "everyone who is called, is justified, everyone who is justified is sanctified, and everyone who is sanctified if glorified." All the called are glorified. The external call is rejectable while the internal call is not and always results in salvation. See Berkhof, *Systematic Theology*, 457–79.

8 Jewett, *Romans*, 579.

foreknowledge as a faithful interpretation of the basis of God's election. God cannot foresee a human choice (which is an action of the
mind) and then claim that his decision was not based on deeds. The
prescient view of election can no more stand up to biblical scrutiny
than the Jewish notion of divine favor.

Paul's point in 9:12 is not merely to speak of the predetermined
destinies of Jacob and Esau, since he already did this in verse 11
(since he already explained in verse 11 that God's choice preceded
their birth). Rather, Paul is stressing that God's choice was not based
upon their behavior, which is why Paul adds οὐκ ἐξ ἔργων ἀλλ' ἐκ τοῦ
καλοῦντος ("Not based on work but based on the one who calls").

Paul goes on to stress his point by citing another proof. This time
he cites Malachi 1:2–3: "'I have loved you,' says the LORD. But you
say, 'How have You loved us?' 'Was not Esau Jacob's brother?' declares
the LORD. 'Yet I have loved Jacob; but I have hated Esau, and I have
made his mountains a desolation and appointed his inheritance for
the jackals of the wilderness.'" Israel was grumbling and doubting
the love of God, and Paul points to the fact that Jacob was no better
than Esau. Yet, Jacob enjoyed God's blessing while Esau didn't. Jewett
recognizes this when he states, "While the original text in Malachi
referred to the nations of Israel and Edom, Paul's interest in this
context is strictly related to the selective quality of God's purpose."[9]

DOUBLE PREDESTINATION IN ROMANS 9:13

In light of the fact that this portion of Scripture has been used
to teach double predestination, many commentators have attempted
to water down the harshness of Paul's citation of Malachi.[10] If the
concept of predestination is deemed offensive by many, the issue of

---

9   Jewett, *Romans*, 580.
10 For example, Dunn writes, "Some form of double predestination can of course be
    deduced from this Malachi passage, as Paul is aware (vv. 18–23), but the thrust of the
    context of the argument needs to be borne in mind. (1) The idea of divine rejection
    arises only as a corollary to the principal claim; it is the assumed or logical converse
    of Israel's sense of election." Dunn, *Romans 9–16*, 545. Schreiner, on the other hand,
    succinctly writes, "Does the text suggest double predestination? Apparently it does."
    Schreiner, *Romans*, 501.

God's hatred is even more offensive. This has led many commentators to interpret "hatred" in many different ways. Leon Morris proposes that "hate" should be understood as "love less."[11] Others have claimed it is merely "ancient Near Eastern hyperbole" and should not be taken as "hatred."[12] Others have claimed that the terms, "love" and "hate" are of little importance because the text is merely, in a Semitic way, expressing God's choice.[13] Some are more vocal in their rejection of predestination in this text. N. T. Wright suggests, "Interpreters have brought to Paul rather than letting him dictate his own terms. Chapter 9 has long been seen as the central NT passage on 'predestination' . . . the theological tradition from Augustine to Calvin (and beyond) did not grasp what Paul was actually thinking about here."[14]

Of those who propose that this text does not teach predestination, many give no warrant for their perspective. For example,

---

11 Morris, *The Epistle to the Romans*, 375. Morris cites that Calvin used the word "reject" when talking about the matter, but it should be observed that Calvin did not specifically say that "hatred" means "rejection." Rather, Calvin was talking about the quote as a proof for God's election and rejection. See Calvin, *The Epistle to the Romans*, 19:352.

12 Furthermore, Fitzmyer explains his position: "The divine choice raises the question of choice, or theodicy. But Paul uses the quotation to stress Israel's role in the salvific plan in contrast to Edom's. Jacob and Esau are the representatives of their ethnic groups." Fitzmyer, *Romans*, 563.

13 Brendan Byrne Jr., *Romans*, Sacra Pagina, ed. Danial J. Harrington (Collegeville, MN: Liturgical Press, 1996), 295; Moo, *The Epistle to the Romans*, 587; Fitzmyer, *Romans*, 563; Kruse, *Paul's Letter to the Romans*, 380.

14 Wright, "Romans," 620. Wright has famously criticized the history of doctrines on many issues claiming that generations of believer have improperly understood Romans. Such examples include his understanding of Second Temple Judaism, his denial of Active Obedience, and his rejection of Imputed Righteousness. See D. A. Carson, Peter T. O'Brien, and Mark A. Seifrid, *Justification and Variegated Nomism*, vol. 1, *The Complexities of Second Temple Judaism* (Grand Rapids: Baker Academic, 2001); Donald A. Hagner, "Paul and Judaism: Testing the New Perspective," in *Revisiting Paul's Doctrine of Justification: A Challenge to the New Perspective*, ed. Peter Stuhlmacher (Downers Grove, IL: InterVarsity Press, 2001); Seyoon Kim, *Paul and the New Perspective: Second Thoughts on the Origin of Paul's Gospel* (Grand Rapids: Zondervan, 2001); Philip H. Eveson, *The Great Exchange: Justification by Faith Alone in the Light of Recent Thought* (Leominster, UK: One Day, 1996); John W. Robbins, *A Companion to the Current Justification Controversy* (Unicoi, TN: Trinity Foundation, 2003); J. V. Fesko, "Justification and Union with Christ," in *Justification: Understanding the Classic Reformed Doctrine* (Phillipsburg, NJ: P&R, 2008), 264–80; most importantly, see John Piper, *The Future of Justification: A Response to N. T. Wright* (Wheaton, IL: Crossway, 2007).

as Mounce suggests, "Paul was not building a case for salvation that in no way involves the consent of the individual. Nor was he teaching double predestination. Rather he was arguing that the exclusion of so many Jews from the family of God did not constitute a failure on God's part to maintain his covenant relationship with Israel."[15]

Yet Mounce seems to misunderstand compatibilism in the Reformed scheme of salvation (since no Reformed theologian has claimed that God removes human volition). He interprets the text to say, "This is merely about God's covenant faithfulness," which in no way aligns with the straightforward reading of the text.

There are others who offer yet another explanation, such as Geisler, who states,

> The Hebrew word for "hatred" really means "loved less." . . . So even one of the strongest verses used by extreme Calvinists does not prove that God hates the non-elect or even that He does not love them. It simply means that God's love for those who receive salvation looks so much greater than his love for those who reject it that the later looks like hatred by comparison. A couple of illustrations make the point. The same loving stroke that makes a kitten purr seems like hatred if she turns the opposite direction and finds her fur being rubbed the wrong way.[16]

---

15   Mounce, *Romans*, 199. For a convincing counter-argument to Mounce's sweeping statement, see Murray: "In accord to what we have found . . . respecting biblical usage it must be interpreted as hate with the positive character which usage indicates, a hate as determinative as the unfailing purpose in terms of which the discrimination between Jacob and Esau took place. In view of what Paul teaches elsewhere respecting the ultimacy of the counsel of God's will, it would not be proper to say that the ultimate destines of Jacob and Esau were outside his purview." Murray, *The Epistle to the Romans*, 23. His case is built between pages 20–23.

16   Geisler, *Chosen but Free*, 83. James White gives an excellent response to this explanation when he states, "With all due respect to Dr. Geisler, this is a 'non-response' that does not focus upon the text at all. There is no exegesis with which to interact." James White, *The Potter's Freedom* (Amityville, NY: Calvary Press, 2000), 217.

In attempting to refute those whom he labels as "extreme Calvinists," Geisler offers two reasons why he rejects the most natural understanding of the word "hate." Only one of his two explanations should be needed to refute the Calvinist position, if such an explanation is indeed accurate.

But these explanations are ultimately unconvincing. The Hebrew word translated "hate" in Malachi 1:3 is שָׂנֵא. Concerning this verb, "The verb *sane'* and its derivatives have the root meaning 'to hate.' It expresses an attitude toward persons and things which are opposed, detested, despised and with which one wishes to have no contact or relationship. It is therefore the opposite of love."[17] Other linguists note,

> The gamut of feelings of dislike are included in the scope of *śn'*; it may express the most intense hatred of the enemies of God (Ps 139:21–22), or that of a violent enemy (25:19). . . . Love (Heb. *'lo*) is the opposite of hate; the two words are found in contrast. . . . When the prophet Malachi says, "I have loved Jacob, but Esau I have hated" (Mal 1:2–3), he is emphasizing the sovereign choice of God; nevertheless, the rejection of Esau leads further to their judgment.[18]

---

17 Gerard Van Groningen, "שָׂנֵא," *Theological Wordbook of the Old Testament,* eds. R. Laird Harris, Gleason L. Archer, and Bruce K. Waltke (Chicago: Moody, 2004), 2:880. Groningen adds a helpful distinction to God's hatred which reflects the thoughts of Johannes Maccovius (mentioned in Appendix One) who distinguished two kinds of hatred in reprobation. Gerard states, "[A]n interesting usage of the word "hate" is found in Rom 9:13 which quotes from Gen 25:13 and Mal 1:2–3. Some have concluded that Paul grounds the reprobation of Esau on a divine decree in which God hated Esau before he was born. It may be helpful to offer an alternative suggestion. The statement in Rom 9:11 that God's choice of Jacob was apart from works may be completely satisfied by the quotation from Gen 25:23 which indeed was spoken before the twins were born. It does not necessarily follow that Esau was hated before he was born. This statement is quoted from Mal 1:3 which was written long after Esau had lived his predominantly secular life. Though the doctrine of election by God's grace alone is widely held, the condemnation of the lost is most widely held to be on account of their own sin" (880). Gerard recognizes a tension which the categories of Maccovinus would be helpful in solving. Maccovinus suggested that there are two kinds of hatred: aA negative, where God does not love someone (He actively withholds love); and a positive, where he peruses and punishes the wicked on account of sin.

18 A. H. Konkel, "שָׂנֵא," *New International Dictionary of Old Testament Theology and Exegesis,* ed. William VanGemeren (Grand Rapids: Zondervan, 1997), 3:1257. Konkel

This has not stopped many from believing that Esau was still within the saving purposes of God. Commenting on Romans 9:13, Cranfield writes,

> We must not read into Paul's argument any suggestion that Ishmael, because he is not chosen to play a positive part in the accomplishment of God's special purpose, is therefore excluded from the embrace of God's mercy . . . it must be stressed that, as in the case of Ishmael, so also with Esau, the rejection is still, according to the testimony of Scripture, an object of God's merciful care.[19]

Schreiner points out (regarding Cranfield's conclusions), "This is an unwarranted reading of the Romans account, for the very purpose of Paul's argument is to explain why some ethnic Israelites are not part of the saved people of God."[20] The fact of the matter is that the word "hate" is offensive to most commentators. As a result many see a need to mitigate against a literal understanding of the text.

A historical-grammatical hermeneutic, applied to Paul's statement in Romans 9:13, leads to the inevitable conclusion that "hate" is not merely "lesser love." An examination of the context of Malachi, from which Paul cites without violating Malachi's authorial intent, makes it incontestable what "hate" means. The full text of Malachi 1:3 reads, "I have hated Esau, and I have made his mountains a desolation and appointed his inheritance for the jackals of the wilderness." It would be hard to imagine this language to mean "love less." Malachi 1:4 con-

---

discusses the use of the term in the other ANE languages and how in Ugaritic there are times when it is used in the context of marriage where one wife is preferred over another, however, that context does not apply here.

19 Cranfield, *Epistle to the Romans*, 2:475, 480. It is also worth mentioning, as was noted earlier, the influence of Neo-Orthodoxy on modern commentators concerning national election and reprobation. Cranfield cites Barth for his proof on the matter (480n2).

20 Schreiner, *Romans*, 497. Furthermore, he states, "Cranfield's understanding of this section is flawed because he posits that there are two different forms of election here, so that no ethnic Israelites are outside the circle of God's electing mercy. This contradicts the exclusionary principle that informs all of Rom. 9:6b–13."

tinues with these words, "Though Edom says, 'We have been beaten down, but we will return and build up the ruins'; thus says the LORD of hosts, 'They may build, but I will tear down; and men will call them the wicked territory, and the people toward whom the LORD is indignant forever.'" God's hatred here does not represent a personal vendetta, but rather his judicial disposition resulting from his decree to condemn.

SUMMARY REMARKS

What can we glean about reprobation from Romans 9:6–13? First, God's choice in the matter of reprobation is eternal. Reprobation is a pretemporal decision on God's part; a discrimination between Jacob and Esau made by God before they were ever born. Romans 9:11 ("though the twins were not yet born") establishes the timing of God's decree for them as being eternal. Second, this expresses the unconditional nature of God's choice in reprobation. Romans 9:11 says God's choice was made before they had "done anything good or bad." This removes the concept of prescient foreknowledge from having any bearing on God's decree of reprobation. The text explicitly states that God's choice was made without consideration of their deeds. Finally, regarding reprobation, the text expresses God's attitude toward the non-elect. This is one of the more offensive elements of reprobation, for Romans 9:13 says, "Esau I hated."

There can be little confusion within the broader text that the expression of God's hatred is in view. The term translated as "indignant" is the Hebrew word זָעַם. "The basic idea is experiencing or expressing intense anger. It would be difficult from the context and lexical meaning of the words employed in Malachi to understand "hate" to mean "love less." There are numerous other passages in the Old Testament which employ the terminology of God's hatred toward persons (Ps. 5:5; 11:5; Prov. 6:16; 8:13; Isa. 1:14; 61:8; Jer. 44:4; Hos. 9:15; Amos 5:21; Zech. 8:17; Mal. 2:16) and in none of them would it be appropriate to imply that God's indignation is passive or merely the denial of blessing.

Based on this, we can deduce that reprobation contains an active attitude of God's judgment toward those whom he righteously hates.

It is important, however, not to impose upon God's hatred the negative elements of sinful men. Murray says, "We must not predicate of this divine hate those unworthy features which belong to hate as it is exercised by us as sinful men . . . we must, therefore, recognize that there is in God a holy hate that cannot be defined in terms of not loving or loving less."[21]

Dunn sees the conclusion of this text pointing toward double predestination and worries it will lead to pride.[22] However, this is precisely the concern Paul addresses in Romans 11:17–24: "But if some of the branches were broken off, and you, being a wild olive, were grafted in among them and became partaker with them of the rich root of the olive tree, do not be arrogant toward the branches; but if you are arrogant, remember that it is not you who supports the root, but the root supports you" (vv. 17–18).

It is essential to observe that Paul addresses the issue of boasting next, because it is a natural concern when the doctrine of predestination is only partially understood.

Further, since this text teaches both election and reprobation, Schreiner reminds interpreters of the need to retain a commitment to compatibilism and human responsibility. He states,

> We need to remember that in the Pauline view predestination never lessened human responsibility (cf. Rom. 1:18–3:20; 9:30–10:21), and the correlation between divine sovereignty and human responsibility is ultimately a mystery that is beyond our finite comprehension. We dare not conclude that human decisions are a charade, insignificant, or trivial. But we must also beware of a rationalizing expedient that domesticates the text by exalting human freedom so that it fits neatly into our preconceptions.[23]

---

21   Murray, *The Epistle to the Romans*, 22; see also Schreiner, *Romans*, 6:500.
22   Dunn, *Romans 9–16*, 545.
23   Schreiner, *Romans*, 501.

Since this text gives no indication as to the means God uses to execute his decree of reprobation, it is important not to insert any into the text, nor to assume, as some do, that reprobation means God is the author of sin or that man's responsibility is undermined. These are unnecessary and unwarranted by the text. But it is possible to glean from the exegetical insights that reprobation is an eternal decree, unconditional in nature, and involves God's active choice and attitude in the matter.

Another critical point to recognize in this text is that Paul presents God's choice as timeless. Paul explains how God's choice, in election and reprobation was made before Jacob and Esau were born, but Ephesians 1:4 indicates that the timing of election and reprobation was even before time began: "He chose us in Him before the foundation of the world." There is no distinction concerning the timing of God's choice between Jacob and Esau, so it can be concluded that God's choice for both individuals was at the same period, before time began.

Paul also further elaborates on the unconditionality of God's choice in the context of Ephesians 1, just as he does in Romans 9. In Ephesians 1:5 he says, "He predestined us to adoption as sons through Jesus Christ to Himself, according to the kind intention of His will." The basis for God's decision was "the kind intention of His will." When it comes predestination in Pauline literature, the basis is always the unconditional will of God—and so it is in Romans.

CHAPTER 6

A DEFENSE OF METICULOUS SOVEREIGNTY

With the outstanding example of Jacob and Esau, Paul assumes his audience will find his argument unnerving. To further establish God's electing sovereignty, Paul elaborates, presenting a defense of God's meticulous sovereignty. The apostle Paul continues in Romans 9:14–18 by writing,

> What should we say then? Is there injustice with God? May it never be! For He says to Moses, "I will have mercy on whomever I will have mercy, and I will have compassion on whomever I will have compassion." So then it is not a matter of him who wills or of him who runs, but of God who shows mercy. For the Scriptures say to Pharaoh, "For this purpose I raised you up, so that I might demonstrate My power in you. And so that My name would be proclaimed throughout all the earth." So then, He has mercy on whomever He wills, and He hardens whomever He wills.[1]

---

1   Translation mine.

EXEGESIS OF ROMANS 9:14–18

Paul brings an imaginary objector into the discussion as a rhetorical device to promote his reasoning. God's claim that he loves one individual while hating the other, not on the basis of anything but his own good pleasure (cf. Eph. 1:5), is a cause for objection in the mind of the average hearer. Paul anticipates this objection by introducing two questions. The first, ("What then shall we say?"), is a rhetorical question indicating that someone may have come to the wrong conclusion based on Paul's previous remarks.[2] Paul's next question is straightforward: ("Is there unrighteousness with God?" or, simply put, "Is God unjust?"). This question refers to the entirety of Paul's answer to the dilemma raised in 9:6, regarding Israel's unbelief and why so many have rejected the Messiah. His answer was given in a series of responses exposing the doctrine of God's unconditional election of individuals in spite of their natural heritage or their behavior. Furthermore, Paul's use of Malachi 1:2, "Jacob I loved and Esau I hated," naturally provokes a strong response.

Paul uses the term ἀδικία ("injustice" or "unrighteousness")[3] to set forth the question in reference to the fairness of God's choice.[4] His response is the emphatic μὴ γένοιτο ("God forbid!"). This phrase is emotionally charged and reflects the contempt Paul feels for even asking such a question. Murray describes it this way: "The thought of injustice with God is so intolerable that it must be dismissed with abrupt and decisive denial."[5]

PAUL'S USE OF EXODUS 33:19 IN ROMANS 9:15

This verse then sets the stage for Paul's explanation, which runs through verse 18. In verse 19 Paul's next objection is raised, making

---

2   Cranfield has noted that this is a similar word play Paul uses throughout Romans (3:5; 4:1; 6:1; 7:7; 8:31; and 9:30), but the only exact wording is found here. Cranfield, *Epistle to the Romans*, 2:481.

3   "ἀδικία," J. P. Louw and Eugene A. Nida, *Greek-English Lexicon of the New Testament: Based on Semantic Domains* (New York: United Bible Societies, 1989), 2:4.

4   Jewett, *Romans*, 581. Fitzmyer states, "Again a diatribic objection is entertained. God might seem to be involved in *adikia*, 'injustice,' in choosing one brother over the other." Fitzmyer, *Romans*, 566.

5   Murray, *The Epistle to the Romans*, 2:25.

verses 14–18 one continuous thought. In verse 15 Paul cites Exodus 33:19. By placing emphasis on Moses here, Paul is appealing to the Jewish understanding of the righteousness of Moses as the administrator of the Law, thereby appealing to their trust in him regarding holiness. Paul stresses the absolute freedom of God to show mercy on whomever he wishes; it is not contingent on anything in human beings. Commentators have recognized that this is not merely talking about God's will in the matter of salvation but rather his freedom to show mercy on whomever he chooses.[6]

The term used for "having compassion" is οἰκτίρω, used as a verb only here in the NT.[7] The companion term Paul uses with οἰκτίρω is ἐλεέω ("mercy"). The fact that "mercy" is only used by Paul in reference to salvation is of great importance and should be understood this way in this context. God's uninfluenced mercy not only places his free choice in the realm of predestination, but it removes any notion that "election" in Romans 9 could refer to an exalted position of a nation. Because of this, many commentators who take a national election view of Romans 9:10 have been forced to at least recognize the unconditional nature of election.

THE INABILITY OF HUMANS AND THE LIBERTY OF GOD (9:16)
Verse 16 is Paul's conclusion to the implications of the text he just cited to prove unconditional election. Paul further elaborates on the nature of God's freedom to dispense mercy. Paul's citation of Exodus followed by his explanation amplifies the freedom of God in salvation. He gives two proofs of human inability to influence God's decision in predestination, followed by an ultimate conclusion. The phrase reads, "Not on the man who wills or the man who runs, but on God who has mercy." This phrase removes the idea of anything within humans influencing God's decision.

Three key words help to explain the text in more detail: θέλοντος ("willing"), τρέχοντος ("running"), and ἐλεῶντος ("mercying").

---

6 Cranfield, *Epistle to the Romans*, 2:438.
7 "In the NT the verb οἰκτίρειν occurs only at R. 9:15 in a quotation from Ex. 33:19, and, as in the original, it stands parallel to ἐλεεῖν." Rudolf Bultmann, "οἰκτίρω, οἰκτιρμός, οἰκτίρμων," *TDNT* 5:161.

The series of negatives οὐ ("not"), οὐδὲ ("or"), ἀλλὰ ("but") sets the first two phrases in contrast with the third. The phrase "not of the man who wills" has great theological importance in this text. The Arminian position asserts that God's predestination is predicated on his foresight of human belief or unbelief. Arminius explains, "Eternal life was prepared for all men, on condition of that obedience which they could render. Therefore, eternal life could not be denied to some men, by the sure and definite decree of God, that is, by preterition, except on account of their foreseen disobedience."[8] Will is a necessary requirement of faith. On the other hand, the Reformed position affirms that God regenerates the heart and will, which precedes and produces faith.[9] We cannot exercise faith

---

8   Arminius, *Works*, 3:199.
9   "The Reformed view . . . teaches that before a person can choose Christ . . . he must be born again . . . one does not first believe and then become reborn. . . . A cardinal doctrine of Reformed theology is the maxim, "Regeneration precedes faith." R. C. Sproul, *Chosen by God* (Wheaton, IL: Tyndale House, 1986), 10, 72. "A man is not regenerated because he has first believed in Christ, but he believes in Christ because has been regenerated." Arthur W. Pink, *The Sovereignty of God* (1930; repr., Grand Rapids: Baker Books, 1984), 55. "Regeneration logically must initiate faith." John MacArthur, *The Gospel According to the Apostles* (Nashville: Thomas Nelson, 2000), 62. "When Christ called to Lazarus to come out of the grave, Lazarus had no life in him so that he could hear, sit up, and emerge. There was not a flicker of life in him. If he was to be able to hear Jesus calling him and to go to Him, then Jesus would have to make him alive. Jesus resurrected him and then Lazarus could respond. [Similarly,] the unsaved, the unregenerate, is spiritually dead (Eph. 2). He is unable to ask for help unless God changes his heart of stone into a heart of flesh, and makes him alive spiritually (Eph. 2:5). Then, once he is born again, he can for the first time turn to Jesus, expressing sorrow for his sins and asking Jesus to save him." Edwin H. Palmer, *The Five Points of Calvinism* (Grand Rapids: Baker, 1972), 18–19. "Abraham Kuyper observed that, prior to regeneration, a sinner 'has all the passive properties belonging to a corpse. . . . [Therefore] every effort to claim for the sinner the minutest co-operation in this first grace destroys the gospel, severs the artery of the Christian confession and is anti-scriptural in the highest degree.' Like a spiritual corpse, he is unable to make a single move toward God, think a right thought about God, or even respond to God—unless God first brings this spiritually dead corpse to life." James Montgomery Boice and Philip Graham Ryken, *The Doctrines of Grace: Rediscovering the Evangelical Gospel* (Wheaton, IL: Crossway, 2002), 74.
          Even Arminian theologians recognize this is taught by Reformed theologians, "Calvinists put the new birth before faith, since they believe that spiritually dead humans cannot exercise faith and, therefore, need to be born again before they can believe." C. Gordon Olson, *Beyond Calvinism and Arminianism: An Inductive, Mediate Theology of Salvation* (Springfield, MO: Global Gospel, 2012), 39.

without the will to yield it. Arminius believed the exact opposite of what Paul states here.

A sharp dichotomy is drawn between the human will in verse 16 and the divine will in verse 18. God's will is determinative, causative, and supreme over human will. Because human will is dead in sin, it cannot be the determinative agent in eternal salvation. The human will is incapable of choosing God, so it is left to God to choose us.

Not only is human salvation not based on human will, but it is not based on human effort. Paul describes this using the substantival participial phrase τοῦ τρέχοντος ("him who runs"). This is a term for human effort and using the analogy of a runner it is expressed as, "The negative point is that things do not depend on the man who puts forth all the power of his will in an ultimately autonomous attempt to win salvation. Hence they do not depend on the one who accomplishes such brilliant and yet superfluous achievements as the runner in the arena."[10] The determiner of salvation is not found in humans, but in God.

THE HARDENING OF PHARAOH (9:17)

Paul turns to another supporting text in verse 17 to further illustrate his point about God's absolute sovereignty. Paul cites Exodus 9:16: "But, indeed, for this reason I have allowed you to remain, in order to show you My power and in order to proclaim My name through all the earth."

In Exodus God confronts Pharaoh after the sixth plague. Rather than obliterating Pharaoh, God allowed his existence and continued disobedience for a specific purpose. It was God's plan all along. Paul's textual change captures the context of Exodus 9:16 and stresses God's active choice in the matter.

Paul uses the account to highlight God's power over Pharaoh. Pharaoh's disobedience did not catch God by surprise, nor was it weighing on his patience. It was all according to God's sovereign power. John Murray affirms this when he states, "The adamant

---

10   Otto Bauernfeind, "τρέχω, δρόμος, πρόδρομος," *TDNT* 8:232.

opposition of Pharaoh became the occasion for the display of God's great power in the plagues visited upon Egypt and particularly in the destruction of Pharaoh's hosts in the Red Sea and the passage of Israel as on dry land."[11] Paul could have chosen any of the instances prior to the sixth plague in which God confronts Pharaoh. However, this demonstrates that it was always God's plan to display his power over Pharaoh, even to the bitter end.

Like Romans 9:13, this text shows that God's plan does not merely include the elect or the blessings of salvation. There is no indication here that anything good was ordained for Pharaoh. Rather, the context from which Paul is citing (Exod. 9:16) says just the opposite. God ordained that Pharaoh would undergo all the plagues and not grant him repentance beforehand (cf. Exod. 4:21–23). This parallels verse 15, where God explains he has the liberty to withhold mercy in order to demonstrate his power.

THE FREEDOM OF GOD TO HARDEN (9:18)

In verse 18, Paul naturally draws these comments into a concluding summary, "So then He has mercy on whom He desires, and He hardens whom He desires." Here, Paul's repetition of the phrase θέλει ("He wills") is significant to show that there is no distinction in God's choice to have mercy or to harden. By the same faculty of will by which God shows mercy in election, he hardens in reprobation. It is important to also emphasize that θέλει, in both instances of having mercy and hardening, is in the active voice. When God wills either the elect to mercy or the reprobate to hardening it is an active will.

God's active choice regarding the hardening of the reprobate is of great importance in regard to predestination. Because of the paramount nature of this text, commentators found on extreme ends of the spectrum. Dodd goes so far as to say that Paul makes a "false step" and even questions the ethical nature of Paul's presentation of God.[12] Some commentators merely gloss over the hardening element of this

11   Murray, *The Epistle to the Romans*, 2:28.
12   Dodd, *The Epistle of Paul to the Romans*, 157–58.

text.[13] Many others present an apology or explanation that seeks to remove the roughness of Paul's expressions here. Or, commentators offer qualifications after rightly recognizing what Paul is saying. James Dunn says,

> In drawing this conclusion from Exod 9:16 Paul shows very clearly that he is conscious of its context, since the word ("harden") is particularly prominent in this section. . . . Paul for his part clearly has in view the divine initiative. So to look for reasons for God's hardening in Pharaoh's "evil disposition" or previous self-hardening is a rationalizing expediency.[14]

However, Dunn himself makes unnecessary qualifications to try and explain away eternal reprobation.[15]

Cranfield is another example of a commentator who recognizes the unconditional nature of God's choice but attempts to condition its implications.[16] Like others, he attempts to qualify the teaching of the text when he states, "The assumption that Paul is here thinking of the ultimate destiny of the individual, of his final salvation or final ruin, is not justified by the text. The words εἰς ἀπώλειαν are indeed

---

13 Jewett, *Romans*, 585. He claims, "Well-meaning theologians have expended far more ink in dealing with the hardening side of this antithesis, even though that was widely accepted throughout biblical literature." This is not only incorrect, but irresponsible of a serious commentator to merely gloss over half of an entire text, especially one of such paramount importance, and only deal with the parts of it that are more palatable to sensitive ears.

14 Dunn, *Romans 9–16*, 554–55.

15 Dunn, *Romans 9–16*, 555.

16 Cranfield, *Epistle to the Romans*, 2:488. Cranfield proves he does not understand Reformed compatibilism or unequal ultimacy double predestination when he states, "We are not free to understand it in the sense in which it has very often been understood, namely, of an altogether unqualified, indeterminate, absolute will, which moves nor in one direction, not in another, capriciously." There is nothing capricious about Reformed predestination, which he later villainizes in his unwarranted critique of Calvin. Furthermore he states, "Both the ἐλεεῖ and σκληρύνει, though so different in their effects, are expressions of the same merciful will." It is hard to justify such a conclusion because there is nothing merciful about God's judicial hardening.

used in v. 22; but we have no right to read them back into v. 18."[17] The nature of divine hardening is thoroughly discussed in chapter 13. However, it is important to note that apart from the conjunctions, the two relative clauses that comprise Romans 9:18 are grammatically identical (ὃν θέλει ἐλεεῖ; ὃν θέλει σκληρύνει).

The language indicates that the understanding of God's role in "mercy" is the same as his role in the "hardening." Since this text does not indicate a means by which God dispenses both, but only his will, this must be speaking of God's decision in the matter, not how he brings that decision to pass. A level of symmetry in God's sovereign decision is demanded by the text. Murray states, "The hardening, it should be remembered, is of a judicial character. It presupposes ill-desert and, in the case of Pharaoh, particularly the ill-desert of his self-hardening."[18] There is no warrant to discuss means of hardening at this point; it is not Paul's main issue here.

Primarily, Paul is speaking of God's freedom to unconditionally decide the destiny of the elect and the reprobate. The context of Paul's entire argument needs to be kept in mind. In Romans 9:11, Paul already established the basis for his discrimination among men when he gave the example of Jacob and Esau: "not on the basis of birth or deed good or bad" but (based on the ὅπως purpose clauses) "in order that" Pharaoh might display God's power (9:17). If Paul had intended to locate the basis for God's decision to harden Pharaoh in something negative Pharaoh had done, all of Paul's surrounding arguments would be for nothing. Rather, Paul establishes God's choice in the matter of election and reprobation in his purpose alone, therefore unconditional in respect to man.

---

17 Cranfield, *Epistle to the Romans*, 2:489. Cranfield is correct that as a principle of hermeneutics one cannot read one text into another text, in a manner which violates the original text. However, his conclusion that it is out of the context to discuss eternal destiny in this text is unsustainable, because the entire context about salvation. In fact, to conclude that Paul is not talking about eternal destinies here ignores those key elements of the context leading up to Romans 9:18 and following it.

18 Murray, *The Epistle to the Romans*, 2:29. Piper explains, "Not once in Ex 4–14 is the assertion of God's hardening of Pharaoh *grounded* in any attitude or act of Pharaoh. Instead, again and again the reason given for the hardening is God's *purpose* to demonstrate His power and magnify His name." Piper, *Justification of God*, 174.

SUMMARY REMARKS

While it is true that in some respects God judicially hardens based on sin (Rom. 1:22–32), here Paul's emphasis is on God's choice made apart from anything in man. God's decision to have mercy or harden is parallel to his decision to love or hate, as Paul previously outlined (9:13). In neither instance is there a cause given apart from God's sheer liberty. John Calvin explains this precisely when he says,

> Paul, as we have already reminded you, speaks these things in his own person, namely, that God, according to His own will, favors with mercy them whom He pleases, and unsheathes the severity of His judgment against whomsoever it seemeth Him good. That our mind may be satisfied with the difference which exists between the elect and the reprobate, and may not inquire for any cause higher than the divine will.[19]

From the text, it is unwarranted to conclude that God was merely reacting to Pharaoh.[20] If God were merely sealing people in a situation that had no origin in him, who would object to God's fairness? God's judgment would simply be their merited recompense. However, because the question of fairness with God is raised by the objector it must be maintained that God's eternal choice is made independent of temporal human actions.

---

19   Calvin, *The Epistle to the Romans*, 19:361.
20   Dunn, *Romans 9–16*, 555; Fitzmyer, *Romans*, 568; Jewett, *Romans*, 590. Whether the objection raised is from an opponent or a friendly exchange is of no consequence because this opponent is not real. What matters is that this objection is brought about in light of Paul's previous conclusions regarding God's sovereignty in 9:18. Jewett recognizes when he states, "The sharply formulated conclusion of the preceding verse, in fact, was intended to provoke these questions and thus to move Paul's argument forward" (Jewett, *Romans*, 590). Calvin states, "[T]he word hardens, when applied to God in Scripture, means not only permission, (as some washy moderators would have it,) but also the operation of the wrath of God." Calvin, *The Epistle to the Romans*, 19:362. Compare Morris, *The Epistle to the Romans*, 361, who states, "Neither here no anywhere else is God said to harden anyone who has not first hardened himself."

CHAPTER 7

THE PLAN OF GOD

*P*aul elicits a negative response from his audience when he explains the reason some believe and some reject the gospel (9:1–5) is because of God's sovereign choice (9:6–13). One would anticipate after their first response Paul would be quickly offering qualifying remarks or back peddling so as to not offend his audience. Instead, he gives even more examples of God's sovereignty over the mightiest leaders (Moses and Pharaoh, 9:14–18). Paul doubles down on his claims in Romans 9:19–23:

> You will then say to me, "Why does He still find fault? For who has resisted His will?" On the contrary, who are you, O man, who talks back to God? What is molded does not say to the Molder, "Why have you made me like this?" Or does the potter have no power over the clay, to make from the same lump one vessel for honor and the other for dishonor? If God is willing to demonstrate His wrath and make His power known, He endures with great patience vessels of wrath prepared for destruction. In order that He might make known the richness of His glory upon the vessels of mercy, which He prepared beforehand for glory.[1]

---

1 Translation mine.

EXEGESIS OF ROMANS 9:19–23

The next section of Paul's argument concerning God's sovereignty is, like the previous sections, introduced by an objection. Verse 19, then, is the introduction to the response Paul gives in 9:20–23. Its purpose is to help move Paul's argument forward. This objector plays the role of a skeptic and asks two questions, with the second being a further extrapolation of the first. The first question contains a direct personal address to Paul, which intensifies the question raised and makes it more personal.

These questions follow Paul's comments based on the Exodus account, in particular regarding Pharaoh (based on the conjunction οὖν, "then"). The first question is, "Why does He still find fault?" Once again, God's justice is brought into question. This follows the same question raised in 9:14, "There is no injustice with God, is there?" This continues developing the theme of God's selectivity, to love or hate, to have mercy or harden. It begs the question, Is this right? Is this fair? How can God fault Pharaoh if Pharaoh had no choice in the matter?

The term used for "fault" is μέμφεται, occurring only twice in the New Testament (here and in Hebrews 8:8). Greek scholar Walter Grundmann, in explaining this term, states,

> History is brought to pass by God, and it serves His purpose, namely, the demonstration of His power and the declaration of His name throughout the world. Both His mercy and His hardening serve this end. . . . Paul rejects the question with a reference to the fact that man has no right to dispute with God. The problem is that of the omnicausality of God and the fault of man.[2]

The idea of fault-finding, or blaming, has a judicial connotation and therefore brings into question God's justice once again.

---

2   Walter Grundmann, "μέμφομαι, μεμψίμοιρος, ἄμεμπτος, μομφή," *TDNT* 4:572–73.

The second question further objects to God's justice by disputing God's legitimacy to condemn someone as a result of something irresistible. Because the theme of God's will is pervasive throughout the context, being mentioned just a verse earlier, the question takes on a near sarcastic tone.

Paul's response to the one who questions the integrity of God is to draw them into the line of fire. Paul would not allow God's justice to be put on trial by men. Rather, he reverses the objection and puts the skeptic under the weighty scrutiny of divine wisdom. Paul's questions paint a vivid contrast between human authority and divine authority.[3] Mounce states, "The contrast between humans and God in v. 20a (ὦ ἄνθρωπε . . . τῷ θεῷ) serves to remind us that as created beings we are in no position to question our Creator."[4] Paul's response emphasizes the inferiority of humanity against the backdrop of divine supremacy.[5] The audacity of frail humans to question God is communicated as "Who are you, O man, to answer back to God?" The littleness of humans and the illegitimacy of their attempted rebuke of God is stressed by the emphatic position of "you" within the phrase.

To illustrate the futility of mortal humans to question the holiness of God, Paul sets forth the analogy of the potter and the clay. This illustration is drawn from the Old Testament (Isa. 29:16; 45:9–11;

---

3 Cranfield, *Epistle to the Romans*, 2:490. "An antithesis between man and God is intended, as the setting of the words at the places of emphasis in the sentence (beginning and end) makes clear." Dunn, *Romans 9–16*, 556.

4 Mounce, *Romans*, 201. It is interesting to see how Mounce changes his opinion regarding God's sovereignty in predestination from what he previously had said regarding 9:10–13 (199), possibly because he believes Paul did not address the matter there, but does so here. There are some who suppose that Paul is here correcting his own theology from verse 19. Piper gives ample evidence as to why that is unreasonable in *Justification of God*, 191–92. Schreiner simply and sufficiently notes, "verses 20b–23 do not support the claim that human beings have the capacity ultimately to resist God. He is the potter who exercises complete authority over the clay. Any attempt to carve out ultimate human self-determination in these verses is eisegesis." Schreiner, *Romans*, 514–15.

5 Sanday and Headlam, *The Epistle to the Romans*, 259; and Dunn, *Romans 9–16*, 566, both refute the notion that Paul doesn't give an answer to the objector.

Jer. 18:1–6).[6] The terms used to express God's absolute sovereignty, τῷ πλάσαντι ("the one who formed"), ὁ κεραμεύς ("the potter"), and τὸ πλάσμα ("the thing molded," referring to humans), put God in the seat of supreme authority.

THE RIGHT OF GOD (ROM. 9:20–21)

The term used for "form or mold" (πλάσσω) shows that Paul has in mind the passage found in Isaiah 29:16, where the first half of the rhetorical question is taken almost word for word from the LXX.[7] Verse 21 introduces a major area of disagreement among commentators in respect to the σκεῦος ("vessel") and whether this text refers to salvation. Some believe it does not,[8] including Jewett: "It would therefore be inappropriate to conclude from Paul's use of the sharply formulated antithesis between 'honorable' and 'dishonorable' vessels that he is dealing here with the predestination of individuals."[9]

Jewett, like many other commentators who are convinced of this position, comes to his conclusions based on his previous line of reasoning for national election. However, this fails to capture the sense of Paul's distinction in 9:6 and here. Instead, commentators who recognize the distinction understand that this section is speaking of eternal salvation.[10]

Before coming to a conclusion about God's intention in creating vessels of wrath and vessels of honor, it is helpful to examine the key phrases Paul uses to establish his argument. First, the term φύραμα is the common word for "lump of clay." It has been described as "a three-dimensional object with irregular rounding contours—'lump.'"[11] While the term itself is not unique, Paul asserts that

---

6   Paul does not rely on any individual text for his illustration. See Schreiner, *Romans*, 516.
7   Herbert Braun, "πλάσσω, πλάσμα, πλαστός," *TDNT* 6:260. Romans 9:20–22 becomes the basis for the element of reprobation known as predamnation, which is defined and discussed in chapter 2.
8   Cranfield, *Romans*, 492, 495; Dunn, *Romans 9–16*, 557; Fitzmyer, *Romans*, 569. These commentators take it to be historical in relationship to their interpretation of previous texts about national/corporate election.
9   Jewett, *Romans*, 594.
10 Sanday and Headlam, *The Epistle to the Romans*, 261; Murray, *The Epistle to the Romans*, 2:33; Piper, *Justification of God*, 200.
11 "φύραμα," L&N, 1:702.

the two products made by God originate from the "same" (αὐτοῦ) lump. This continues Paul's illustration from earlier, where he spoke of Jacob and Esau having origins from the same mother and the same father (Isaac). Paul intends to keep this important connection to stress the freedom of God's choice in the matter, otherwise he would not need to qualify the source of the material the Potter used. Sanday and Headlam rightly observe this when they state, "The potter is represented not merely as adapting for this or that purpose a vessel already made, but as making out of a mass of shapeless material one to which he gives a character and form adapted for different uses, some honorable, and some dishonorable."[12]

Many have noted that the term often translated as "dishonorable" can be used for "common" vessels.[13] However, this could be misleading, as "common" does not carry the reproachful or disdainful nature that is associated with ἀτιμία. Most have commented on this when speaking to the lexical meaning: "a state of dishonor or disrespect as a negative of τιμή 'honor, respect' (87.4)—'dishonor, disrespect.'" This would often refer to a vessel used to dispose of waste, and to compare anyone to this lowly sort of vessel in the Ancient Near East culture would be a dishonorable position. This is doubly true when it is used in the same context as τιμὴν ("honorable").

The term for "honor" is synonymous to δόξα ("glory") in the Greek New Testament.[14] Linguistic scholar Johannes Schneider explains this when he says, "As the potter makes vessels εἰς τιμήν and others εἰς ἀτιμίαν from the same clay, so God in the sovereignty of his creative power has the freedom in execution of his purposes in human history to make some into vessels of wrath and others into vessels of mercy; σκεῦος εἰς τιμήν is the vessel to which the use for which it is destined brings honor."[15]

---

12   Sanday and Headlam, *The Epistle to the Romans*, 260.
13   This is how the NASB translators have rendered the term. While the ESV translators have rendered it correct as "dishonorable."
14   "The word τιμή (*timē*, honor) designates eternal life in 2:7, 10, where it parallels the term δόξα." Schreiner, *Romans*, 518.
15   Johannes Schneider, "τιμή, τιμάω," *TDNT* 8:176.

THE POTTER METAPHOR (ROM. 9:22–23)

Paul's entire frame of thought is united here. The conjunction δέ connecting verse 21 with 22–23 demonstrates that Paul sees the εἰς τιμὴν σκεῦος ("a vessel unto honor") and σκεῦος . . . εἰς ἀτιμίαν ("a vessel unto dishonor") as being one and the same as the σκεύη ἐλέους ("vessels of mercy") and σκεύη ὀργῆς ("vessels of wrath"). Paul gives no indication he has changed subjects or has a different meaning in his illustration between 21 and verses 22–23.

Paul's explanation for the purpose of God's freedom as a potter makes little sense if verse 21 and the explanation in verse 22 are not connected.

In addition, there are three elements of Paul's final argument to consider. The first is the purpose of God in creating two destinies and appointing all men to life or death. The second is determining how to understand the phrases "vessels of wrath" and "vessels of mercy." The third is to grasp what is meant by "prepared" and God's role in the matter.

God's purpose is expressed in the phrase θέλων ὁ θεὸς ἐνδείξασθαι ("the will of God to demonstrate"), as he seeks to demonstrate his wrath, power, and patience.

Election and reprobation are intended to display the attributes of God. Verse 22 parallels God's desire in predestination, further highlighting that the end goal for enduring vessels of wrath was always to demonstrate his rich glory in mercy upon vessels of honor. By placing the role of the elect to glorify God, it helps to add emphasis to the statement. Schreiner states, "Those with whom he is patient are σκεύη ὀργῆς heading for eschatological judgment in contrast to the σκεύη ἐλέους in verse 23 who will experience eschatological salvation."[16] This parallel mirrors all of Paul's previous examples between the elect and reprobate.

WHAT IS MEANT BY "PREPARED FOR DESTRUCTION"?

The phrase σκεύη ὀργῆς κατηρτισμένα εἰς ἀπώλειαν ("vessels of wrath prepared for destruction") has been explained differently by many

---

16   Schreiner, *Romans*, 520.

commentators. The meaning of the individual terms within the phrase is simple enough. The most hesitation for commentators is what it means in terms of God's relationship to sin. Many commentators feel the need to explain Paul's words in a manner which, in their opinion, justifies God's actions by describing his choice as a response to human sin. For example, Mounce states, "They are σκεύη ὀργῆς, 'objects of wrath.' They are 'prepared for destruction' in the sense that by their life and conduct they have determined their own destiny."[17] Furthermore, Murray states, "There is an exact correspondence between what they were in this life and the perdition to which they are consigned. This is another way of saying that there is continuity between this life and their lot of the life to come."[18]

Instead of referring to quality, this word should be understood as a genitive of origin; meaning that the vessel is destined to be destroyed by wrath. The genitive of origin fits with Paul's previous statements about a vessel designed for dishonor.

However, the genitive quality position is highly dubious. Nowhere does Paul give the impression that the pot can change itself. On the contrary, the fact that Paul uses a pot in this illustration demonstrates its inability to do so, and that it is at the disposal of the one molding it (v. 20). The verb in the phrase προητοίμασεν εἰς δόξαν ("prepared beforehand for glory") is in the active voice. Other commentators desire a more ambiguous interpretation of the participle and take it as an adjective, "fit for destruction," which leaves the active agent uncertain.

What is the best solution to understanding the passive participle? Should its contrast with the active "prepared beforehand for glory" be taken to imply that God has no active involvement in the preparation of the vessels of wrath? The real question is the question of agency: who is doing the action and who is being acted upon? The option of taking the participle as a middle, "they fitted themselves for destruction," is impossible for several reasons. If Paul intended to express man's self-determination, he could have been clearer. For

---

17   Mounce, *Romans*, 202.
18   Murray, *The Epistle to the Romans*, 2:36.

a context where God's sovereignty is shown over unborn children, over powerful men like Moses and Pharaoh, and most of all in the illustration of a potter over clay, it seems impossible that this could be Paul's intention.

Further, how can an inanimate object act upon itself? It is absurd to think that the God of the universe would sit as a potter waiting for clay to fashion itself for his purposes. The vessels of dishonor are being prepared, namely, as vessels of wrath prepared for destruction—reprobation. John Piper says, "If ἀπώλεια means an eternal, inglorious existence in hell, then the objection that God could not make persons for such ἀπώλεια, since potters do not do that sort of thing, is not true. For potters do make vessels which are fit for inglorious uses."[19]

The precise language of the text expresses the designation of the reprobate in terms of their eternal resting place. This distinction is by God, to reject them from the blessings of election and to purposefully visit upon them the punishment their sins warrant. Furthermore, ἀπώλεια is contrasted with eternal glory. So, as the elect are prepared for glory, the reprobate are prepared for judgment.

SUMMARY REMARKS

The evidence that Paul most likely is teaching double predestination with the use of the passive participle (in 9:22) is expected, based on all his previous examples: Romans 9:13 ("Jacob I loved, but Esau I hated"), Romans 9:18 ("He has mercy on whom He desires, and He hardens whom He desires"), Romans 9:21 ("Making from the same lump a vessel for honor and a vessel for dishonor"). Contextually, Paul's most likely intention is to express that God is in control of the destiny of the vessel of wrath, fashioned from the same lump. It follows that God hardens the dishonorable vessel (in some fashion), as seen in the example of Pharaoh, and that this determination was made concerning the reprobate before they were ever born, from to the example of Esau.[20]

---

19   Piper, *Justification of God*, 201–2.
20   John Piper provides an excellent comparison between Paul's use of καταρτίζω in relation to the Qumran tradition and the Essene doctrine of predestination. See Piper, *Justification of God*, 212–13.

Likewise, this text indicates that there is an action of divine agency in the preparation of vessels of wrath. The passive participle indicates that the vessel is passively being acted upon. God is presented as the one performing the action.

It seems likely that Paul intends to emphasize God's activity in the election of the vessels of mercy, reiterating that he is the only active agent in the matter. "If this is the case, Paul would be implying that not wrath but mercy is the greater, overarching goal for which God does all things."[21] This is likely why Paul also switches his parallelism throughout Romans 9. First, it was Jacob followed by Esau (9:13). Next, it was Moses (9:15) and Pharaoh (9:17). Then it was mercy followed by hardening (9:18). Then it was honor and dishonor (9:19). Finally, for emphasis, Paul swaps what would be the anticipated order and lists vessels of wrath (9:22) first, before concluding with vessels of mercy (9:23).

Throughout this passage, Paul expresses how God works in election and reprobation. God's involvement in orchestrating the destiny of the elect is by direct agency (expressed through the active verb προητοίμασεν). It naturally follows that Paul's use of the passive participle expresses that God's work in bringing to pass the reprobate's condemnation is done according to his sovereign will and plan.

WHAT CAN BE LEARNED?

After looking at reprobation in Romans 9, a number of elements can be highlighted for a proper definition of reprobation. Not only does this text provide support for the doctrine of reprobation, it also delineates the key aspects of the doctrine. It explains God's role in reprobation and the motivating cause in God's distinction between the elect and non-elect. It articulates God's desire for and affections toward the non-elect. It provides believers with a proper context to discuss reprobation and even gives parameters for discussing it.

---

21   Piper, *Justification of God*, 241.

In the first five verses, Paul establishes the proper context for its teaching, raising the question as to why God's chosen nation rejected their Messiah. In the verses that follow, Paul answers that question using the doctrine of reprobation, demonstrating that Israel's rejection is part of God's sovereign plan.

The first five verses also reveal the proper attitude that should characterize believers when contemplating this doctrine. Paul knew that it was not within his purview to know who is numbered among the elect or reprobate. Because God has not revealed this to humanity, but has concealed the matter in his eternal counsel, believers should respond with compassion and a desire to see unbelievers brought to saving faith and into the blessings of God. Verses 1–5 provide both the proper setting for discussing the doctrine of reprobation—as the explanation for why not all men believe—and the proper response believers ought to have toward it.

From Paul's explanation in 9:6–13, God's choice in reprobation is pretemporal, unconditional, and not a matter of indifference. Paul explains how God's choice in election and reprobation was made before Jacob or Esau were born. Other New Testament passages indicate that God's electing choice was, in fact, made before time began. For example, Ephesians 1:4 states, "He chose us in Him before the foundation of the world."

This passage also demonstrates that God's choice in both election and reprobation was not conditioned on prescient foreknowledge regarding any performed actions by Jacob or Esau. Romans 9:13 establishes God's unconditional choice; it was not influenced by the order of their birth, nor their faithfulness or rejection, nor their deeds of any kind. Finally, God's choice in reprobation is not a matter of indifference. It is not as if God simply neglected to speak regarding Esau, or that he did not have any interest. Rather, God hated Esau, even as a preborn entity. Esau was rejected by God and, in time, brought to punishment.

Romans 9:14–22 provides invaluable insight into God's ability (and prerogative) to harden whomever he wishes and to have mercy on whomever he wishes. The root cause of God's choice rested in his desire to demonstrate his attributes of mercy and wrath. This final portion of Romans 9 gives the foundation for what is known as the doctrine of predamnation, which will be given more attention in the following chapter. This is highlighted in the example of Pharaoh and the vessels prepared for destruction (9:20–22). Both of these examples depict God's involvement in the matter as not merely passive, but rather, his decree is an active decree, even if he is not the active agent in its execution.

While Romans 9 depicts God's unconditional choice in both individual election and reprobation, chapter 10 reveals elements of the means of the execution of those decrees in "belief" (10:4, 9, 11, 14, & 16), "faith" (10:6, 8, 17), "confession" (10:9–10), "the preaching of the gospel," the gospel preacher himself and those who send him (10:14–15). The responsibility of human agency is consistently maintained in election, and likewise in reprobation. Romans 10 and 11 both speak to those who are "disobedient" (10:21; 11:30–32), "obstinate" (10:21), in "a spirit of stupor"(11:8), and with "blind eyes" (11:8, 10), "deaf ears" (11:8), "unbelief" (11:20, 23), all because they are "rejected" (11:15),[22] "broken off" (11:19–20), and "hardened" (Rom. 11:25)—once again stressing God's use of secondary causes and human responsibility for God's ultimate purpose to occur. This is the salvation of his remnant throughout all redemptive history, the ingrafting of the Gentiles into the promises of God's people, and the future restoration of Israel. God's decree does not nullify but rather establishes human responsibility, for both vessels of wrath and mercy.

---

22 It is important to notice that Paul says both, "God has not rejected His people" (11:1–2) and "their rejection is the reconciliation of the world" (11:15). How can both of these be true? The only way to maintain that both are true is to recognize that God has an elect remnant which constitutes true Israel, while He also has a rejected and reprobated remnant who are the "natural" Israel. This is consistent with Paul's previous statement, "not all of Israel are Israel" (Rom. 9:6) and answers his concern as to why so many ancestral Jews were rejecting the Messiah, which is why he discusses reprobation in the first place.

CHAPTER 8

PARTS OF PREDESTINATION, PART ONE

*T*he doctrine of reprobation has been plagued with a negative reputation, primarily from misunderstandings of its actual teaching. Most opponents of the doctrine of reprobation either fail to understand the doctrine correctly or dismiss the clarifications and definitions offered by those who believe it. Many historical opponents fall into one of these two categories—ranging from those who just do not understand it to others who purposefully ignore the clarifications provided by theologians seeking to define it. It is important to clarify any misconceptions by defining reprobation and all of its subsequent parts.

A CONTINUED HISTORY OF MISUNDERSTANDING

From the earliest years of the Reformation to today, misconceptions have continued, unfortunately sterilizing the teaching of this important doctrine throughout church history. How have such errors undermined the true teaching of reprobation within much of Christendom?

Jacobus Arminius, in his dialogue with Calvinist Franciscus Junius, failed to properly define reprobation according to the Reformed view. Recognizing this to be the case, Junius points it out to Arminius, stating, "That, in this statement of views (which are apparently, not really, contradictory) you have, in some manner, fallen into error, we shall, in its own place, demonstrate."[1] He goes on to define reprobation, preterition, and condemnation. However, Arminius never seems to take his distinctions into account. Junius, having read one of Arminius's replies, comments, "Before I treat the subject itself, it is necessary to refer to the ambiguity which was alluded to. . . . In the whole of your letter, to reprobate is to damn, and reprobation is damnation. But in my usage, reprobation, and preterition or non-election are the same."[2] Arminius either failed to recognize the distinctions Junius made, or refused to accept them even for the sake of dialogue. His approach is representative of the very problem that plagues this entire discussion between Arminians and Calvinists, even to this day.

This kind of intellectual dishonesty seemed to continue in the discussion throughout subsequent years. Episcopius represents another example. Historians have recognized that Episcopius portrayed reprobation in as vile terms as possible in order to demonize the entire system of Calvinism. Fredrick Calder has noticed this, stating, "And while such excitements must have been felt by the Dutch [Calvinist] divines, they likewise knew that it was possible for the Remonstrants to present their doctrines and especially that of reprobation, in such a point of light as to shake the confidence of the people in other parts of the system."[3]

Another champion of the Arminian tradition who misunderstood and misrepresented both predestination and reprobation is John Wesley. He and George Whitefield ministered together for some time, but when Whitefield left for America (in what would become the Great Awakening), he left Wesley with his church and instructed him not to preach on predestination. He considered Wesley's views to be lacking in understanding in respect to the nature of election and reprobation.

However, while Whitefield was away, Wesley preached against Calvinism and predestination, turning the entire congregation against

---

1   The dialogue between Arminius and Junius is preserved in Arminius, "A Discussion on the Subject of Predestination," in *Works*, 3:20.
2   Arminius, *Works*, 200.
3   Arminius, *Works*, 352.

Whitefield almost immediately.[4] In his 1739 sermon "Free Grace," which instigated public debates with Whitefield, Wesley wrote, "So directly does this doctrine tend to shut the very gate of holiness in general, to hinder unholy men from ever approaching thereto, or striving to enter thereat."[5] Wesley believed that the Calvinist position removed a need to pursue holiness. He saw little reason for anyone to seek obedience if their salvation or damnation was unconditionally established by God's eternal decree.

This disputation quickly became public once Wesley published his sermon and called "the Calvinist god" the devil.[6] When Whitefield returned, he confronted Wesley, and, according to Wesley, "He [Whitefield] told me [Wesley], he and I preached two different Gospels, and therefore he not only would not join with, or give me the right hand of fellowship, but has resolved to preach against me and my brother, wheresoever he preached at all."[7] This lead to a series of public disputes and sermons between the two.

Whitefield's public letters to Wesley demonstrate that he believed Wesley had an improper view of predestination all along. He writes: "Infidels of all kinds are on your side of the question. Deists, Arians, and Socinians arraign God's sovereignty and stand up for universal redemption. I pray to God that dear Mr. Wesley's sermon, as it has grieved the hearts of many of God's children, may not also strengthen the hands of many of His most avowed enemies!"[8]

---

4   Whitefield recounts this when he wrote, "many of my spiritual children . . . who at my last departure from England would have plucked out their own eyes to have given them to me, are so prejudiced by the dear [Mr. Wesley's] dressing up the doctrine of election in such horrible colors, that they will neither hear, see, nor give me the least assistance: Yes, some of them send threatening letters that God will speedily destroy me." Arnold A. Dallimore, *George Whitefield: God's Anointed Servant in the Great Revival of the Eighteenth Century* (Wheaton, IL: Crossway, 1990), 98.

5   Wesley, "Free Grace," in *Works* 1:484.

6   "[Your] God is worse than the devil; for the devil can only tempt a man to sin; but if what you have said be true, God forces a man to sin; and, therefore, on your system, God is worse than the devil." W. H. Daniels, *The Illustrated History of Methodism in Great Britain, America, and Australia* (New York: Phillips & Hunt, 1883), 192.

7   Daniels, *Illustrated History of Methodism*, 192.

8   George Whitefield, "A Letter from George Whitefield to the Rev. Mr. John Wesley in Answer to Mr. Wesley's Sermon Entitled 'Free Grace,'" in *The Revived Puritan:*

It is important to note how Whitfield positions Wesley as being on the side of the Deists, Arians, and Socinians on the matter. This is not an uncommon line of reasoning among Calvinists who often attribute the Arminian position to the heretic Pelagius. While in some cases those associations may be unfounded, broad-sweeping, and unfair, it was clear that Wesley found no problem with Pelagius. He even though they taught similar doctrine in respect to the human will and predestination. In a letter to an Arminian colleague, Wesley reveals his severe ignorance as to the historical development of the doctrine of predestination. He believed Augustine created it out of spite for Pelagius, whom Wesley claimed, "probably held no other heresy than you and I do now."[9]

Although Whitefield tried to persuade Wesley toward a proper view of predestination and reprobation, it was to no avail. Instead, as Randy Maddox has observed, "The fundamental difference between Wesley and his Calvinist opponents really lies more in their respective understandings of the nature of God than in their evaluation of the human situation."[10] This fundamental difference is perhaps the reason why so many speak past each other on the matter; their presuppositions concerning the nature of God are different.

Similar challenges to the doctrine of reprobation, stemming from misunderstanding, have continued throughout history. A more modern opponent to the Reformed view of reprobation is Harry Boer, who challenged the scriptural basis of reprobation as it was laid out in the Synod of Dort. In 1965, through a series of articles in *The Reformed Journal*, Boer himself suggested that the traditional Reformed view of reprobation was insufficient.[11] However, he did not deny its existence

---

Select Works of the Reverend George Whitefield (London: Lewes, 1829), 683–92. Hereafter *Works*.

9   John Wesley, "To John Fletcher," in *The Letters of John Wesley*, ed. John Telford (London: Epworth, 1931), 6:378–79.

10   Randy L. Maddox, *Responsible Grace: John Wesley's Practical Theology* (Nashville: Kingswood, 1994), 55–56.

11   For more on the history of Harry Boer and James Daane's critiques of the Reformed view of reprobation, see David F. Wells, *Reformed Theology in America: A History of Its Modern Development* (Grand Rapids: Eerdmans, 1985), 147–49. For a thorough argument containing their position, see R. B. Kuiper, *God Centered Evangelism* (Grand Rapids: Baker, 1957), and "Professor Dekker on God's Universal Love," *Torch and Trumpet* 13 (1963): 4–9.

nor offer an alternative. His main argument was simply that it was unbiblical. He believed it was a doctrine deduced from mere logic and not found in Scripture.[12] Although Boer believes that reprobation was purposefully left out of the confessions because it was not universally held, this is not the case. The omission of reprobation in the Heidelberg Catechism and Belgic Confession was not a denial of its existence. As Hoeksema says, "In the mind of all Reformed men, Luther and Calvin and Ursinus and Olevianus and all the fathers of Dordrecht included, it is absolutely impossible to breathe the word 'election' without saying by implication 'reprobation.'"[13] While Boer's complaints were heard by the church, his conclusions were rejected.

The same line of reasoning persists even to this day. In fact, more serious than historical misunderstanding is the more heinous misrepresentation which exists amongst modern scholars. Norman Geisler has presented a view of what he calls "Calvinism and hyper-Calvinism," which are not historically accurate and, as a result, have led to even more confusion regarding the nature of reprobation.[14] Geisler attempts to offer an alternative to traditional Calvinism. However, in doing so, he presents a historically inaccurate form of Calvinism.

Geisler does not use terms in their historical context but rather redefines terms. Geisler presents the Calvinist acrostic of TULIP and labels it "extreme Calvinism," allegedly synonymous with "hyper-Calvinism." He states, "We use the term 'extreme' (or strong) rather than 'hyper' since hyper-Calvinism is used by some to designate a more radical view known as supralapsarianism, which entails double predestination (that God predestines some to heaven and others to hell), denies human responsibility . . . or nullifies concern for missions and evangelism."[15]

12   Harry R. Boer, *The Doctrine of Reprobation in the Christian Reformed Church* (Grand Rapids: Eerdmans, 1983).

13   H. C. Hoeksema, "The Heidelberg Catechism and Reprobation," *The Standard Bearer* 55, no. 20 (1979): 462.

14   Norman Geisler considers his view a "middle" ground position, however, many Reformed critics of Geisler could categorize him as holding a weakened form of Arminianism.

15   Norman Geisler, *Chosen but Free: A Balanced View of God's Sovereignty and Free Will*, 2nd ed. (Minneapolis: Bethany House, 2010), 32.

By conflating terms, Geisler makes a categorical error that permeates his entire perspective. Geisler's conflation of terms becomes evident when he provides a chart showing "hyper-Calvinism" alongside "strong Calvinism." His chart is as follows:

CHART 10.1: NORMAN GEISLER ON POSITIONS OF CALVINISM	
Hyper Calvinists	**Other Strong Calvinists**
Elect and non-elect are actively predestined	Only elect are actively predestined
God is active in choosing both	God is passive in not choosing the non-elect
Unbelief given to the non-elect	Faith given to the elect
Symmetrical relation	Asymmetrical relation
Predestination is positive in both	Predestination is positive of the elect and negative of the non-elect
Equal ultimacy	Unequal ultimacy[16]

Geisler claims that he is using a similar chart to R. C. Sproul's *Chosen by God*, which is as follows:

CHART 10.2: R. C. SPROUL ON POSITIONS OF CALVINISM	
Hyper Calvinism	**Calvinism**
Positive-positive	Positive-negative
Symmetrical view	Asymmetrical view
Equal ultimacy	Unequal ultimacy
God works unbelief in the hearts of the reprobate	God passes over the reprobate[17]

---

16   Norman L. Geisler, *Systematic Theology*, vol. 3, *Sin/Salvation* (Minneapolis: Bethany House, 2004), 565. A similar chart is found in his book *Chosen but Free*, 3:263.

17   R. C. Sproul, *Chosen by God* (Wheaton, IL: Tyndale House, 1994), 143. R. C. Sproul's chart was flipped so that it would align with Geisler's for comparison purposes.

Geisler is severely mistaken on his definitions of Calvinism, hyper-Calvinism, and predestination. He uses different definitions for each of the terms he employs. He claims that by believing that God makes an active choice for the reprobate, such a person is a hyper-Calvinist, which could not be further from the truth. Furthermore, he shows an inability to properly differentiate between hyper-Calvinism and historic Calvinism when he states, "Moderate Calvinists call the active predestination of both the elect and reprobate 'double predestination.' Those who maintain it are called hyper-Calvinists."[18]

This is contrary to what Calvinists have historically taught. R. C. Sproul explains:

> Unless we conclude that every human being is predestined to salvation, we must face the flip side of election. If there is such a thing as predestination at all, and if that predestination does not include all people, then we must not shrink from the necessary inference that there are two sides to predestination. It is not enough to talk about Jacob; we must also consider Esau.[19]

Additionally, Geisler demonstrates a misunderstanding of equal and unequal ultimacy. Sproul provides a historically correct definition of the terms, which differs from what Geisler previously set forth: "Equal ultimacy is based on a concept of symmetry. It seeks a complete balance between election and reprobation. The key idea is this: Just as God intervenes in the lives of the elect to create faith in their hearts, so God equally intervenes in the lives of the reprobate to create or work unbelief in their hearts."[20]

Ultimacy refers to the destiny God chose for men, not the means employed to bring about that destiny. Both Calvinists and hyper-Calvinists affirm that God ordains the ends of the elect and the non-elect.

---

18 Geisler, *Systematic Theology*, 3:564.
19 Sproul, *Chosen by God*, 141.
20 Sproul, *Chosen by God*, 142.

Where they differ is in the means God employs to bring about his double decree. Hyper-Calvinists affirm a symmetrical view, in which God works unbelief and evil into humans directly, while Calvinists believe God is not the direct agent responsible (also known as the efficient cause). The Calvinist maintains that God directly intervenes in regenerating the elect to bring them to salvation, but does not have to directly intervene in the non-elect in order for them to receive condemnation.

The hyper-Calvinist, on the other hand, asserts that God directly intervenes in the lives of the elect via regeneration, as well as directly intervening in the lives of the non-elect (via what has sometimes been called "degeneration"). This is where secondary causality becomes vital to understand. Because Geisler does not distinguish among the types of causality, he has mistakenly lumped true and balanced Calvinism into the same camp as hyper-Calvinism. As a result of the wide publications of Geisler (and others like him), any meaningful discussion on reprobation have been hindered, by working with definitions which do not stand the test of historical accuracy.

CLASSIFICATIONS AND DEFINITIONS

Because misconceptions concerning reprobation are pervasive throughout history, it is necessary to use proper definitions before addressing objections.

HOW IS REPROBATION RELATED TO PREDESTINATION?

Within predestination, God determines each person's eternal resting place in one of two places: heaven or hell. The act of God choosing men to salvation and heaven is known as election. The act of God choosing men to eternal perdition and hell is known as reprobation. When it comes to predestination there are many views, but most people fall into one of four categories: (1) single predestination, (2) equal ultimacy double predestination, (3) unequal ultimacy double predestination, and (4) no view at all.

Since the Bible explicitly uses terms for predestination and election, it is necessary to reject view four outright. Though an individual may be in the process of developing his or her convictions regarding the matter, it is unbiblical to simply have no view at all. The first view asserts that God only predestines some individuals to salvation and leaves the rest up to the "free will" of the individuals. In this view, God does not intend, want, or plan for any individual to go to hell. Therefore, double predestination "refers to positions which explicitly speak of predestination to life and to death, or as consisting of election as well as reprobation. 'Single predestination' refers to positions which equate predestination with election."[21]

The second view is "equal ultimacy double predestination," held by hyper-Calvinists. This view describes the predestination of both the elect and the reprobate as being "positive-positive," which is to say that God works as extensively in the life of the reprobate as he does in the life of the elect to bring about their determined ends. Equal ultimacy teaches that just as God is the sole active agent working directly to bring about the salvation of the elect, he is also in orchestrating the damnation of the reprobate. With equal ultimacy, just as God changes the hearts of the elect to believe, he also works unbelief in the hearts of the reprobate.[22] This view is problematic, because it makes God the infuser of evil and the author of sin. By directly working unbelief into the hearts of the reprobate, he is forcing them to do evil.

The third view represents the best way to explain how God predestines individuals to heaven and hell. This perspective is given in the book *Chosen by God*, in which Sproul defines the process of double predestination as "positive-negative," also known as "unequal ultimacy."[23] In this view, God actively decrees the eternal ends (heaven

---

21   Donald W. Sinnema, "The Issue of Reprobation at the Synod of Dort (1618–19) in Light of the History of this Doctrine" (PhD diss., University of St. Michael's College, Toronto School of Theology, 1985), 4.

22   Almost all major Reformed theologians reject equal ultimacy; see Herman Bavinck, *Reformed Dogmatics*, ed. John Bolt, trans. John Vriend (Grand Rapids: Baker Academic, 2008), 2:396; Francis Turretin, *Institutes of Elenctic Theology*, ed. James T. Dennison (Phillipsburg, NJ: P&R, 1993), 4:14; Heinrich Heppe, *Reformed Dogmatics: Set Out and Illustrated from the Sources*, rev. and ed. Ernst Bizer, trans. G. T. Thomson (London: Willmer Bros., 1950), 132.

23   Sproul, *Chosen by God*, 143.

or hell) of both individuals; elect and reprobate. This is what is meant by "ultimacy." But in this view, God determines the secondary means of bringing about those ends, regarding his direct involvement.[24]

The Reformed view of predestination is that God in election is the only active agent involved in bringing sinners unto salvation. In reprobation, however, God has determined not to be directly involved in their unbelief. An overview of the doctrine of election is helpful here, as doctrine of reprobation is only properly understood in contrast to the doctrine of election.

ELECTION

The Bible defines election in three major categories. The first point is that in the Old Testament, God had a chosen people: the Israelites. Amos 3:2 reads, "You only have I chosen among all the families of the earth; Therefore I will punish you for all your iniquities." This is known as "national election."[25] The second kind of election is toward an office or vocation. Examples of this include King David who was chosen to be God's representative ruler over the nation of Israel, and the apostles who were chosen for their offices. This can be referred to as "vocational election."[26] The third biblical category of election, the most prominent in the New Testament and arguably the most important, is God's choice of certain individuals unto salvation. Taking place before the foundation of the world, this is known as "individual election." This third category helps bring into focus the doctrine of reprobation.

Individual election is God's predetermined choice, resting solely on his will, of particular individuals unto salvation.[27] His choice of particular persons was not based on any foreseen response or obedience

---

24   John MacArthur and Richard Mayhue, eds., *Biblical Doctrine: A Systematic Summary of Biblical Truth* (Wheaton, IL: Crossway, 2017), 505–6.

25   John Frame, *Systematic Theology: An Introduction to Christian Belief* (Phillipsburg, NJ: P&R, 2013), 210. MacArthur, *Biblical Doctrine*, 494–95 (there called "corporate election").

26   Frame, *Systematic Theology*, 209. MacArthur, *Biblical Doctrine*, 494.

27   Berkhof, *Systematic Theology*, 114–15; Bavinck, *Reformed Dogmatics*, 2:399; A. A. Hodge, *Outlines of Theology* (1861; repr., Carlisle, PA: Banner of Truth, 1991), 218.

on their part. God does not elect to save those whom he first *sees* exercising faith and repentance. On the contrary, God grants faith and repentance to those individuals whom he first elected to save. Romans 9:11–12 says, "For though the twins were not yet born and had not done anything good or bad, so that God's purpose according to His choice would stand, *not because of works but because of Him who calls*, it was said to her, 'The older will serve the younger.'"[28] God's mercy is not contingent upon anything foreseen in man, since the choice was made "before the foundation of the world" (Eph. 1:4). Men do not determine their election; God does. This is also described in John 1:13, speaking of rebirth: "who were born, not of blood nor of the will of the flesh nor of the will of man, but of God."

Election is not a choice made by humans but by God. If we were given the choice in any way, we would choose sin (resulting in hell) every time.[29]

The Purpose of Election

God elects some unto salvation because in his most wise counsel, he has decided to display his glory in this way.[30] God's glory is the primary purpose, not only in creating the world, but also in his saving work. The salvation of the elect is a manifestation of many of God's attributes, his mercy being at the forefront.

Paul states that the purpose for this divine favor upon one son and divine disapproval of the other has nothing to do with them, but depends on God. Since Jacob and Esau had not yet done anything yet when God's disposition toward them was settled, their example served to demonstrate God's predetermined purpose to display his sovereign election. God can then say, as he does in Exodus 33:19, "I will be

---

28 Italics added.
29 See also Deut. 7:6–7; 10:14–15, Ps. 33:12; 65:4; 106:5; 115:3; 135:6; Haggai 2:23; Matt. 11:27; 19:26; 20:15; 22:14; 24:22, 24, 31; Mark 13:20; Luke 18:7; John 6:43–44, 64–68; Rom. 8:28–30, 33; 9:10–24; 10:20; 11:4–6, 28, 33–36; 16:7, Col. 3:12; 1 Thess. 5:9; Titus 1:1; 1 Peter 1:1–2; 2:8–9; and Rev. 13:8; 17:8.
30 John Brown, *Systematic Theology: A Compendious View of Natural and Revealed Religion* (Grand Rapids: Reformation Heritage, 2002), 148–50; Turretin, *Institutes of Elenctic Theology*, 1:329; Berkhof, *Systematic Theology*, 115.

gracious to whom I will be gracious, and I will show compassion upon whom I will show compassion." God's choice of the sinner, not the sinner's choice of Christ, is the ultimate cause of salvation: "They are elected because they were called according to the purpose—the purpose, however, not their own, but God's . . . that they have been elected before the foundation of the world, not because they were foreknown as men who would believe and would be holy, but in order that by the means of that very election of grace they might be such."[31]

The reason God is the only agent in salvation is because men simply cannot have any involvement in their own salvation. In their fallen nature, they are dead, blind, deaf, and dumb to the things of God. Otherwise, it would rob God of his glory. The manifestation of his grace is by definition dependent upon the utter inability of mankind to contribute to salvation.

The Means of Executing Election

God brings about the results of election through the death of Christ, the miracle of regeneration, and the response of faith through hearing the gospel. This means of election follows a predictable pattern. First, the death of Christ, according to election, intentionally takes away the punishment due to the elect. Once the gospel has been heard, the Spirit's act of regeneration changes the disposition of the sinner's heart, resulting in faith and repentance. Imputed righteousness then is applied at the moment of faith to those who have been set apart according to election.

Through Christ's substitution, he purchased the right for the elect to be called sons of God. He took the punishment due them on the cross, as Romans 3:24 says: "being justified as a gift, by his grace through the redemption which is in Christ Jesus." Individuals are justified by the redeeming work of Christ.

Regeneration (which immediately precedes faith) is also a means through which election is brought to fruition. On account of Christ's

---

31   Augustine, "On the Predestination of the Saints," in *The Works of Saint Augustine*, in *NPNF,* trans. Peter Holmes and Robert Ernest (Peabody, MA: Hendrickson, 1999), 5:498.

atonement, the Spirit applies the fruit of that labor to the hearts of the elect. Acts 13:48 says, "When the Gentiles heard this, they began rejoicing the word of the Lord; and as many as had been appointed to eternal life believed." The result of being appointed to eternal life is always belief. As God has determined the ends, he has also determined the means.[32] This is seen in Romans 8:30, which says, "and those whom He predestined, He also called; and these whom He called, He also justified; and these whom He justified, He also glorified." Who are the glorified? Those who are glorified are the ones who have been justified. Who then are justified? Those who are justified are the ones who have been called. Then who are the called? The effectually called are only those whom God determined (predestined), on the basis of his own pleasure, to bring to eternal glory. Therefore, all who are called are justified and then on the last day glorified.

---

32   See also 1 John 5:1; Acts 16:14b; John 10:24–26; Ezekiel 36:26–27; John 6:37; John 1:13; 1 Cor. 4:7; 15:10; James 1:17; John 3:27.

CHAPTER 9

PARTS OF PREDESTINATION, PART TWO

*T*he biblical doctrine of reprobation is "that eternal decree of God whereby he has determined to pass some men by, with the operations of His special grace, and to punish them for their sins, to the manifestation of His justice."[1] This doctrine is one to be handled with great care. Because the Bible was written to the elect, it speaks far more about election to salvation than about reprobation. This has resulted in people speculating to the point of grievous error. Scripture unmistakably teaches the doctrine of reprobation, but not to the same detail as election. Calvin calls this doctrine the "dreadful decree."[2] He did not believe it was bad, but sobering, and to be handled with great wisdom.

Reprobation is not purely passive—God's choice to reprobate is an active choice. It is not an afterthought or simply the logical byproduct of neglecting to assign an eternal destination for the non-elect. This positive choice of God is taught in Romans 9:22–23, which states, "What if God, although willing to demonstrate His wrath and to make His power known, endured with much patience vessels of wrath prepared for destruction? And He did so to make known the riches of His glory upon vessels of mercy, which He

---

1 Louis Berkhof, *Systematic Theology* (Grand Rapids: Eerdmans, 1996), 116.
2 Calvin, *Institutes*, 2:955.

prepared beforehand for glory." Jude 4 similarly states, "For certain persons have crept in unnoticed, those who were long beforehand marked out for this condemnation, ungodly persons who turn the grace of our God into licentiousness and deny our only Master and Lord, Jesus Christ." They were "marked out" and prepared for destruction. It is their "nature" to be children of destruction. First Peter 2:8 is another example of this (emphasis added): "'A STONE OF STUMBLING AND A ROCK OF OFFENSE'; for they stumble because they are disobedient to the word, and to this *doom* they were also appointed." In this passage, the apostle Peter notes that the unbeliever rejects the "word" (apostolic testimony) in accordance with how they have been "appointed" (based on a form of τίθημι, which means "to put in place," "to fix," or "to establish"). By pairing an act in time (stumbling in disobedience to God's Word) with the divine appointment that brought it about, Peter perfectly illustrates the relationship between ends and means.

God predestines the reprobate unto condemnation because, as with election, he desires to display his glory. God's glory is displayed by manifesting his attributes, and justice is at the forefront in the case of reprobation. God, intending to display the riches of his glory, endures with patience the vessels of wrath so that for all eternity, his glory will be made known through mercy shown to the elect as well as justice shown to the reprobate. A. W. Pink captures this concept well, stating,

> It must be God Himself who "fits" unto destruction the vessels of wrath. Should it be asked how God does this, the answer necessarily, is, objectively,—He fits the non-elect unto destruction by His fore-ordaining decrees. Should it be asked why God does this, the answer must be, to promote His own glory, i.e., the glory of His justice, power, and wrath.[3]

---

3   Pink, *The Sovereignty of God*, 96–97.

What Reprobation Is

Reprobation is not merely a doctrine based on deductive reasoning but is explicitly taught in Scripture. As the exegesis of Romans 9 indicated, Paul gave just as much attention (if not more) to the issue of the reprobation as to election. He speaks just as much concerning Esau and Pharaoh as it does about Jacob and Moses. With an abundance of material, it is evident that while reprobation may be hard to accept, it is not hard to understand. In fact, the emotional reticence caused by this topic in Romans 9 could be what undergirds Peter's comments about Paul's teaching being "difficult" (as in 2 Peter 3:16).

The Westminster Confession gives a very basic definition of reprobation after discussing election, stating, "The rest of mankind God was pleased, according to the unreachable counsel of His own will, whereby He extendeth or withholdeth mercy as He pleaseth, for the glory of His sovereign power over His creatures, to pass by, and to ordain them to dishonor and wrath for their sin, to the praise of His glorious justice."[4] Edwin Palmer gives a more thorough definition when he says, "[Reprobation is] God's eternal, sovereign, unconditional, immutable, wise, holy, and mysterious decree whereby, in electing some to eternal life, He passes others by, and then justly condemns them for their own sin—all to His own glory."[5]

God's design for reprobation is not merely non-election. Even the most basic definition of reprobation contains two elements: the decree and its execution. Both the decree and the execution also contain two elements.

Within the decree there is preterition and predamnation (also known as precondemnation) and within the execution there is causality and condemnation.[6] These elements need to be examined

---

4   WCF 3.7.
5   Palmer, *The Five Points of Calvinism*, 97.
6   Turretin, *Institutes of Elenctic Theology*, 1:380–81; MacArthur, *Biblical Doctrines*, 505–6; Loraine Boettner, *The Reformed Doctrine of Predestination* (Phillipsburg, NJ: P&R, 1932), 104–8; Robert L. Reymond, *A New Systematic Theology of the Christian Faith* (Nashville: Thomas Nelson, 1998), 345; Berkhof, *Systematic Theology*, 116.

in order to fully comprehend reprobation. "Essentially *reprobation* includes two elements, *praeteritio* or the denial of grace not due, and *praedamnatio* or the appointment of punishment due."[7] These two elements are important to distinguish from one another to understand man's culpability and God's glory.

THE DECREE OF REPROBATION

The two elements of the *decree* of reprobation are known as the negative and positive sides of reprobation.[8] The negative element (preterition) is considered negative, not because God refrains from making a choice (because he does), but because he has chosen to exclude every individual who is not elect from the eternal benefits of salvation. This first negative element is that of preterition, which means that God chooses to pass by the non-elect.[9]

Preterition is "a word derived from the Latin *praeter*, meaning beyond or past, and *praeteritus*, meaning that which is passed over. In theology it is used to refer to God's passing over of the non-elect, whom he allows to go their own way and perish for their sins."[10]

The individuals under consideration were not yet born (they did not exist), hence, God first decreed that they would exist and then that they would be individuals reserved for justice. This passing by is the choice of God to not elect them to salvation, to not send Christ to be their substitute, nor give them the Holy Spirit to regenerate their hearts and believe the gospel. Ultimately, preterition is the act of God to leave individuals to themselves. It is a purely sovereign act by God, made according to the wisdom of his own will, apart from any consideration of the creature.

---

7   Heppe, *Reformed Dogmatics*, 180.
8   Berkhof, *Systematic Theology*, 116–17; Reymond, *A New Systematic Theology*, 345; Turretin, *Institutes of Elenctic Theology*, 1:380–81; A. A. Hodge, *Outlines of Theology*, 222; Boettner, *The Reformed Doctrine of Predestination*, 107;
9   Geerhardus Vos, "The Biblical Importance of the Doctrine of Preterition," *The Presbyterian* 70, no. 36 (1900): 9–10.
10 W. S. Reid, "Preterition," in *Evangelical Dictionary of Theology*, ed. Walter A. Elwell (Grand Rapids: Baker Books, 2001), 952.

The second element of the decree of reprobation is known as predamnation.[11] Predamnation "refers to God's eternal will to decree to damn or punish with eternal death. This is distinct from actual damnation or punishment."[12] This is known as the positive side of the decree of reprobation, not because it is something optimistic, but because it is an affirmative choice of God to hold men accountable to justice. The fact that God determines to hold anyone according to the standard of his holy standard is strict justice. Predamnation, different from damnation, is rightly called "pre-" because it is a decision by God to hold men accountable without consideration to the lives they will live (as opposed to damnation, which is the accountability that does take into account the lives that men have lived). Predamnation is God's determination that certain individuals will be held to the strict standards of justice and receive unbiased judgment.

Frame articulates these aspects well: "Traditionally, within reprobation theologians have distinguished between preterition, in which God determines not to choose certain persons for salvation, and precondemnation, in which he determines to justly punish them for their sin."[13] Predamnation is not God's decree to punish men before they sin, as if they were still innocent and without fault. It is a positive decree by God to hold them responsible to the standards of justice. Predamnation is purely judicial in that God will not hold someone else responsible for their actions (as he does for the elect when he counts Christ as accountable for their demerits), but predamnation is God's decision to hold the non-elect accountable for everything they do.

In summary, preterition is a negative decree in which God passes over, or rejects someone. Predamnation is a positive decree in which God determines to hold individuals responsible.

---

11   Perhaps a better term, that is not as easily given to misunderstanding, would be pre-justice. However, because "pre-justice" is not the historic term, predamnation will be used in its place.

12   Donald W. Sinnema, "The Issue of Reprobation at the Synod of Dort (1618–19) in Light of the History of this Doctrine" (PhD diss., University of St. Michael's College, Toronto School of Theology, 1985), 5.

13   Frame, *Systematic Theology*, 221.

Remember that reprobation is different from damnation, since damnation is the execution of the just results of the reprobation decree. John Calvin observed this when he says, "Their perdition depends on the predestination of God in such a way that the cause and occasion of it are found in themselves."[14] Similarly William G. T. Shedd carefully argues that,

> Preterition is a sovereign act; condemnation is a judicial act. God passes by, or omits an individual in the bestowment of regenerating grace, because of his sovereign good pleasure (εὐδοκία). But he condemns this individual to punishment, not because of his sovereign good pleasure, but because this individual is a sinner. To say that God condemns a man to punishment because he pleases, is erroneous; but to say that God omits to regenerate a man because he pleases, is true.[15]

THE EXECUTION OF REPROBATION

Having understood the dual nature of reprobation as negative-positive (preterition and precondemnation), it is important to resolve the second aspect: the execution of that eternal immutable decree. Michael Horton properly warns against mixing these two aspects when he writes, "We must distinguish carefully the decree in eternity from its execution in history. . . . Purposes are different from their fulfillment; determinations are different from their accomplishment. God has not only determined the ends but the means by which He will achieve them."[16]

God's execution of the decree of reprobation in time is divisible into two elements: causality and condemnation. Causality can be briefly defined as a description of the means God employs in

---

14   Calvin, *Institutes*, 2:957.
15   William G. T. Shedd, *Dogmatic Theology* (Grand Rapids: Zondervan, 1971), 433.
16   Michael Horton, *For Calvinism* (Grand Rapids: Zondervan, 2011), 70. This distinction can be slightly observed in William Twisse when he states, "Reprobation includeth the will of God of permitting sin, and of inferring damnation for sin." William Twisse, *A Discovery of Doctor Jackson's Vanity* (London, 1631), 305.

bringing about all he has ordained. A. W. Pink summarizes causality when he states,

> It must be God Himself who "fits" unto destruction the vessels of wrath. Should it be asked how God does this, the answer is necessarily, is, objectively,—He fits the non-elect unto destruction by His fore-ordaining decrees. Should it be asked why God does this, the answer must be, to promote His own glory, i.e., the glory of His justice, power and wrath.[17]

Causality with respect to sin is always done via secondary agency, whereby it is important to remember that "God is the Creator of the wicked, not their wickedness; He is the Author of their being, not the Infuser of their sin. God does not (as we have been slanderously reported to affirm) compel the wicked to sin, as a rider spurs on an unwilling horse."[18] God's relationship to sin in the doctrine of causality raises the most questions concerning the issue of theodicy, or the problem of evil. In short, Calvin states, "But how it was ordained by the foreknowledge and decree of God what man's future was without God being implicated as associate in the fault as the author and approver of transgression, is clearly a secret so much excelling the insight of the human mind, that I am not ashamed to confess ignorance."[19]

The second element of God's execution of reprobation is condemnation. Condemnation is a judicial act of God in which he chooses to give the sin of unbelievers their due consequences. This is how God holds men responsible. "The terms 'damnation' or 'condemnation' refer to God's final judgment of the wicked at the end of history."[20] This is the aspect of reprobation whereby God actively and justly holds men responsible. Proverbs 11:21 says, "Assuredly, the evil man

---

17 Pink, *The Sovereignty of God*, 96–97.
18 Pink, *The Sovereignty of God*, 101.
19 John Calvin, *Concerning the Eternal Predestination of God*, trans. J. K. S. Reid (London: James Clarke, 1961), 124.
20 Sinnema, "The Issue of Reprobation at the Synod of Dort," 5.

will not go unpunished." It is against God's nature to allow any sin to escape justice. God is One who is "of purer eyes than to behold evil, and canst not look on iniquity" (Hab. 1:13, KJV), and whose wrath is "revealed from heaven against all ungodliness and unrighteousness of men" (Rom. 1:18). Exodus 34:7 reads, "who keeps lovingkindness for thousands, who forgives iniquity, transgression and sin; yet He will by no means leave the guilty unpunished, visiting the iniquity of fathers on the children and on the grandchildren to the third and fourth generations." This is the reason why Christ came to die—to acquit the elect of their sins.

However, the reverse is also true. God justly chooses to not send a substitute for the reprobate, leaving them to themselves, and justly condemning them. God has the right to do this to everyone—no one deserves to escape an assigned punishment. But it is amazing grace that God chooses to send an advocate and sin-bearer for the elect. This is something he reserves the right to do for whomever he desires. And he also reserves the right to not send the sin-bearer for others if he so desires. Every one either has Christ as their substitute to bear their sins, or they will bear their own.

Condemnation, then, is God's declaration at the end of one's life that they deserve damnation on account of their sin. When God condemns someone, it is always on account of their sin, which has been historically maintained since the early discussions of reprobation.

CHART 10.3: DEFINING REPROBATION AND ITS PARTS		
Term	**Definition**	**Biblical Texts**
Reprobation	God's will to pretemporally decree, to pass by the individuals who are non-elect unconditionally. And to hold each one accountable to his justice for the purpose of displaying the glory of his justice.	Romans 9:6–23

CHART 10.3: DEFINING REPROBATION AND ITS PARTS		
Term	**Definition**	**Biblical Texts**
Preterition	God's choice to pass by and to reject or exclude from the eternal benefits of salvation every individual who is not elect.	Romans 9:6–23 Every time election is mentioned preterition is assumed of those not elected.
Predamnation	The affirmative decision of God to hold the non-elect to the standards of his justice.	Romans 9:22 1 Peter 2:8 Jude 4
Condemnation	The judicial act of God in which he chooses to visit the penalty for the sin of unbelievers upon them.	Hebrews 9:27 2 Timothy 4:1 1 Peter 4:5 Psalm 9:7 Mark 9:44 etc.
Causality	The means God employs in bringing about all that he has ordained. Furthermore, causality with respect to sin is always done via secondary agency.	Acts 2:23; 4:27

What Reprobation Is Not

With the essential elements of God's decree and execution of reprobation in mind, it is easier to discuss what reprobation is not. Lack of clarity in the definitions related to reprobation (and man's natural aversion to it) has led many to improperly equate reprobation with hyper-Calvinism. Oftentimes, the distortions of hyper-Calvinism lead many to equate terms like *double predestination*, *reprobation*, or even *sovereignty* with being solely associated with hyper-Calvinism.[21] This

---

21 It has been recognized that the majority of Arminians and four-Point Calvinists often label everyone to their right as "hyper-Calvinists," which is precisely what George

has created difficulty not only in discussing these important doctrines, but in even labeling what hyper-Calvinism is. Jim Ellis points this out when he states:

> Hyper-Calvinism is a term of derision that today is often used to negatively label anyone with a strong theological view of God's sovereignty in the affairs of men. . . . For example, Arminians regard any who hold to unconditional election as hyper-Calvinists. The four-point Calvinist views the five-point Calvinist as "hyper" because he holds to a limited atonement.[22]

Reprobation, when properly understood in the Reformed tradition, should not be associated with hyper-Calvinism.[23] There are five aspects associated with reprobation that are distinct from hyper-Calvinism: (1) Reprobation does not hinder the free offer of the gospel to all men, since we do not know who the elect are. (2) Reprobation does not hinder the assurance of believers, since assurance is not based on understanding eternal decrees. (3) Reprobation is not symmetrical to election. (4) Reprobation does not teach that God has no benevolence toward the reprobate. (5) Reprobation does not deny common grace.[24] A brief examination of these will be helpful to clarify the doctrine of reprobation and distinguish it from hyper-Calvinism.

These five tenets have summarized the error of hyper-Calvinism since its inception. Phillip R. Johnson offers five key tenets that

---

Bryson does in *The Five Points of Calvinism: "Weighed and Found Wanting"* (Costa Mesa, CA: Word for Today, 1996). Norman Geisler was also quick to do likewise.

22 Jim Ellis, "What Is Hyper-Calvinism?" *Reformed Perspectives Magazine* 10, no. 15 (2008): 1.

23 Ellis, "What Is Hyper-Calvinism?," 1. Ellis also highlights that the difficulty of labeling hyper-Calvinism is because it is a subtle distortion or blurring of the traditional teachings of Calvinism.

24 When defining reprobation many Reformed systematic theologians are careful to make this definition, Heinrich Heppe explains, "[B]ut while by *praeteritio* God refuses His redeeming grace to the rejected He does not deprive them of His common grace." Heinrich Heppe, *Reformed Dogmatics*, trans. G. T. Thomson (Eugene, OR: Wipf & Stock, 1950), 185.

indicate whether a person can be classified as a hyper-Calvinist (or at least have hyper-Calvinist tendencies). A hyper-Calvinist is someone who either:

1. Denies that the gospel call applies to all who hear, or
2. Denies that faith is the duty of every sinner, or
3. Denies that the gospel makes any "offer" of Christ, salvation, or mercy to the non-elect (or denies that the offer of divine mercy is free and universal), or
4. Denies that there is such a thing as "common grace," or
5. Denies that God has any sort of love for the non-elect.[25]

The only thing that could be added is the tendency of hyper-Calvinists to stress God's sovereignty over men and even sin, without any qualifications about man's responsibility or culpability. This often takes the form of equal ultimacy, or any similar scheme in which God is said to actively coerce (or even force) men to sin to bring about their predestined demise. Peter Toon defines hyper-Calvinism as:

> A system of theology framed to exalt the honour and glory of God and does so by acutely minimizing the moral and spiritual responsibility of sinners. . . . It emphasizes irresistible grace to such an extent that there appears to be no real need to evangelize; furthermore, Christ may be offered only to the elect . . . thus it undermines the universal duty of sinners to believe savingly in the Lord Jesus with the assurance that Christ actually died for them; and it encourages introspection in the search to know whether or not one is elect.[26]

---

25 Phillip R. Johnson, "A Primer on Hyper-Calvinism," *Sword and Trowel* 1 (March, 2002), 11. This is the most helpful article on the matter which covers all the main tenets, tendencies, and historical developments of hyper-Calvinism. Much of my work on the matter is owed to the sources and further research stemming from this article.

26 Peter Toon, "Hyper-Calvinism," in *The New Dictionary of Theology*, eds. Sinclair B. Ferguson, David F. Wright, and J. I. Packer (Downers Grove, IL: InterVarsity Press, 1988), 324. A similar definition is found in his work *The Emergence of Hyper-Calvinism*

Toon highlights the major tenets of hyper-Calvinism and how it often distorts true elements of doctrine (such as God's sovereignty, predestination, and irresistible grace) so greatly that it neglects other important doctrines (such as the instrumental agency of man's responsibility, faith, and evangelism). These distortions by hyper-Calvinists overemphasize sovereignty to the point that they are comfortable claiming God is the author of sin, without qualification—something the Westminster Confession of Faith and the Synod of Dort both outright deny.

In today's society, hyper-Calvinism is left to the unchecked corners of the internet and does not find a prominent place in academics or pulpit ministry, which leaves much of modern discussion on hyper-Calvinism to historical theology.[27]

The most heinous part of hyper-Calvinism is that it is willing to claim that God is the author of sin, without any clarifications or reservations. Hyper-Calvinism teaches the aforementioned perspective of equal ultimacy. This is a view of double predestination which sees God's work in salvation as being symmetrical to his work in reprobation. It stresses the sovereignty of God in reprobation to the point that humans are no longer responsible for sin.

Part of the difficulty in defining the error of hyper-Calvinism is that equal ultimacy has been taken to mean two different things.

---

in English Nonconformity 1689–1765 (1967; repr., Weston Rhyn, England: Quinta, 2003), 144–45. It is important to notice how Toon recognizes that hyper-Calvinists are often times supralapsarian, however, not all Supralapsarians are hyper-Calvinists. This distinction is important in order to distinguish those who are within an acceptable Christian tradition and those who are downright heretical.

27   For an excellent work on the history of hyper-Calvinism among the English Puritans, see Toon, *The Emergence of Hyper-Calvinism In English Nonconformity.* Another exceptional summary and refutation of hyper-Calvinism is Curt Daniel, "Hyper-Calvinism and John Gill" (PhD diss., University of Edinburgh, 1983). I disagree with Daniel's conclusion that John Gill was a hyper-Calvinist. While his presentation and refutation of hyper-Calvinism in general is superb, he overlooks some essential elements of John Gill which would remove him from this category. One key element was his financial support of George Whitefield and the Great Awakening, yet a hyper-Calvinist is one who discourages or avoids evangelism, not one who supports one of the greatest Calvinist evangelists of all time. Perhaps some of the things Gill said could lead people to think he was hyper-Calvinistic, yet it is an unfounded label.

For some, such as Van Til, it simply means that God has effectually determined the eternal resting place of both the elect and non-elect.[28] However, Van Til is not a hyper-Calvinist and does not employ the term "equal ultimacy" in the same manner as hyper-Calvinists. Instead, he means that God is the ultimate cause of everything but not necessarily the chargeable cause. For others, such as G. C. Berkouwer, equal ultimacy is understood to teach a symmetrical relationship between reprobation and election, making God the author of sin, and coinciding with the view found in hyper-Calvinism.[29] It is because of these monstrosities leveled against the Reformed tradition that clarity is absolutely vital. Without the clarity brought about by the nuances of the Reformed tradition the Christian is left with gaping holes in their theology and ability to accurately handle all of God's Word. Therefore, with so much at stake, these distinctions are important to consider in finding the true meaning of the doctrine of reprobation.

---

28   John M. Frame, *Cornelius Van Til: An Analysis of His Thoughts* (Phillipsburg, NJ: P&R, 1997), 86–88.

29   G. C. Berkouwer, *Divine Election* (Grand Rapids: Eerdmans, 1960), 172–217; *The Triumph of Grace in the Theology of Karl Barth* (Grand Rapids: Eerdmans, 1956), 390; see also Sproul, *Chosen by God*, 142–43.

CONCURRANCE, COMPATIBILISM, AND THE ORIGIN OF OBJECTIONS

*A*n element commonly missed by opponents of double predestination is the key principle known as compatibilism. James Daane assumes, "Once one commits himself to the decree of decretal theology, it is theologically impossible for him to allow, justify, or explain preaching the gospel to all men."[1] However, this misses the essential element of compatibilism—God uses means (such as preaching the gospel) to fulfill his predetermined ends. Compatibilism is how "God cooperates with created things in every action, directing their distinctive properties to cause them to act as they do."[2]

Another interchangeable term for compatibilism is concurrence. Berkhof says that concurrence is "the cooperation of the divine power with all subordinate powers, according to the pre-established laws of their operation, causing them to act and to act precisely as they do."[3] Both of these definitions require an understanding of God as sovereign and humans as responsible.

Richard Muller states that concurrence "defines the continuing divine support of the operation of secondary causes (whether free,

---

1   James Daane, *The Freedom of God: The Study of Election and Pulpit* (Grand Rapids: Eerdmans, 1973), 33.
2   Grudem, *Systematic Theology:* 317.
3   Berkhof, *Systematic Theology*, 170.

contingent, or necessary). For any contingent being to act in a free, contingent, or a necessary manner, the divine will which supports all contingent being must concur in its act."[4]

The question to be asked is, "Is God's sovereignty compatible with human responsibility?" Compatibilist theologians have consistently affirmed this. D. A. Carson has demonstrated this by answering the question in two proposals. First, God's sovereignty is never shown in Scripture in a manner that would remove human responsibility. Second, Scripture shows that humans are responsible for their actions. They choose to believe, disobey, to act one way or another, and their decisions and actions have significant moral consequences. However, human choices are never portrayed in Scripture in a manner that diminishes God's sovereignty or reduces God to being contingent on anything in creation.[5]

Compatibilism is another term for both truths in Scripture, that God's meticulous predetermination and governance are "compatible" with voluntary human choice. Scripture presents human choices as being exercised voluntarily but not independent of God. The compatibilist believes that human desires determine human choices which occur through divine determinism (see Acts 2:23 and 4:27–28). Human choice in Scripture is not presented as being coerced, but human actions are always in accordance with desire.

On the other hand, libertarian freedom is an incompatibility framework that presents humans as agents of free choice in a manner that is uninfluenced, apart from inclination or ability to go contrary to disposition. Libertarianism holds onto a concept of free will that requires humans to be able to take more than one possible course of

---

4   Richard Muller, *Dictionary of Latin and Greek Theological Terms: Drawn Principally from Protestant Scholastic Theology* (Grand Rapids: Baker, 1985), 76.

5   See D. A. Carson, "A Sovereign and Personal God" in *A Call to Spiritual Reformation: Priorities from Paul and His Prayers* (Grand Rapids: Baker, 1992), 145–66; "The Mystery of Providence," *How Long, O Lord? Reflections on Suffering and Evil* (Grand Rapids: Baker, 1990), 199–228. His most thorough treatment can be found in the fruit of his doctoral dissertation *Divine Sovereignty and Human Responsibility: Biblical Perspective in Tension* (Eugene, OR: Wipf & Stock, 1994).

action under a given set of circumstances.[6] Compatibilism teaches voluntary choice, not libertarian choice. Voluntary choice means the ability to choose based on desires, not the ability to choose contrary to desires.[7] Therefore, humans can only choose within their sin nature. Carson suggests, "Hundreds of passages could be explored to demonstrate that the Bible assumes both that God is sovereign and that people are responsible for their actions. As hard as it is for many people in the Western world to come to terms with both truths at the same time, it takes a great deal of interpretative ingenuity to argue that the Bible does not support them."[8]

Compatibilism defines how God is able to ordain evil events by evil people in such a way that maintains their complete responsibility. God determines all things, including evil (Eph. 1:11), and he uses them for his sovereign purposes (Isa. 45:7). However, God's predetermination of sin is always in such a way that he remains blameless and humanity remains blameworthy (Acts 2:23; 4:27). Compatibilism distinguishes Christianity from deism (an impersonal god who allows events to unfold without purpose) or open theism (a god whose knowledge does not extend to future events). Biblical Christianity believes that God not only knows whatever has or ever will happen in creation but actually ordains them so they accomplish his purposes in creating them in the first place. Despite God's determination of all events, every secondary cause (actions performed by God's creation) is truly real. Both of these truths intertwine to make the double helix of compatibilism. God's predetermined plan is compatible with human will and actions. So humans never act contrary to God's eternal plan, and humans never act contrary to his own desire.[9]

---

6   Robert Kane, "Libertarianism," *Four Views on Free Will* (Oxford: Blackwell, 2007), 39.

7   The Arminian view of Libertarian freedom is known as contrary choice; the Calvinist view of volitional freedom is known as free agency. So, compatibilism denies that the will is free to choose contrary to its desires because the desires influence the will and the human desire is dead in sin and the corruption of original sin. Furthermore, compatibilism does not teach that the human will is free from God's decrees.

8   Carson, *A Call to Spiritual Reformation*, 150.

9   Antony Flew, "Compatibilism, Free Will, and God," *Philosophy* 48, no. 185 (July 1973): 232–33.

Compatibilistic Middle Knowledge?

Some, misunderstanding compatibilism, call themselves Calvinists but adhere to a form of Molinism to explain God's role in reprobation. Thinkers like Erickson exhibit this Molinism, or middle knowledge, by saying, "In our scheme, however, God has a foreknowledge of possibilities. God foresees what possible beings will do if placed in a particular situation with all the influences that will be present at that point in time and space. On this basis he chooses which of the possible individuals will become actualities and which circumstances and influences will be present."[10]

Another strong proponent is Bruce Ware, who states, "God, through his middle knowledge, can know whether he should permit an agent to choose according to his greatest desire or whether to alter the circumstances."[11]

Compatibilist middle knowledge is, at best, an aberration of true compatibilism.[12] While it is true that God knows all things, including what he has decreed would never happen but he could have done (possibilities), to say that God's decree of reprobation is contingent on such knowledge is an affront to the historical understanding of compatibilism.[13] The Westminster Confession of Faith states,

---

10   Millard Erickson, *Christian Theology* (Grand Rapids: Baker Books, 1985), 387.

11   Bruce A. Ware, *God's Greater Glory: The Exalted God of Scripture and the Christian Faith* (Wheaton, IL: Crossway, 2004), 121. For a thorough critique of compatibilist middle knowledge, see John D. Lang, "The Compatibility of Calvinism and Middle Knowledge," in *Journal of the Evangelical Theological Society* 43, no. 7 (2004): 455–67.

12   There are some who think that compatibilist middle knowledge is the way to reconcile Calvinism and Arminianism, e.g., William Lane Craig, "Middle Knowledge: A Calvinist-Arminian Rapprochement?," in *The Grace of God and the Will of Man*, ed. Clark H. Pinnock (Minneapolis: Bethany House, 1989), 161.

13   God's knowledge can be a complicated labyrinth for many people. The two main Categories are God's knowledge of himself and God's knowledge of external things. Under God's knowledge we can further distinguish God's knowledge of necessary things (such as the truths of mathematics (for example, 2+2=4). It is also the knowledge of truths such as the whole is greater than the part and no circle can be a square). Second, God's Free Knowledge is his knowledge of his decree (of that which, in his wisdom, God freely and unchangeably ordained to come to pass). That which God decrees is obviously a subset of all the possibilities that are known to him. His decree also has its source solely in his mind and will. This category can be separated further into two subcategories: (a) knowledge of things he chooses to bring into reality we

"Although God knows whatsoever may or can come to pass upon all supposed conditions, yet hath He not decreed anything because He foresaw it as future, or as that which would come to pass upon such conditions."[14] Further, Charles Hodge writes,

> The knowledge of God is not only all-comprehending, but it is intuitive and immutable. He knows all things as they are, being as being, phenomena as phenomena, the possible as possible, the actual as actual, the necessary as necessary, the free as free, the past as past, the present as present, the future as future. Although all things are ever present in his view, yet He sees them as successive in time. The vast procession of events, thoughts, feelings, and acts, stands open to his view.[15]

The greatest distinction between compatibilism and Molinism rests in how one understands God's knowledge of possibilities. While God has a knowledge of possibilities (divine counterfactual knowledge), nevertheless, it has always been part of God's natural knowledge, not distinct from it nor dependent on man.

Middle knowledge necessitates that God knows the "possibilities" of libertarian free creatures (creating a third kind of knowledge in God). This limits God's knowledge of possibilities not by God's knowledge of counterfactuals, but by man's choices in those counterfactuals. Although unstated by proponents, this theological position assaults both God's omnipotence (making his choices subject to a set of possible circumstances, regardless of how numerous those possible circumstances may be) and his omniscience (as it, necessarily involves God "looking" into the future and analyzing a potential situation outside of his own decree). David Basinger writes,

---

call this his Definite Knowledge; (b) knowledge of things he chooses not to bring into reality sometimes called his Simple Knowledge.

14   WCF 3.2.

15   Charles Hodge, *Systematic Theology* (Grand Rapids: Eerdmans, 1981), 1:897.

> But since a God with middle knowledge cannot control
> what we will choose to do in any situation in which we pos-
> sess meaningful freedom, it can hardly be said that middle
> knowledge allows God to "plan" the world he wants in the
> sense that he can insure that the most desirable "ends and
> purposes" of which he can conceive will always be achieved. [16]

Those who support a compatibilist middle knowledge often do so
with a libertarian view of the will in mind, while those who reject it
do so with a compatibilist view of the will.

It is either true that counterfactuals exist in the mind of God
rationally, or that his knowledge is based on human free actions. But
both cannot be true! If counterfactuals exist in the mind of God and
how he chose to create a creature, then compatibilism is true. If God's
knowledge of counterfactuals is determined by human liberty in a
given situation, then libertarian free will is true. Both cannot be true
at the same time because they contradict one another. So compatibilist middle knowledge cannot logically exist. While it is true that
there is divine counterfactual knowledge, it is part of God's natural
knowledge, not human libertarian choice.

Compatibilism Properly Defined

The chief objection to compatibilism is that God is still responsible
for human sin because he is in control of the factors which influence
a person's choice. However, compatibilism has always maintained that
God cannot directly commit evil, and that he cannot force anyone to do
evil. James 1:13 says, "Let no one say when he is tempted, 'I am being
tempted by God'; for God cannot be tempted by evil, and He Himself
does not tempt anyone." What James says is that God's holiness and
justice will not allow for him to author sin nor commit it in any manner.
"His work is perfect, for all His ways are just; a God of faithfulness and
without injustice, righteous and upright is He" (Deut. 32:4).

---

16   David Basinger, "Divine Control and Human Freedom: Is Middle Knowledge the
      Answer?," *JETS* 36 (1993): 62.

These two truths are taught in Scripture: God ordains all things, and humans are the only ones who can be chargeable for sin. That statement on its own can seem misleading if left unqualified. It must be understood that God doesn't force anyone to sin and then blame them for it. Instead, God's ordinance is compatible with the human agency which willfully commits sin. Regarding the crucifixion, Acts 2:23 says, "this Man, delivered over by the predetermined plan and foreknowledge of God, you nailed to a cross by the hands of godless men and put Him to death." It is obvious here that God predetermined the crucifixion event, yet it was carried out by the "hands of godless men." It is important in this matter to affirm everything Scripture teaches without squelching one doctrine with another, or distorting Scripture.

Martin Luther shows an understanding of compatibilism time and again as he discusses human responsibility and the doctrine of reprobation. He uses the examples of Pharaoh, Esau, and Judas to prove that God, by his unconditional will, chose to reprobate certain individuals. He states,

> On your view [Erasmus], God will elect nobody, and no place for election will be left; all that is left is freedom of will to heed or defy the long-suffering and wrath of God. But if God is thus robbed of His power and wisdom in election, what will He be but just that idol, Chance, under whose sway all things happen at random? Eventually, we shall come to this: that men may be saved and damned without God's knowledge! For He will not have marked out by sure election those that should be saved and those that should be damned; He will merely have set before all men His general long-suffering, which forbears and hardens, together with His chastening and punishing mercy, and left it to them to choose whether they would be saved or damned, while He Himself, perchance, goes off, as Homer says, to an Ethiopian banquet.[17]

---

17   Martin Luther, *The Bondage of the Will*, trans. J. I. Packer and O. R. Johnston (1517; repr., Grand Rapids: Baker Books, 1957), 199–200.

Luther highlights that the main failure of this perspective is the unwillingness to grant that God's sovereignty marks out and unconditionally predestines both the elect and the reprobate. Luther understands this issue as connected not only to God's sovereignty but also to God's knowledge. God cannot be rightly said to be omniscient if he does not know with certainty who the elect and the reprobate are. If there is even the remotest possibility that God does not know this then he cannot be said to be omniscient. This concern becomes the driving force behind Luther's understanding of the necessity that flows from God's sovereignty. Regarding this matter as it pertains to Judas, Luther writes,

> If God foreknew that Judas would be a traitor, Judas became a traitor of necessity, and it was not in the power of Judas or of any creature to act differently, or to change his will, from that which God had foreseen. It is true that Judas acted willingly, and not under compulsion, but his willing was the work of God, brought into being by His omnipotence, like everything else. . . . If you do not allow that the thing which God foreknows is necessarily brought to pass, you take away faith and the fear of God, you undermine all the Divine promises and threatenings, and so you deny Deity itself![18]

It is no surprise that Luther's work on the matter is offensive to many modern audiences. The sort of polemic that was acceptable in academic society in his time is something of a legend by today's standards.

While at first glance Luther's statements concerning Judas might seem to affirm a form of equal ultimacy or hyper-Calvinism, his qualification that "Judas acted willingly, and not under compulsion," proves that Luther was working within a compatibilistic framework. What really separated Luther from Erasmus (and later, Calvinists from Arminians) was the issue of compatibilism. By "compatibilism" it is meant that God's will and the human will are compatible. It shows God

---

18   Luther, *Bondage of the Will*, 213.

operates in such a manner that the human will is not violated, even when he decrees their actions from before the foundation of the world.

Noncompatibilists such as Erasmus (and Arminians after him) believe that man's "free will" is not compatible with divine determinism. To explain the discrepancy between God's sovereignty and man's freedom, they often resort to the idea that God somehow relinquishes his sovereignty.[19] The compatibilist position realizes that there is an aspect of mystery behind how God's absolute sovereignty does not destroy human responsibility.[20] It is under the compatibilist framework that Luther can claim at the same time that, "Judas became a traitor by necessity," and "Judas acted willingly." In order to make this clear, and to resolve God's justice in damning the reprobate, Luther says,

> You may be worried that it is hard to defend the mercy and equity of God in damning the undeserving, that is, ungodly persons, who, being born in ungodliness, can by no means avoid being ungodly, and staying so, and being damned, but are compelled by natural necessity to sin and perish; as Paul says: "We were all the children of wrath, even as others" (Eph. 2.3), created such by God Himself from a seed that had been corrupted by the sin of the one man, Adam. But here God must be reverenced and held in awe, as being most merciful to those whom He justifies and saves in their own utter unworthiness; and we must show some measure of deference to His Divine wisdom by believing Him just when to us He seems unjust.[21]

Without being cold and calculating, Luther addresses what might be a stumbling block for some and comforts them with trusting God's justice in the matter of reprobation (even when it might not seem

---

19   This position will be discussed in the "Objections" section to follow.
20   The Arminian view eventually appeals to mystery as well. They ultimately appeal to mystery to explain how God can foreknow libertarian free actions and they still be free.
21   Luther, *Bondage of the Will*, 314.

fair). The caution Luther emulates when discussing this matter is one which should always accompany a proper discussion of reprobation.

WHERE DO OBJECTIONS ORIGINATE?

Reprobation is a difficult doctrine. The numerous sub-standard definitions make discussions even more difficult. Also, because there are many necessary qualifications, it is often discouraging to new believers, making it easier for them to neglect it rather than pursue a comprehensive knowledge of it. However, it is the responsibility of faithful ministers to guide people in the study of God's Word, so they do not neglect even difficult matters. The full counsel of God, including this difficult doctrine, requires both intentionality and precision.

In summary, reprobation is a matter of God's eternal, unconditional decree regarding the destiny of the non-elect. This unconditional decree is divisible into two elements, a negative element and a positive element. The negative element is known as preterition, whereby God chooses to exclude the non-elect from election unto salvation; to reject them and to leave them to justice. The positive element of God's decree is known as precondemnation. This is God's active decision before time began, that the non-elect would be held accountable for all their actions; that there would be no mercy or forgiveness given to them but rather that they would be held accountable to his holiness and justice.

Distinct from the decree of reprobation (which is resigned to eternity past) is the execution of reprobation (which occurs in time and space). The execution of God's decree can also be subdivided into two elements: causality and condemnation. The first, causality, is enveloped in the concept of compatibilism. This refers to the compatibility between the human will and God's sovereign eternal plan. These two concepts are so compatible that God's decree is executed in such a manner that the creature always does what is in his heart to do, what he wills to do, leaving him willfully responsible. With regard to evil, God always brings it to pass through secondary means. This brings about the second element of the execution of the decree of reprobation, condemnation, which involves man's culpability and therefore worthiness of condemnation. Condemnation is the act God goes through with holding humans accountable for their sins; and the just consequence of this is damnation.

Based on the aforementioned components of reprobation, it is inaccurate to say that God reprobates humans to hell without any further qualification. This simplistic manner of speaking disregards many essential elements to a proper understanding of reprobation, which in turn lends itself to the false caricature of hyper-Calvinism. When careful attention is not given to the teaching of reprobation, the errors of hyper-Calvinism can easily creep in. But with proper considerations given, it is easy to address common objections to the doctrine of reprobation—most are founded on a false understanding of what it actually teaches.

The claim of hyper-Calvinism is not the only objection raised against the Reformed view of reprobation. Many objections are traditionally raised, but, the main issue, regarding free will, is addressed by the doctrine of compatibilism.[22] While libertarian free will is a primary objection, other objections are often leveled against reprobation and predestination. Two major categories of objections are that reprobation is fatalism, and that God limits his sovereignty. These two objections are based either on misconceptions of what reprobation logically concludes, or contain a presupposition about why it cannot be in the first place. However, because biblical fidelity is on the line, and faithfulness to the Lord, it is of paramount importance that each potential error is considered and any conclusion that is less than biblical is eradicated.

---

22   Luther, *The Bondage of the Will*; John Calvin, *The Bondage and Liberation of the Will: A Defense of the Orthodox Doctrine of Human Choice Against Pighius*, ed. A. N. S. Lane, trans. G. I. Davies (Grand Rapids: Baker Books, 1996); Jonathan Edwards, *The Freedom of the Will*, vol. 1, in *The Works of Jonathan Edwards*, ed. Paul Ramsey (1834; repr., Edinburgh: Banner of Truth, 1995); Scott Christensen, *What about Free Will?: Reconciling Our Choices with God's Sovereignty* (Phillipsburg, NJ: P&R, 2016).

OBJECTIONS CONSIDERED, PART ONE

*T*hroughout history, there have been numerous objections to the doctrine of double predestination, specifically reprobation. These objections span a wide spectrum. Some presuppose a libertarian free will and from there find the doctrine of predestination in general to be odious. Others have an objection on the basis of their understanding of God's holiness. Some, such as Rice, object to it outright, calling election "a bad teaching, a false doctrine."[1] The range of objections is broad.

However, these objections chiefly assume that reprobation demands some conclusions that are not necessarily true. Arminians and Calvinists both need to give an account for the fact that God does not save all men. God is omnipotent enough to create and save, omniscient enough to comprehensively know the destiny of all men, and sovereign enough to refrain from creating those who he knows will eternally perish. But it is clear by the creation of the non-saved that God willed them to exist. Both camps simply must address this perceived dilemma. Reformed theologian Loraine Boettner recognized exactly this when he wrote, "The chief difficulty with the doctrine of Election, of course, arises in regard to the unsaved; and the Scriptures

---

1   John R. Rice, *Predestined for Hell? No!* (Murfreesboro, TN: Sword of the Lord Foundation, 1958), 85.

have given us no extended explanation of their state."[2] The coexistence of sinful, unsaved people with an omnipotent, holy God brings the issue of theodicy to the forefront of every believer's mind.

What should the Christian's response be? It is of the utmost importance that neither human responsibility nor divine sovereignty be denied in favor of the other. These two doctrines are the bedrock for the believer to properly understand God's great plan in a sin-cursed world. They are inseparable.

The question is straightforward: "If God elects, what happens to those he does not elect?" No one should believe in election and reprobation just because it provides a nice and coherent system (though it does do that). Rather, believers are obligated to study and understand the truths of election and reprobation because they are revealed in Scripture.

Most objections are simply based on a faulty or mistaught definition of one of the elements of reprobation (previously discussed). These various objections can be collected into three main categories: It is fatalism, God limits his sovereignty, or it demeans God's holiness.

One of the chief arguments against unconditional, predetermined reprobation of the non-elect is that it appears to be fatalism.[3] There are many who do not properly understand reprobation and often associate it with this philosophical idea. In Scripture, the Hebrew and Greek words בָּחַר and ἐκλέγω are synonyms, and when used in regard to human destiny they speak of God picking certain individuals from the human race to be the beneficiaries of his sovereign grace.[4]

The Greek term for predestination (προορίζω) unquestionably means "to fix beforehand."[5] In other contexts (outside of those

---

2   Loraine Boettner, *The Reformed Doctrine of Predestination* (Philadelphia: P&R, 1972), 104–5.

3   Although predestination is often charged with fatalism, it is outside the scope of this book to give a lengthy discussion on the matter. A cursory explanation surveys the purpose of the book, however, supplemental material can be found in the footnotes throughout this section.

4   "בָּחַר," *BDB*, 103–4; Lothar Coenen, "Elect, Choose," *NIDNTT*, 1:536–43.

5   G. Abbott-Smith, *A Manual Greek Lexicon of the New Testament* (Edinburgh: T&T Clark, 1937), 382. K. L. Schmidt, "προορίζω," in *TDNT*, eds. Gerhard Kittle and Gerhard Friedrich (Grand Rapids: Eerdmans, 1967), 5:456. Paul Jacobs and Hartmut Krienke, "Foreknowledge, Providence, Predestination," in *TNIDNTT*, ed. Colin

which speak of human destiny), it and its word family always refer to initiating a preplanned action.[6] When applied to the context of human destinies, it indicates an intentionality on God's part prior to human creation and interaction. Because predestination inherently deprives humans of their autonomy (particularly regarding election and reprobation), it is often viewed as most offensive.

Often, the objection to reprobation on the basis that it teaches fatalism comes from two major groups. The first are those who concede that the Christian Bible teaches predestination. However, they reject the Christian Bible and the Christian God. They believe that a God who could predetermine anything is equivalent to fatalism. The second group consists of those who believe that predestination is fatalism and that the Bible does not teach individual election and reprobation. This group believes that the Bible does not teach predestination because it would thereby remove human autonomy. This ends up requiring a redefinition of biblical predestination.

What Is Fatalism?

Because predestination teaches that God ordains all things, it is often associated with fatalism. It is important to define and distinguish the two concepts. First, fatalism is a philosophical idea that teaches that no matter what someone does, a particular outcome will occur. Fatalism teaches that humans are powerless to do anything other than what they are "fated" to do, irrespective of any actions they perform in their lives. Included in this is the belief that humans have no power to affect the future outside of fate.[7]

A famous historical illustration of fatalism is found in what is known as the Idle Argument.[8] The basis of the argument has been

---

Brown (Grand Rapids: Zondervan, 1975), 1:695–96. K. L. Schmidt, "προορίζω," *TDNT*, 5:456. Paul Jacobs and Harmut Krienke, "Foreknowledge, Providence, Predestination," *NIDNTT*, 1:695–96.

6   "προτίθημι," A-S, 380, 390.

7   Richard Taylor, "Fatalism," *PR* 71, no. 1 (1962): 56–66.

8   This took place between Origen and Cicero. See Origen, *Contra Celsum*, 2:20; it is also called "The Lazy Argument." Translated by Henry Chadwick, *Origen: Contra Celsum* (Cambridge: Cambridge University Press, 1980).

succinctly recounted by Susanne Bobzien, who summarizes it as follows:

> If it is fated that you will recover from this illness, then, regardless of whether you consult a doctor or you do not consult [a doctor] you will recover. But also: if it is fated that you won't recover from this illness, then, regardless of whether you consult a doctor or you do not consult [a doctor] you won't recover. But either it is fated that you will recover from this illness or it is fated that you won't recover. Therefore, it is futile to consult a doctor.[9]

The following example displays the thought process of fatalism. Suppose someone is fated to die of sickness or to recover from a sickness; it does not matter what they do because their fate has already been determined. If they are fated to die, they could take medicine, go to a doctor, get surgery, or pursue any other means of recovery, and it would not change the reality that they are going to die from the sickness. Fatalism is concerned with a solitary, unavoidable event that disregards human action.

In fatalism there are two forms. The first is materialistic fatalism, in which "fate" is an impersonal force of nature, found in ancient astrology and some strains of atheism. The second version of fatalism is found in Stoic philosophy, claiming that written within the natural law of creation there is a particular "fate" for everything. This version of fatalism is often associated with pantheism.

With that said, the word "fate" does occur in Scripture. One example is found in Ecclesiastes 2:14–15, which states, "The wise man's eyes are in his head, but the fool walks in darkness. And yet I know that one fate befalls them both. Then I said to myself, 'As is the fate of the fool, it will also befall me. Why then have I been extremely wise?' So I said to myself, 'This too is vanity.'" The term used for "fate" is

---

9 Susanne Bobzien, *Determinism and Freedom in Stoic Philosophy* (Oxford: Oxford University Press, 1998), 182.

מִקְרֶה, which means, "what happens by itself without any assistance or wish of person involved."[10] But this word is not intended to teach blind, impersonal fate. Solomon is speaking of the reality that humans cannot add any more time to their lives no matter what they do; theirs is a common end (Matt. 6:27). Death is a "fate" which awaits everyone. Far different from philosophical fatalism, what is spoken of here is merely humans facing reality. Death itself has been foreordained (Heb. 9:27). This term is used in Hebrew for an occurrence in life that is an inescapable reality, not the impersonal force of fate. It is a description of the general happenings of life.

In contrast to fatalism, Christianity teaches absolute predestination. For example, the doctrine of predestination essentially teaches that God determines a man's destiny from before creation, that God is the ultimate cause in realizing it, utilizing the exercise of human volition on the part of the individual predestined. Fatalism is an impersonal, meaningless entity which somehow delimits the outcome of all of reality, whereas predestination is the intentional plan of the triune God for a specific purpose; namely, the manifestation of his own glory throughout eternity.

Calvin distinguishes Christian predestination from fatalism when he states,

> Fate is a term given by the Stoics to their doctrine of necessity, which they had formed out of a labyrinth of contradictory reasoning; a doctrine calculated to call God Himself to order, and to set Him laws whereby to work. Predestination I define to be, according to the Holy Scriptures, that free and unfettered counsel of God by which He rules all mankind, and all men and things, and also all parts and particles of the world by His infinite wisdom and incomprehensible justice.[11]

---

10 William Lee Holladay and Ludwig Köhler, "מִקְרֶה," *A Concise Hebrew and Aramaic Lexicon of the Old Testament* (Leiden: Brill, 2000), 213.

11 John Calvin, *A Defense of the Secret Providence of God*, vol. 2, *Calvin's Calvinism*, trans. Henry P. Cole (London: Paternoster-Row, 1856), 261–62.

Loraine Boettner, in his book *The Reformed Doctrine of Predestination*, explains how the only line of agreement between predestination and fatalism is that there is an absolute destiny for every person, yet he points out that there many lines of demarcation. Boettner explains that Christian predestination affirms a personal, holy, and infinitely wise God. Within this paradigm, God may be the first cause (ultimate cause), but not the efficient cause of evil. Christian predestination is not only concerned with the determined end, but also the means to that end. These means include human volition and actions; a distinction which establishes morality and human responsibility in regard to their actions.

Is Christian Predestination Similar to Islamic Predestination?

Some who misunderstand Christian predestination will associate it with Islamic predestination. The Islamic doctrine of predestination is very similar to fatalism (as it has been defined). Islam teaches a form of fatalism that has no regard for human volition, saying, "Allah has written for the son of Adam his inevitable share of adultery whether he is aware of it or not."[12] By a statement such as this, it can be observed that there is no concern for secondary causes, human volition or responsibility; only an inevitable and unavoidable end. Samuel Zwemer, a Christian missionary to Muslims, describes Islamic predestination: "This kind of Predestination should be called fatalism and nothing else. For fatalism is the doctrine of an inevitable necessity and implies an omnipotent and arbitrary sovereign power."[13] Essentially, Islam takes the pagan philosophy of fatalism and simply attributes it to the will of Allah. Like "Fate," Allah's decrees have no regard for morality or human volition. Furthermore, Allah does not have any gracious purpose in his plans or decrees.

---

12   Muhammad Ibn Ismail Bukhari and Muhammad Muhsin Kha, *Ahadith: The English Translation of Sahih Al-Bukhari with the Arabic Text* (Alexandria, VA: Al-Saadawi, 1996), 8:397–98 (§8.77.609).

13   Samuel M. Zwemer, *Moslem Doctrine of God: An Essay on the Character and Attributes of Allah according to the Koran and Orthodox Tradition* (New York: American Tract Society, 1905), 97.

This is why Islamic predestination leads to hopelessness. Islamic predestination introduces a hopeless skepticism that undermines human volition. Within this framework, there is no reason to act either good or bad, to desire good over evil, because in the end Allah (fate) has assigned an unavoidable destiny to everyone regardless to human volition and actions. Charles Hodge explains how this mentality is the opposite of the Christian doctrine of predestination when he states, "The Sovereignty of God is the ground of peace and confidence to all his people. They rejoice that the Lord God omnipotent reigneth; that neither necessity, nor chance, nor the folly of man, nor the malice of Satan controls the sequence of events and all their issues."[14]

Islamic predestination engenders a blind resignation to the "fate" of Allah within its adherents. Allah's determinations have no regard for the agency of the creature; as such, they are whimsical, arbitrary, absent of grace, and contrary to justice. Because Islamic predestination ignores these essential elements of predestination it cannot rightly be associated with Christian predestination (which is concerned with the holiness of God and the culpability of volitional agents).

Evaluating the First Category of Objections

The Bible teaches that an all-wise and holy God determines all things with the consideration of human agency. To ascribe the Christian doctrine of predestination to fatalism is inaccurate. It not only undermines the Word of God but it twists what is taught by predestination to make it appear heinous when, in fact, it is just the opposite. The Christian Scriptures teach that while God has decreed the destiny of every human, he has done so in such a way that humans are always accountable for their actions and do everything their hearts desire. No one goes to hell while desiring righteousness and forgiveness, nor is anyone forced into heaven while still harboring hatred for God. Rather, the means by which humans go to hell is on account of their own sinful heart's ambitions. Humans are personal agents and God is a personal God who holds personal agents accountable. Thus,

---

14   Hodge, *Systematic Theology*, 1:440–41.

predestination is not "fatalism" and God is not blind fate. Rather, God is purposeful in all he does.

In contrast, fatalism is an impersonal blind force; it has no regard for morality, human volition, or divine holiness. Fatalism teaches the futility of human volition or actions because of fatalistic necessity. Predestination, however, is the work of a personal, holy, wise God who is just in all his ways, purposing the destiny for each individual for a very specific (and ultimately, greatest) reason: the manifestation of his attributes. Fatalism is only concerned with finality and not causality. It is not concerned with the steps to the end, only the end itself (and had concern for the end only insofar as that it comes to pass; not for any particular reason or purpose).

While fatalism denies human responsibility, predestination establishes it. Since one of the purposes of predestination is to manifest God's justice and holiness against sin, this necessarily demands that human action (namely, sin) and responsibility for such action are both integral to the bringing about such destinies. Fatalism has no such concern. This is why D. A. Carson rightly concludes, "Christians are not fatalists. The central line of Christian tradition neither sacrifices the utter sovereignty of God nor reduces the responsibility of his image-bearers."[15] Ultimately God's predestination remains the key element.

REPROBATION IS NOT TRUE BECAUSE GOD LIMITS HIS SOVEREIGNTY

A second denial of reprobation rests in the idea that God limits himself in some manner or another.[16] This view manifests itself in three major categories: (1) those who affirm only a single predestination but deny reprobation (prominently found in Lutheranism); (2) those

---

15   D. A. Carson, *The Difficult Doctrine of the Love of God* (Wheaton, IL: Crossway, 2000), 50–51.

16   While predestination is often denied because God "limits His sovereignty," it is outside the scope of this book to give a lengthy discussion on the matter. A cursory explanation surveys the purpose of the book however supplemental materials can be found in the footnotes throughout this section.

who believe that God limits his sovereignty in such a way that he does not determine the destiny of anyone or everyone (Arminianism); or (3) those who believe God limits his sovereignty to such a degree that he restrains his knowledge of future events (open theism). Of those who hold to predestination, errors exist on one of two ends of the spectrum. On one end are those who teach that predestination is merely single-sided (that reprobation only happens passively and by divine permission). On the other end of the spectrum are those known as hyper-Calvinists, who teach equal ultimacy double predestination, that God is the author of sin in the same manner that he is the author of faith in the elect.

Those who adhere to single predestination incorrectly affirm that reprobation is exclusively a "passive" activity. The most famous and thorough theologian to present this position is Augustus Strong. Strong has been rightly critiqued for promoting a merely "passive" understanding of God's decree in relation to evil. he says, "The decree of reprobation is not a positive decree, like that of election, but a permissive decree to leave the sinner to his self-chosen rebellion and its natural consequences of punishment."[17]

Those who espouse single predestination assign the result of the condemnation of the non-elect to mere permission. First, the presupposition that permission alleviates the issue of theodicy will be evaluated. Second, the assertion that single predestination is less offensive than reprobation will be inspected.

Permissive Language and Theodicy

Many of those who espouse single predestination according to permissive language do so because their chief presupposition is that reprobation is both unbiblical and offensive. Being generally

---

17   Augustus Hopkins Strong, *Systematic Theology* (Philadelphia: American Baptist Publication Society, 1907), 3:789–90. B. B. Warfield after describing the differences between Fatalism and predestination says, "That is the difference between fate and predestination. And all the language of men cannot tell the immensity of the difference." "What Fatalism Is," in *Selected Shorter Writings of Benjamin B. Warfield*, vol. 1, ed. John E. Meeter (Phillipsburg, NJ: P&R, 1970), 1:7–8.

dissatisfied with how reprobation answers the issue of theodicy, they would attempt to alleviate this problem by proposing the concept of permission (rather than predestination) regarding sin. Many of these theologians ultimately land on a version of single predestination or prescient foreknowledge when discussing predestination. However, before these concepts can be addressed, it is important to ask, "Is the concept of permission acceptable?"

Augustus Strong writes, "Men are not 'appointed' to disobedience and stumbling in the same way that they are 'appointed' to salvation. God uses positive means to save, but not to destroy."[18] Strong affirms that election is 'positive' but denies it regarding reprobation. Instead, he invokes the "passive" view in order to solve the issue of theodicy and reprobation that are raised.[19]

Even Arminius's chief objection to reprobation is due to its relationship to sin (although the prior historical analysis demonstrated that he did not actually understand the concept entirely). However, his concern is similar to that of many, who wonder how God can be the ultimate cause of all things, including evil, and yet not be the chargeable cause of sin. Many, like Arminius, attempt to alleviate the tension of theodicy by appealing to divine permission.

Jonathan Edwards offers a rebuttal by arguing that the notion of "permission" is illogical because it undermines the will of God. He begins by explaining the chief definition of permission: "To permit is not to hinder what has, or appears to have, a tendency to take place."[20] Noninterference is the chief principle of permission by every standard of the definition. Arminian theologian Jack Cottrell states, "God simply allows these agents to produce what they will. This is true permission, i.e., not efficaciousness but noninterference."[21]

---

18   Strong, *Systematic Theology*, 3:790.
19   It is important to note that Strong misses the fact that there is a distinction between the decree and its execution, for Scripture does say people are appointed to disobedience and stumbling (1 Peter 2:8).
20   Editor's note in Jonathan Edwards, "Concerning the Divine Decrees," in *The Works of Jonathan Edwards* (1835; repr., Peabody, MA: Hendrickson, 2005), 2:530.
21   Jack Cottrell, "The Nature of Divine Sovereignty," in *The Grace of God and the Will of Man*, ed. Clark H. Pinnock (Minneapolis: Bethany House, 1995), 110.

However, such a concept is fallacious; it is impossible for there to be noninterference on God's part (especially when eternal matters are concerned).

Johnathan Edwards exposes the illogical nature of mere permission as a means to explain theodicy on two accounts. First, it assumes something is "destined" to occur which God did not decide. Second, it undermines the will of God in what transpires in time. God's decrees take place before the foundation of the world and, because there is no independent force outside of God, it is impossible for there to be any notion of noninterference before time began (with whom or what would God be interfering?).[22] Since God's will determined all things to occur in the manner they do (evil included), it would be improper to say that God did not will it to occur (again, that would necessitate the existence of something opposing the will of God, that he allows). In other words, to say that God doesn't "interfere" is to imply that the universe and all of its operations occur apart from God's sustaining hand; that he is a third-party observer who may or may not disrupt what is inevitably going to occur.[23]

The conclusion that divine permission is more tolerable than ordination in respect to evil is ultimately a distinction without a difference. Rather than alleviating the issue of predetermined sin, it merely redirects it to an impersonal force (reminiscent of fatalism) that God is simply given the luxury of either allowing or prohibiting. Who or what set in motion such a disposition towards evil, which God then passively permits for the non-elect, is an entity that exists not in Scripture, but only in the minds of those willing to philosophically speculate.

---

22   "The idea of permission is possible only where there is an independent force. . . . But this is not the situation in the case of the God of the universe. Nothing in the universe can be independent of the Omnipotent Creator, for in him we live and move and have our being. Therefore, the idea of permission makes no sense when applied to God." Gordon H. Clark, *Religion, Reason, and Revelation* (Phillipsburg, NJ: P&R, 1961), 205.

23   "His will is supreme, underived, and independent on anything without himself; being in everything determined by His own counsel, having no other rule but his own wisdom." Edwards, "The Freedom of the Will," in *The Works of Jonathan Edwards*, 1:71.

It is only natural to ask why the Reformed position is so insistent that "permission" is an unacceptable way of speaking of God's predetermined plan for evil. Outside of the logical inconsistencies, the key problem with the permissive language is that there are many times in which Scripture puts God's active sovereignty over evil on display. While Scripture teaches that God is impeccably holy and beyond reproach when it comes to sin, it also speaks of his predetermined plan for sin and evil.

It is helpful to consider one scriptural example that shows the insufficiency of the divine permission view in respect to sin. Genesis 50:20 serves as a powerful passage for consideration: "As for you, you meant evil against me, but God meant it for good in order to bring about this present result, to preserve many people alive." Those who propose divine permission as the answer to theodicy have used two arguments from this text.

The first is presented by David Hunt: "The Bible does not say that God decreed that Joseph's brothers would hate him, desire to kill him, sell him into Egypt, and then lie to their father. It is clear that their evil intent came from jealous hearts. God foreknew their hearts and restrained and channeled their wicked desire to accomplish His will."[24] To begin with, this idea of foreknowledge does not fit with his own concept of free will. If free will is man's ability to choose either good or evil at any given moment, this concept may suffice to some degree in a surface-level Arminian understanding of libertarian free will however, it ends up as open theism when taken to its logical conclusion.

The second (and more internally consistent) argument is that God takes a bad situation and makes it good. Roger Olson explains Genesis 50:20 as God turning evil into good:

> Arminians are well aware of Calvinist arguments based
> upon the Genesis narrative where Joseph's brothers meant

---

24   David Hunt and James R. White, *Debating Calvinism: Five Points, Two Views* (Sisters, OR: Multnomah, 2004), 52.

his captivity for evil but God meant it for good (Gen 50:20). They simply do not believe this proves that God ordains evil that good may come of it. Arminians believe God permits evil and brings good out of it. Otherwise, who is the real sinner?[25]

However, once one begins to examine the text he will find that this interpretation does not stand up to the scrutiny of the historical-grammatical hermeneutic. In context Joseph understands that God is just as responsible for his bondage into slavery as his brothers. When Joseph reveals himself to his brothers he comforts them with these words: "Now do not be grieved or angry with yourselves, because you sold me here, for God sent me before you to preserve life" (Gen. 45:5). Joseph repeats the phrase "God sent me" to describe his slavery in Egypt (Gen. 45:7). In case it wasn't clear the first two times, Joseph associates his predicament with God a third time: "Now, therefore, it was not you who sent me here, but God." Nowhere does Joseph give the idea that God simply took the bad situation his brothers put him in and made it good; he associates his brothers' sinning with God's sending.

The manner in which Joseph's brothers planned evil was the very plan of God in using that evil for his good purposes. Compatibilism, in a superior manner, explains this text in a way that is consistent with the lexical usage of "meant." This text demonstrates how the divine will incorporates the human will in respect to evil.[26] A plethora of other texts and examples could be provided, such as Amos 3:6 ("If a calamity occurs in a city has not the LORD done it?"), Lamentations 3:38 ("Is it not from the mouth of the Most High that both good and ill go forth?"), and Isaiah 45:7 ("The One forming light and creating

---

25   Olson, *Arminian Theology*, 100.
26   In a similar discussion on this matter, James White, using the example of the Assyrians in Isaiah 10:5, states, "This is compatibilism with clarity: God uses the sinful actions of the Assyrians for the good purpose of judging His people, and yet He judges the Assyrians for their sinful intentions." Dave Hunt and James R. White, *Debating Calvinism: Five Points, Two Views* (Sisters, OR: Multnomah, 2004), 44.

darkness, Causing well-being and creating calamity; I am the LORD who does all these").

However, the most prominent example is the crucifixion of Jesus and his betrayal at the hands of Judas. In this one example, Scripture speaks of both to the predetermined plan of Jesus's death and the responsible parties of human agency (Acts 2:23 and 4:28). Erwin Lutzer summarizes compatibilism well by explaining God's role in Judas' betrayal of Jesus. He writes, "Scripture explicitly teaches that God actually ordains the evil choices of men. In the case of Judas, for example, God allowed (or used) Satan to put the idea of the betrayal in his heart."[27]

Ultimately, permissive language is inadequate to explain God's relationship to evil in the world. It simply does not alleviate any of the "problems" people have with God's relationship to evil. To present divine permission as the answer to the question of theodicy actually creates more problems than it solves. It either introduces a force outside of God from which he permits evil to proceed, or it undermines the will of God.

In this case, God's will would be allowing something outside of himself to act (leading either to dualism or open theism).

Permission does not alleviate God of any responsibility from evil, but clouds what Scripture teaches about his relationship to evil. Lutzer once again states, "Nonetheless, his permission necessarily means that He bore ultimate responsibility for it. After all, He could have chosen 'not to permit' it."[28] Thus, rather than explain God's relationship to evil in the manner compatibilism does, it does not properly explain where the blame of sin is due.

Single Predestination

While some turn to divine permission to explain the existence of evil in the world, others opt to promote a view of permission that results in what would be called single predestination. Single predestination teaches that God only determined certain individuals (the elect) unto

---

27   Lutzer, *The Doctrines That Divide*, 190–91.
28   Lutzer, *The Doctrines That Divide*, 210.

salvation, but did not determine the (non-elect) unto damnation. The core teaching of single predestination is that God only chose certain people unto salvation and the rest of humanity is left to their free will. That is to say that, "God predestines and elects some to salvation while those who are not saved condemn themselves because of their sin and unbelief."[29]

Theologians who find this acceptable advocate it on the basis that since all humans are sinners, those who are not elected are simply left to themselves; it is not that God predestined them to judgment in any manner. This view is sometimes called "single predestination." Millard J. Erickson explains this position: "The effect is the same in both cases, but the latter view [single predestination] assigns the lostness of the non-elect to their own choices of sin rather than to the active decision of God, or to God's choice by omission rather than commission."[30]

The major group of theologians who hold this position are modern Lutherans in various camps. Lutherans believe that reprobation is a result of the unbeliever's sins, rejection of the forgiveness of sins, and unbelief.[31] While Luther had more in common with Calvin than many want to admit (especially if they consider *Bondage of the Will*), it is not Luther, but Melanchthon, who questioned the doctrine of reprobation.[32] Furthermore, within Lutheranism there are some who

---

29 George Thomas Kurian, "Predestination, Single," in *Nelson's New Christian Dictionary: The Authoritative Resource on the Christian World* (Nashville: Thomas Nelson, 2001), 9309.

30 Millard Erickson, *Christian Theology* (Grand Rapids: Baker Books, 1985), 918. It is not as precise to lump those who hold to single predestination into the camp of Calvinism. Although some are (as in the case with Strong) there are others who are not (as in the broader Lutheran tradition).

31 Some following the semi-Pelagian version of Melanchthon espouse a version of prescient foreknowledge similar to the Remonstrants and Arminius. See J. T. Mueller, *Christian Dogmatics* (St. Louis: Concordia, 1934), 637.

32 This is also why Philip Melanchthon received sharp criticism from the first generation of Lutherans. For a survey of the history on the Formula of Concord on this matter, see Charles Porterfield Krauth, *The Conservative Reformation and Its Theology* (Minneapolis: Augsburg, 1963), 322–24. For those who adopted the synergistic single predestination of Melanchthon, see Heinrich Smid, *Doctorinal Theology of the Evangelical Lutheran Church*, trans. Charles A. Hay and Henry E. Jacobes (Minneapolis: Augsburg, 1889), 272.

take a more Barthian view, believing that salvation itself is predestined for those who seek God.[33]

Concerning the claim of single predestination itself, it may be recognized that election is a more prominent theme in Scripture. However, this does not diminish the parts of Scripture which speak concerning reprobation. On the contrary, the same text which explicitly teaches concerning election (Romans 9) also explicitly teaches reprobation as the parallel.[34] Those who propose a single predestination do so neither on the basis of Scripture nor logical deduction. In fact, this is why many scholars concede with Chafer that "it is impossible actively to choose some from a company and not, at the same time and by the same process, actively reject the remainder."[35] This is the logical conclusion that is often ignored by proponents of single predestination.

The parallels between election and reprobation are logical and often appealed to on the basis of rational argumentation. Rational arguments are not necessarily alien to Scripture; in fact, as is the case with reprobation, they stem from it. John Frame summarizes this concept well when he states, "When it is used rightly, logical deduction adds nothing to Scripture. It merely sets forth what is there. Thus we need not fear any violation of sola scriptura as long as we use logic reasonably. Logic sets forth the meaning of Scripture."[36]

The parallel between the two stems from Romans 9 and this is why Augustus Toplady insists, "So that, from His actually leaving some men in final impenitency and unbelief, we assuredly gather that it was His everlasting determination so to do, and consequently that He reprobated some from before the foundation of the world. And as this inference is strictly rational, so is it perfectly Scriptural."[37]

---

33 Mueller, *Christian Dogmatics*, 585–89; Engelder, *Popular Symbolics*, 124–28.

34 Romans 9:10–23 presents "the chief text about reprobation." John M. Frame, *Salvation Belongs to the Lord: An Introduction to Systematic Theology* (Phillipsburg, NJ: P&R, 2006), 180.

35 Lewis Sperry Chafer, "Biblical Theism: Divine Decrees," *Bibliotheca Sacra* 96 (1939): 268.

36 John M. Frame, *The Doctrine of the Knowledge of God* (Phillipsburg, NJ: P&R, 1987), 247.

37 Girolamo Zanchi, Augustus Toplady, and Justus Lipsius, *The Doctrine of Absolute Predestination* (Grand Rapids: Baker, 1977), 72.

It is on the basis of the scriptural support (which was examined in chapter 1) that the parallel is logical and natural. This is what Reformed scholars have consistently appealed to. William Shedd serves as an example of this when he writes, "Consequently, whoever holds the doctrine of election, must hold the antithetic doctrine of reprobation."[38] Berkouwer, and those who claim that reprobation is merely a "logical" doctrine, are either mistaken or simply ignoring the literature on the matter. It is impossible to suppose one without the other (at least on the most basic premise that God chose not to elect those whom he reprobated).

Evaluating the Second Category of Objections

Considering the objections that God limits his sovereignty in some measure, and implements either bare permission or single predestination, these propositions offer no satisfactory solution to the issue of theodicy. With divine permission, it not only creates a competitor to God, proposing that some external force is at work which God merely allows, but it also creates a division in the very will of God.

Not only is permissive language absent in Scripture in respect to the decree of reprobation, but such a concept does severe injustice to what Scripture says about the nature of God. The solution offered by single predestination is one presented not because of the veracity of Scripture, because of the sentimentalities of men. Single predestination introduces issues with human culpability (by assuming a libertarian free will—which is violated once God chooses a particular reality), logic (since it disregards the reality that God cannot choose one without purposefully not choosing the other), and the teaching of Scripture on the matter (which addresses both aspects of predestination). Finally, it introduces a serious problem with respect to the wisdom of God because choice and non-choice both require a willful, intentional, deliberate concentration of the mind to decide what is best in choosing some and not choosing others. To assume God chooses some, and just does nothing with regard to the rest, makes God thoughtless, careless, and foolish.

---

38   Shedd, *Dogmatic Theology*, 430.

CHAPTER 12

OBJECTIONS CONSIDERED, PART TWO

REPROBATION DEMEANS GOD'S JUSTICE

The greatest (and most frequent) accusation leveled against reprobation regards God's justice, righteousness, his moral nature. Those who deny reprobation do so because they believe that it makes God unjust, unfair, and cruel. This objection is often raised in two broad categories: those who claim that reprobation makes God unjust and those who claim that it makes God the author of evil. Both of these positions are primarily based on emotionally charged arguments. However, they nevertheless bring to light one of the key misconceptions and assumptions regarding the doctrine. It demonstrates that those who deny reprobation often misunderstand or disregard compatibilism and secondary causality.

Reprobation Makes God Unjust

The argument that reprobation makes God unjust is often based on a concept of God needing to conform to a certain standard of fairness. This arbitrary standard of fairness is then pressed against all of God's attributes, demanding that his love, grace, and mercy (among other attributes) be equally bestowed upon every individual without partiality or else he would be unjust.

163

Thinkers in this camp state that if God did not show mercy to all, when all were equally guilty and worthy of death, then he perverts justice, because mercy must be given to all.[1] George Bryson says, "Even those Calvinists who believe God loves all people have redefined that love, in their thinking and theology, to exclude any kind of saving grace for some of the people they say God loves."[2]

This concept of equity in all of God's attributes to all his creatures is the engine that arbitrarily drives this argument. It is not an argument based on Scripture, because God is shown to exercise his love to his creatures in different relations, while at the same time choosing to love some and hate others. God exercises his love in different expressions depending on his relationship to various people—love for his elect, love for the non-elect—is not the same because these relationships are not the same. This indicates that these sorts of arguments do not appeal to the context of terms such as "love," "mercy," or "grace" according to their context in Scripture. For example, there are many terms in Greek for "love." So when determining what it means, it is important to consider the semantic range of the particular term and the context.

This is even true in the English language: humans can be said to love sandwiches, love their children, and love their spouses, but they do not necessarily love them all in the same way. In fact, if someone loved a sandwich in the same manner as they loved their children, their values and priorities would be questioned. Context and semantic range matter when interpreting Scripture.

Additionally, many who oppose reprobation do so using circular reasoning regarding what they believe God ought to do in order to be just. For example, Jos Salins proposes his reasoning for rejecting predestination when he states, "Primarily, it is because this doctrine as promulgated by Calvinists distorts the character of God and portrays

---

1   Dave Hunt, *What Love Is This?: Calvinism's Misrepresentation of God* (Bend, OR: Berean Call, 2002), 115. He continues saying, "Calvinism presents a God who fills hell with those whom He could save but instead damns because He doesn't love them" (116).

2   George Bryson, *The Dark Side of Calvinism: The Calvinist Caste System* (Santa Ana, CA: Calvary Chapel, 2004), 26.

him as an unloving, arbitrary, capricious, an unjust monster, and not the God who is portrayed in the Bible—a God who is loving, compassionate, and absolutely just, showing no partiality."[3] Salins, like many others, presupposes that if God is going to be loving and compassionate he has to be so to everyone without distinction or exception.

However, those who claim that predestation is unfair present predestation in an unfair manner. The irony of desiring fairness is found in the unfair caricatures presented by opponents of reprobation. This misrepresentation is not uncommon, however what is sad regarding the matter is the insensitive way they present the position of their opponents. While Calvinists are not always innocent in the manner, that does not excuse such behavior. Another example is Micah Coate, who tells a story as a means to describe the Calvinist positions of unconditional election and reprobation when he states,

> Imagine if a killer walked into a church of 300 members, including young children, adults, and the elderly, and held them hostage at gunpoint. With reasons unknown to anyone in the church, the killer approaches a middle-aged man, and pulls the trigger. The Killer repeats this action over and over, killing many people within the church: men, women, kids, babies, and the elderly. Finally, after he has murdered 275 of the churchgoers, he tells the remaining that not only are they free to go, but that they are invited to his house for a celebratory feast. Would the survivors be rejoicing over the gunman's graciousness upon them, or horror-stricken by his cruelty toward the others? Would they be filled with joy that they were set free, or would they be so plagued by what happened that they wished death upon themselves? Would they take his invitation? Would they run into the killer's arms, or run from him?

---

3   Jos Salins, *Satan's Big Lie: The Doctrine of Predestination* (Grand Rapids: Xlibris, 2013), 15.

Note the logic that "he didn't have to save anyone" applies to this scenario. The few people who had nothing to do with their deliverance or salvation would most likely not be too thrilled to take the invitation to the killer's banquet feast. Although the reasoning that God didn't have to save any of us is true, it fails to make coherent sense of an all-loving god.[4]

Here it can be seen that the driving factor to this story is the author's view of an "all-loving god." This line of reasoning is inaccurate and unhelpful. In order to make his point more appealing he resorts to making God into a killer in his analogy. This sort of reasoning is not only offensive but it is downright unscholarly. In order to make the case for "fairness," supporters of this objection present Calvinism in an odious fashion—but is this fair? Can dialogue be had when scholars ignore the legitimate distinctions of the opposing view and resort to name-calling? No, it cannot. J. I. Packer explains the basic assumptions behind such demands of fairness when he writes,

> The idea of fairness, which forms itself unbidden in every child's mind and has more recently become big in Western political discourse, is a facet of the larger idea of justice. Fairness is held to require, first, that other things being equal, resources, benefits, privileges, and immunities should be distributed evenly (sausages at a cookout, for instance) and, second, that penalties and rewards should be proportioned to what people actually deserve. . . . The complaint here [to predestination] is that God appears to appoint destinies arbitrarily, treating human beings as pieces on a chessboard or robots to be programmed, and ignoring the reality of free will which (so it is claimed) is the true determiner of the direction and destination of one's life. This, it is said, is unfair, and so indeed it would be if things were as stated—but they are not.[5]

---

4   Micah Coate, *A Cultish Side of Calvinism* (Collierville, TN: Innovo, 2011), 283.
5   J. I. Packer, "Is God Unfair?" *Modern Reformation* 15, no. 5 (2006): 21–22.

If "fairness" means an individual receives the exact wages, no more and no less, that he has earned in his life, then by that definition God would have to punish every single individual for their sins (cf. Rom. 6:23). Scripture teaches that all have sinned and fall short of the glory of God (Rom. 3:23) and are therefore worthy of death. If mankind "fairly" received what they deserve, it would result in the lake of fire for all humanity (Rev. 20:14–15). In fact, the Bible states that God is actually fair in his judgment—Romans 2 outlines the justice of God and states that God will render to each person according to his deeds; eternal life to those who have sought it in perfection, and condemnation to those who have not obeyed the truth.

Humanity ought not to seek fairness; humanity ought to seek mercy. The problem is that the natural bent of the fallen mind is to go one step further and not only seek mercy, but demand it. This poses a problem definitionally and theologically—if God must show mercy to everyone in the same measure then he is no longer freely bestowing it, but it is forced upon him by a standard of fairness to which requires his submission.[6] This assaults the definition of mercy as well as the nature of God. Furthermore, Paul's response to this same objection is raised in Romans 9:14, in which he says, "What shall we say then? There is no injustice with God, is there? May it never be!"

Reprobation Makes God the Author of Evil

The second argument that relates to the holiness of God in respect to reprobation is the charge that it makes God the author of evil. This argument is very common. It assumes that if God planned sin then he is the chargeable cause of sin.

This argument (proposed against an infralapsarian position) is similar to the one made by Salins. The view claims that God is responsible for evil and is unjust to send people to hell on account of sin which he ordained. Like many of the opponents of reprobation,

---

6   This is why many Reformed accurately define preterition as "a denial of grace not due," and precondemnation as "the appointment of punishment due." Heinrich Heppe, *Reformed Dogmatics*, trans. G. T. Thomson (Eugene, OR: Wipf & Stock, 1950), 178.

this view assume a libertarian free will that is more characteristic of open theism than classical Arminianism.

The chief issue with this critique of reprobation is that it neglects to recognize the fact that Reformed scholars have already accounted for this accusation as far back as the Synod of Dort and have demonstrated in every Reformed confession that God is not the chargeable cause of sin (see Appendix One). For example, The Belgic Confession (1561) states, "[N]othing happens in this world without his appointment, nevertheless, God neither is the author of, nor can be charged with, the sins which are committed."[7] The Canons of the Synod of Dort: "The cause or guilt of this unbelief, as well as of all other sins, is nowise in God, but in man himself."[8] And the Westminster Confession of Faith (1647):

> God from all eternity did, by the most wise and holy counsel of his own will, freely and unchangeably ordain whatsoever comes to pass; yet so as thereby neither is God the author of sin, nor is violence offered to the will of the creatures, nor is the liberty or contingency of second causes taken away, but rather established. . . . The almighty power, unsearchable wisdom, and infinite goodness of God so far manifest themselves in his providence that it extendeth itself even to the first fall, and all other sins of angels and men, and that not by a bare permission, but such as hath joined with it a most wise and powerful bounding, and otherwise ordering and governing of them, in a manifold dispensation, to his own holy ends; yet so as the sinfulness thereof proceedeth only from the creature, and not from God; who, being most holy and righteous, neither is nor can be the author or approver of sin.[9]

---

7   Joel R. Beeke and Sinclair B. Ferguson, "The Belgic Confession (1561)," in *Reformed Confessions Harmonized* (Grand Rapids: Baker Books, 2000), 40 (Article 13).

8   Beeke and Ferguson, "Canons of Dort (1619)," in *Reformed Confessions Harmonized*, 96 (Article 5).

9   WCF 29, 31. Furthermore, see Author C. Cochrane, ed., *Reformed Confessions of the Sixteenth Century* (Louisville: Westminster John Knox, 2003), 236.

Not only have the confessions accounted for this objection, but so have Reformed theologians, as Louis Berkhof explains,

> God's eternal decree certainly rendered the entrance of sin into the world certain, but this may not be interpreted so as to make God the cause of sin in the sense of being its responsible author. This idea is clearly excluded by Scripture (Job 34:10). He is the holy God, Isa 6:3, and there is absolutely no unrighteousness in Him, Deut 32:4; Ps 92:16. He cannot be tempted with evil, and He Himself tempts no man, Jas 1:13. When He created man, he created him good and in His image. He positively hates sin, Deut 25:16; Ps 5:4; 11:5; Zech 8:17; Luke 16:15, and made provision in Christ for man's deliverance from sin. In the light of all of this it would be blasphemous to speak of God as the author of sin.[10]

At the same time, those who hold to a strict symmetrical view (equal ultimacy as found in hyper-Calvinism) makes the mistake of saying "that God is the chargeable cause of the loss of the lost. Hence, their view makes God the author of sin."[11] However, this is not true of traditional Reformed theology, only the repugnant system known as hyper-Calvinism.

Further, the objectors seemingly ignore the phrases in the confessions that claim God is not the author of sin. It would be one thing to disagree with the claims of Reformed theologians, that God is not the author of sin, and question how it can be true. Instead, those who disagree with the doctrine of reprobation simply skip over the statements that God is not the author of sin, and claim that according to reprobation he is. Nevertheless, this concern could raise a fair question, namely, "How is

---

10 Berkhof, *Systematic Theology*, 220.
11 W. E. Best, *God's Eternal Decree* (Houston: South Belt Assembly of Christ, 1992), 23. An asymmetrical system best accords with Scripture. Dabney, *Systematic Theology*, 242–43; Berkhof, *Systematic Theology*, 116–17; Shedd, *Dogmatic Theology*, 433; Sproul, *Chosen by God*, 142; Strong, *Systematic Theology*, 790.

it that God has reprobated individuals, and is yet not the author of sin?" This is a concern that will be raised and answered following this section.

Evaluating the Chief Objection
With the various objections to reprobation, most are based upon either bypassing evidence or mischaracterizing the claims of Calvinists. These tactics often employed by opponents of the doctrine of reprobation are not intellectually fair to the evidence and therefore create a vacuum that eliminates any meaningful discussion on the matter. Those who present these objections often do so because they are attempting to alleviate God of a perceived responsibility for evil. Gregory Boyd articulates such a perspective (which gets dangerously close to a dualistic view of the universe, despite his claim to the contrary):

> Divine goodness does not completely control or in any sense will evil; rather, good and evil are at war with one another. This assumption obviously entails that God is not now exercising exhaustive, meticulous control over the world. In this worldview, God must work with, and battle against, other created beings. While none of these beings can ever match God's own power, each has some degree of genuine influence within the cosmos.[12]

While Boyd and others may admit that God will have the ultimate victory, they ultimately place a heavy amount of influence on the world and eternity in the hands of humans and angelic powers.

On the surface, this might appear to alleviate God of responsibility, yet in doing so, it simultaneously removes his meticulous influence over the world (what is referred to as his sovereignty). If it is the intention of Boyd and others to comfort the believer by asserting that God is not responsible for sin, is it comforting that this paradigm also means that he cannot control evil nor purposes it?

---

12   Gregory A. Boyd, *God at War: The Bible and Spiritual Conflict* (Downers Grove, IL: InterVarsity Press, 1997), 20.

It appears that the charge that reprobation is unjust fails on multiple fronts. It simply cannot account for God's sovereignty in a world full of sin, as Jonathan Edwards masterfully explains,

> They who object, that this doctrine makes God the Author of Sin, ought distinctly to explain what they mean by that phrase, The Author of Sin. I know the phrase, as it is commonly used, signifies something very ill. If by the Author of Sin, be meant the Sinner, the Agent, or Actor of Sin, or the Doer of a wicked thing; so it would be a reproach and blasphemy, to suppose God to be the Author of Sin. In this sense, I utterly deny God to be the Author of Sin; rejecting such an imputation on the Most High, as what is infinitely to be abhorred; and deny any such thing to be the consequence of what I have laid down. But if, by the Author of Sin, is meant the permitter, or not a hinderer of Sin; and, at the same lime, a disposer of the state of events, in such a manner, for wise, holy, and most excellent ends and purposes, that Sin, if it be permitted or not hindered, will most certainly and infallibly follow: I say, if this be all that is meant, by being the Author of Sin, I do not deny that God is the Author of Sin, (though I dislike and reject the phrase, as that which by use and custom is apt to carry another sense,) it is no reproach for the Most High to be thus the Author of Sin. This is not to be the Actor of Sin, but, on the contrary, of holiness. What God doth herein, is holy; and a glorious exercise of the infinite excellency of His nature. And, I do not deny, that God being thus the Author of Sin, follows from what I have laid down; and, I assert, that it equally follows from the doctrine which is maintained by most of the Arminian divines.[13]

---

13   Jonathan Edwards, "On the Freedom of the Will," *The Works of Jonathan Edwards* (1834; repr., Edinburgh: Banner of Truth, 1974), 1:76 (Part 4, Section 9). It can be observed that Edwards uses the term "permitter" here, however, he previously said "permission" used to replace reprobation is "indefensible" (see quote on 172n386).

What Edwards introduces here is an exceptional presentation of God's purposeful involvement with sin while concurrently maintaining God's holiness from it.

CONCLUDING REMARKS

While many objections have been raised against the doctrine of reprobation, each can be appropriately addressed. The first category of objections rejects reprobation because it appears to be fatalism. However, as has been briefly examined, this objection fails to understand the difference between philosophical fatalism and theological sovereignty. A failure to observe this distinction severely confuses a purposeful all-sovereign God (who meticulously ordains everything in history for his redemptive purposes) with an arbitrary, careless, deity (who whimsically forces things in history to happen for no particular reason). Most importantly, the mischaracterization of a sovereign God as a fatalistic deity undermines the important doctrine of compatibilism, which is essential to properly understanding how God fulfills his purposes.

The second category of objections seeks to answer the doctrine of theodicy and reprobation by offering alternative solutions (permission and single predestination). However, both of these alternative solutions fail to account for when Scripture shows God determining the destinies of the wicked (Rom. 9:13–22; 1 Peter 2:8; Jude 4). These solutions to the matter then are only half-measure solutions which miss the key ingredient of God's ordaining of evil.

These "solutions" also introduce other serious issues such as God's knowledge and will in the matter of evil in the world. If God permits evil, how can he purpose it for his good purposes? How does he know with any certainty that it will come to pass? If God only predestines

---

Edwards is likely being inconsistent with his word choice at this point. Permission is not the proper conceptual framework for anything related to God's decree, but can be used to speak of God's actions in time when emphasizing that a particular thing is out of accord with His preceptive will. For example, He let the nations go their own way (Acts 14:16); this doesn't mean that this part of His decree was passive, but that the nations' apostasy (in time) was against the revealed will of God.

some and not all, what are his intentions for the non-elect? Does God neglect to assign them a place? These questions (and many more) seem more alarming to the student of Scripture than having an answer to the issue of theodicy that accounts for all the testimony of Scripture without raising these concerns. As a result, the solution of answering the matter of theodicy by denying reprobation and affirming mere permission or single predestination appears to be less advantageous than it might seem. Therefore, it is not a sufficient answer to the matter at hand.

The objection aimed at God's justice is the most serious concern raised by protestors against reprobation. The objectors' questions are valid; however, the conclusions they draw often ignore the evidence as well as the matters of compatibilism and causality. Many misconceptions can occur when reprobation is mishandled or improperly explained. Therefore, the chief objection which needs to be answered is the matter of how reprobation does not necessarily make God the direct agent of sin. It is an unnecessary conclusion to assume that if reprobation is true God by necessity is the author of sin. This misses all the careful definitions and distinctions made by Reformed scholars concerning compatibilistic predestination and reprobation in particular. If the proper view of Reformed compatibilism is to be understood, it is important to make proper definitions and distinctions so that accuracy may be maintained. As it has been demonstrated, both elements (God's sovereignty and human responsibility) are true when it comes to reprobation. God is in control of determining the ends of the non-elect, before they were born, and humans are held morally responsible for their actions in the execution of that pretemporal unconditional decree.

And because it is a serious claim (and a legitimate one), that God appears to be responsible for evil in a manner which at first glance appears to demean his justice, the final chapter will be devoted to explaining exegetically how secondary causality is necessity to answer this apparent problem.

CHAPTER 13

SOLVING OBJECTIONS

*M*any who object to reprobation do so on the basis of a misunderstanding (or misrepresentation) of compatibilism. They often confuse compatibilism with immediate agency, thereby making God the author of sin.[1] This objection generally does not allow for the distinction between primary and secondary causes, which often leads to even more confusion. Many theologians criticize Calvin and Beza for utilizing causality to explain reprobation, which they in turn view as heinous. In order to evaluate the legitimacy or illegitimacy of these accusations raised by Arminian theologians, it is important to establish what compatibilism is in respect to causality.

While many question the use of philosophical language in Christian thought (such as compatibilism and causality), the real question is whether it accurately expresses the concurrent realities of divine sovereignty and human responsibility. Philosophical categories of

---

1   Alex Prokopenko recognized this in his examination when he stated, "[M]any misjudgments and misconceptions about God's decrees and His sovereign control over the course of history and salvation are stipulated by an overly narrow view of God's providence." Alex Prokopenko, "The Relationship between the Divine Decree and the Human Will in Exodus 1–14" (ThM thesis, The Master's Seminary, 2007), 8. He further explains (p. 10) how the divide between Calvinism and Arminianism rests on different views of direct and indirect providence, which is a simplified explanation similar to what is referred to in this book as compatibilism and causality.

causality do not undermine Sola Scriptura, because without these kinds of causal distinctions, meaningful exegesis of particular biblical passages is impaired. Therefore, this kind of logic is not at odds with the exegetical process, but is subservient to it.

A HISTORICAL SURVEY OF CAUSALITY

One of the common misunderstandings of causality is that it is merely cause and effect. However, this oversimplification is a misunderstanding of the nature of causality. In the philosophy of Aristotle, the word "cause" is used to mean "explanation." Aristotle develops this concept into four categories: the material, formal, efficient, and final "causes." In theology, a failure to recognize different categories of "causes" can lead to pointless debates and misconceptions. It is necessary to understand the history of the doctrine of causality. While causality can be traced through the history of philosophy, it should not be limited there.[2]

The teaching of causality spans across many disciplines: from mathematics, to science, to theology. However, many modern audiences do not understand the depth of the classical understanding of causality, essential to making proper distinctions. These distinctions are what chiefly separate a biblical understanding of God's relationship to evil from the monstrosities of hyper-Calvinism. With the rise of the modern era, the empirical sciences have reduced causality to merely cause and effect (as opposed to the quadripartite distinctions of Aristotelianism). This consequence has rendered most theological thinkers uninformed about the doctrine of causality. Mario Bunge explains precisely this when he states,

> The Aristotelian teaching of causes lasted in the official Western culture until the Renaissance. When modern

---

2   Menno Hulswit, *From Cause to Causation. A Peircean Perspective* (Dordrecht: Kluwer, 2002). While all of Hulswit's conclusions are not always the best, he helpfully traces the history of causation, dealing with misconceptions through the Ancient Greek philosophy (Aristotle and the Stoics), the Middle Ages (Aquinas), and the Modern period (Descartes, Hobbes, Leibniz, Locke, Newton, Hume, Kant, and Mill).

science was born, formal and final causes were left aside as standing beyond the reach of experiment; and material causes were taken for granted in connection with all natural happenings. . . . Hence, of the four Aristotelian causes only the efficient cause was regarded as worthy of scientific research.[3]

The dilemma that Christians face is to explain how God interacts in a world that contains evil. When Christians take a merely secularist, empirical approach to explaining this interaction, they reduce divine causality to physical force. By adopting a purely empirical worldview, God's interaction with creation leaves no room for observable patterns of scientific law. Everything is instead done by divine intervention (similar to fatalism). In turn, this is why Albert Einstein argues that divine causality cannot exist. He explains: "The more man is imbued with the ordered regularity of all events the firmer becomes his conviction that there is no room left by the side of this ordered regularity for causes of a different nature. For him neither the rule of human nor the rule of divine will exists as an independent cause of natural events."[4]

This anti-supernatural conclusion is all that is left to those who ignore the diverse doctrine of causality and simplify it to physical cause and effect. This also explains why so many Arminian theologians have drifted toward open or process theology; it caters to this presupposition.[5] Because empirical science is severely limited to what it can categorize, it leaves no place for other categories of causality other than efficient causality.[6]

---

3   Mario Bunge, *Causality and Modern Science* (New York: Dover, 1979), 32.

4   Albert Einstein, *Out of My Later Years* (New York: Wisdom Library, 1950), 32. Keith Ward also observes, "The scientific world-view seems to leave no room for God to act, since everything that happens is determined by scientific laws." Keith Ward, *Divine Action* (London: Collins, 1990), 1.

5   Philip Clayton says, "The present-day crisis in the notion of divine action has resulted as much as anything from a shift in the notion of causation." Philip Clayton, *God and Contemporary Science* (Edinburgh: Edinburgh University Press, 1997), 189.

6   William Wallace proves how the ancient philosophical categories of causality (material, formal, and final) are virtually unknown or dismissed by modern empirical science. See William Wallace, *Causality and Scientific Explanation* (Ann Arbor: University of Michigan Press, 1972), 2:246.

Aristotle sought to trace back from the purpose of a given object to the creation of it by asking the question, "Why?" This form of discursive reasoning yielded four categories of causes: material, form, agent, and purpose. The material cause describes how the material came into existence. The formal cause explains its operative parts. The agent or efficient cause is the object which produces change. The final cause is the purpose for which it was made. These four causes are not disjointed from one another, but answer a specific element to the great question: "Why?" The common example given is that of a table. A table is solid and brown (matter; the substance it is made of), standing upright and able to support weight because it has four legs of equal length (form). It exists in this fashion because a carpenter made it (agency), so that it could be used by humans (purpose).

Another important element of causality in ancient philosophy is the relationship between the material cause, formal cause, and instrumental cause. Aristotle taught that a product does not have to be generated from something of the same quality. Clay is the example commonly used to express this idea: how does clay become hard? It becomes hard via the process of heating which dries up the moisture in the clay, thereby making it hard. Heat itself is not hard, but hardness is the byproduct or the secondary effect of heat on clay. In this respect, it can be gathered that one entity (heat) can cause a quality (hardness) in another entity (clay) even though the former entity does not possess the quality elicited in the latter.

This distinction becomes important because it establishes that there can be a qualitative distinction between God and what he causes or creates. Dionysius the Areopagite (not to be confused with the man mentioned in Acts 17:34) lived in the sixth century and is considered to be the first Christian to have expressed causality from a Neoplatonist mindset in Christian writing. In discussing the names of God, whom he calls "The Beautiful," he writes,

> From this Beautiful being comes all existing things—that each is beautiful in its own proper order; and by reason of the Beautiful are the adaptations of all things, and

friendships, and inter-communions, and by the Beautiful all things are made one, and the Beautiful is origin of all things, as a creating Cause, both by moving the whole and holding it together by the love of its own peculiar Beauty; and end of all things, and beloved, as final Cause (for all things exist for the sake of the Beautiful) and exemplary (Cause), because all things are determined according to It. Wherefore, also, the Beautiful is identical with the Good, because all things aspire to the Beautiful and Good, on every account, and there is no existing thing which does not participate in the Beautiful and the Good.[7]

In this final phrase, he expresses the difference between that which God causes and God himself, thereby destroying the idea of pantheism. In addition, this creates a distinction between the material and efficient causes.[8]

Thomas Aquinas was the most renowned Christian philosopher in the Middle Ages, one who greatly advanced the discussion on causality. Aquinas took the arguments proposed by Aristotle and traced the series of "why" questions (otherwise known as the principle of sufficient reason) back to the first cause, the ultimate cause: God. In doing so, he created the argument of first cause for the existence of God; the uncaused cause.

Aquinas defined causes as follows: "Those things are called causes upon which things depend for their existence or their coming to be."[9] He believed that the relationship between causes was one of ontological dependency. However, he also believed that there was an ultimate cause for everything that existed. The ancient philosophers believed

---

7   Pseudo-Dionysius, *Pseudo-Dionysius: The Complete Works*, trans. Colm Luibheid (Mahwah, NJ: Paulist Press, 1987), 79.

8   Aquinas had a hierarchy in Aristotle's causes: "final > efficient > material > formal." A thorough treatment of this can be found in William E. May, "Knowledge of Causality in Hume and Aquinas," *The Thomist* 34, no. 2 (1970): 254–88.

9   Thomas Aquinas, *Commentary on Aristotle's Physics*, trans. Richard J. Blackwell, Richard Spath, and W. Edmund Thirlkel (1963; repr., Notre Dame, IN: Dumb Ox, 1999), 3 (Book 1, lect.1, note 5).

this as well, which is why they believed in the material cause upon which the other causes depended. They called this the fundamental material principle or "prime matter."[10]

The whole of Aquinas's *The Book of Causes* is built upon its first thesis which says, "Every primary cause infuses its effect more powerfully than does a universal second cause."[11] He builds on this premise by explaining how material causality is dependent upon prime matter. Prime matter then has priority over secondary matter (also called substances) which depend on it and endure through the changes subjected upon them. This in turn establishes a primary and secondary cause within the category of material cause. This principal carries through the four categories of causes. The primary efficient cause has priority over secondary efficient causes since its power extends over them. Using these philosophical categories for theological understanding, Aquinas then applies the first primary efficient cause to God, saying that God is, "the first exemplary effective and final principle."[12]

Additionally, he adds, "The remote cause is more powerfully the cause of a thing than the proximate cause that follows it . . . the first cause aids the second cause in its activity, because the first cause also effects every activity that the second cause effects, although it effects it in another way [which is] higher and more sublime."[13]

With this, he introduces the concepts of remote cause and proximate cause. By remote cause he is referring to God's involvement in the world (which atheists deny), and by proximate cause he is referring to actions directly performed by entities within the world. By this distinction, he shows how it is that God orders and governs all things without being the proximate cause of all things.

---

10   Frederick Copleston shows how the "prime matter" is not "the simplest bodies of the material sublunary world." Frederick Copleston, *A History of Philosophy*, vol. 1, *Greece and Rome* (New York: Doubleday, 1985), 307–8.

11   Thomas Aquinas, *Commentary on the Book of Causes*, trans. Vincent A. Guagliardo, Charles R. Hess, and Richard C. Taylor (Washington, DC: Catholic University of America Press, 1996), 5. Hereafter, *Commentary*.

12   Thomas Aquinas, *Summa Theologica*, trans. the Fathers of the English Dominican Province (Raleigh, NC: Hayes Barton, 2006), 54.

13   Aquinas, *Commentary*, 6–7.

Many within modern philosophy question the ability of God to interact in time, which is in part because many of them are atheists or agnostics. Every unbeliever's resistance to the God of the Bible is ultimately moral, rather than intellectual. But such an objection is unnecessarily aided by the unwillingness of those in modern Christianity to dialogue about primary and secondary causes. One unaddressed issue raised by philosophers is that for divine agency to be true, there needs to be proof of what is called the "causal joint." A causal joint is the way divine causality intersects with the physical world. However, this question in large part presupposes an antisupernatural worldview. Philip Clayton illustrates this when he states, "If one is to offer a full theory of divine agency; one must include some account of where the 'causal joint' is at which God's action directly impacts on the world. To do this requires one in turn to get one's hands dirty with the actual scientific data and theories, including the basic features of relativity theory, quantum mechanics and (more recently) chaos theory."[14]

By demanding that a causal joint be measured by empirical science, such a statement assumes a nonsupernatural worldview.[15] Such a demand, then, is unreasonable, because it supposes that an invisible being must be true by manifesting itself in a visible fashion to be measured by modern empirical science. This would be analogous to going outside and seeing a windmill moving and refusing to believe that wind exists because you cannot see it. Such a perspective ignores theological categories of transcendence and immanence, which are essential to understand divine causality.

Modern philosophers who reject the concept of divine activity call into question the ability of God to interact in time without interfering with creation. This presupposes that God cannot interfere with creation, which is a purely subjective and unsustainable assertion for any Christian. Aquinas, along with the Reformers, believed that God's activity in creation was compatible with how creation was

---

14   Clayton, *God and Contemporary Science*, 192.
15   The notion of the "causal joint" will be further discussed later.

made. He writes, "The first cause itself produces or moves the cause acting secondarily and so becomes the cause of its acting."[16] Aquinas is not saying that divine activity removes human activity, but rather establishes it.

However, some misunderstand what Aquinas and the Reformers believed about causation, such as Brian Shanely, who asserts, "The primary mode of divine causation is creative and constitutive, not controlling and compelling. God is not rival or auxiliary to created causes, but rather the One who makes all causes be causes."[17]

While it is true that Aquinas believed that God created the secondary causes, for there to be causes does not remove his ability to interact directly in the world as the ultimate cause himself. This reimagining of Aquinas too narrowly constrains the doctrine of causality by implying that God cannot act in creation without violating either human volition or the laws of science. Shanely is operating with this misunderstanding when he says God's actions are "not controlling and compelling." He affirms this because as he has asserted, "[D]ivine motion is not the effecting of a change in something with independent existence." This statement utterly fails in a Christian worldview because Scripture is replete with testimony that nothing exists independent of God (cf. Gen. 1:1; Isa. 66:2; John 1:3; Col. 1:16; Rev. 4:11). Aquinas states,

> The divine will must be understood as existing outside of the order of beings, as a cause producing the whole of being and all its differences. . . . And according to the condition of these causes, effects are called either necessary or contingent, although all depend on the divine will as on a first cause, which transcends the order of necessity and contingency. This, however, cannot be said of the human will, nor of any other cause, for every other cause already

---

16   Aquinas, *Commentary*, 10.
17   Brian Shanely, "Divine Causation and Human Freedom in Aquinas," *ACPQ* 72 (1998): 105.

falls under the order of necessity or contingency; hence, either the cause itself must be able to fail or, if not, its effect is not contingent, but necessary. The divine will, on the other hand, is unfailing; yet not all its effects are necessary, but some are contingent.[18]

Aquinas establishes a series of categories based upon the traditional Aristotelian concept of causality (matter, form, agency, and purpose) designated as the following: ultimate, necessary, and dependent causes. God is the first cause (or more accurately, the ultimate cause), who transcends the order of causes in creation (necessary and dependent). This transcendent distinction is an essential aspect of causality which many in modern philosophy ignore.[19] A necessary cause is one which God has established in such a way that it must occur. A dependent cause (also called a contingent cause) is a cause which is dependent upon another. Although God is the ultimate cause of all things, his transcendence does not nullify secondary causes. The following chart: (3.1) illustrates the relationship between these distinctions:

---

18   The term "dependent" is understood to be interchangeable in philosophy with "contingent" in respect to causes. The term "dependent" will be used to refer to this category throughout. See Thomas Aquinas, "Commentary on Aristotle's *On Interpretation*," trans. Jean T. Oesterle, in *Aristotle: On Interpretation: Commentary by St. Thomas and Cajetan* (Milwaukee: Marquette University Press, 1962), 118–19.

19   The action of the ultimate cause upon the creaturely causes is sometimes called "double agency." John Polkinghorne denies the legitimacy of what is known as "double agency" most likely because he does not consider the theological categories of transcendence and imminence. See *The Faith of a Physicist: Reflections of a Bottom-Up Thinker* (Princeton, NJ: Princeton University Press, 1994), 81–82. Austin Farrer is the chief proponent of the concept of double agency in philosophy. See his work in Austin Farrer, *Faith and Speculation* (New York: New York University Press, 1967). Other contributions can be found in: Thomas F. Tracy, "Divine Action, Created Causes, and Human Freedom," in *The God Who Acts: Philosophical and Theological Explorations*, ed. Thomas F. Tracy (University Park: Pennsylvania State University Press, 1994), 77–102; Paul Gwynne, *Special Divine Action: Key Issues in the Contemporary Debate (1965–1995)* (Rome: Pontificia Universita Gregoriana, 1996), 83–87; Mats J. Hansson, *Understanding an Act of God* (Uppsala: Acta Universitatis Upsaliensis, 1991), 63–66. Unfortunately, there is such a major disconnect between theology and philosophy in modern scholarship that none of these individuals sufficiently considers or handles a Reformed perspective of causality.

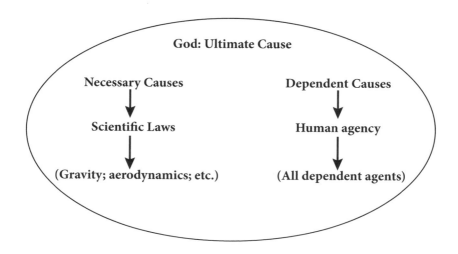

Chart 13.1: Diagram of Causes

Modern philosophers refer to the concept of compatibility (within the chain of causality) as homogeneity. This chain of causality describes the logical connection from the ultimate cause, to the effect (purpose).

A necessary cause produces an effect that is unavoidable; it happens by necessity. For example, an apple falls from a tree (effect) because of gravity (necessary cause). A dependent cause is a cause which produces a dependent effect. For example, someone plucks (dependent cause) an apple from a tree (effect). Another example of a dependent cause is when a sharpshooter shoots a target (cause) and hits the mark (effect). In this example, just because a sharpshooter shoots at a target does not mean that they will hit the mark, demonstrating an example of a dependent cause and effect. Human agency falls into the category of dependent causes, because many variables influence their actions. In contrast, the divine cause exists outside of all secondary (created) causes, as previously mentioned.

The relationship between causes can be broken down almost indefinitely into a long line of events. Philosophers and theologians have lumped this string of causes into two main categories: proximate and efficient causes. A proximate cause is a cause which influences, directs, or enables the efficient cause. An efficient cause is the agency that carries out the particular action. There can be more than one proximate or efficient cause to an effect, depending on the circumstance. For example, the following illustration (Figure 13.2), while imperfect, can help explain:

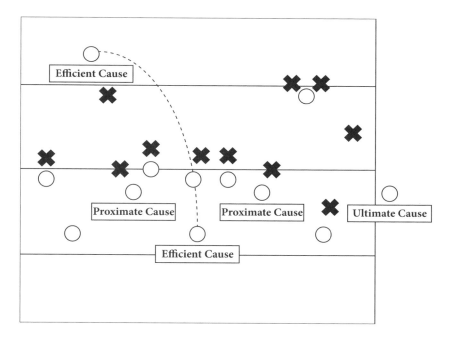

Figure 13.2: Football Analogy

In the above illustration, the circles represent football players who are on the offensive side of the game, while the Xs represent the players on the defensive side of the game. Suppose there is an infallible football coach who brings to fruition every play he calls exactly as he intended. In this case, the infallible coach would be the ultimate cause of the touchdown for the football team. He called the perfect play to perfection. The proximate causes would be the offensive linemen on the football team, who were indirectly associated with the scoring of the touchdown by providing blocks for their teammates who scored with the ball. The efficient cause would be the offensive players, who directly touched the ball in order to score.

There are multiple levels of accountability. These categories allow for distinctions to be easily recognized on the basis of respective accountability. Thus, these categories (ultimate, proximate, efficient) serve as the most precise way theologians use to express divine responsibility in respect to sin. While some have questioned the veracity of these concepts, it is important to consider if these categories of causation are legitimate based on the testimony of Scripture.

BIBLICAL NECESSITY FOR CAUSALITY

To consider the need for categories of causality, the question that should be asked is, "Does Scripture give any indication of God's relationship to evil that would warrant further categorization between God and evil?" This question can be relevant to a number of categories, such as God's relationship to natural disasters, animals, disease, death, war, evil people and evil spirts. All of these exist ultimately in relation to the existence of sin. Death, pain, and suffering only exist on account of sin. Therefore, if God has control over them, what is his relationship to them?

A. W. Pink, in his work *The Sovereignty of God*, demonstrates God's sovereignty over every category of sin and evil.[20] These can be summarized in a few examples. First, natural disasters are various threats which occur in nature from droughts, floods, earthquakes, and wildfires. Hundreds die from famine, which Scripture says God superintends. Psalm 105:16 explains, "And He called for a famine upon the land; He broke the whole staff of bread." Additionally, his sovereignty can be observed over the sea in the flood of Genesis 6 which killed everyone on earth (aside from eight people). Furthermore, he controls every conceivable natural calamity (Ps. 78:26; 104:4;

---

20   Pink, *The Sovereignty of God* (1930; repr., Grand Rapids, Baker Books, 1984), see "The Sovereignty of God in Creation," 28–32; "The Sovereignty of God in Administration," 33–48; "The Sovereignty of God in Salvation," 49–80; and "The Sovereignty of God in Reprobation," 81–108.

135:7; 147:18; 148:8). Hymn writer Isaac Watts famously coursed this reality when he wrote, "There's not a plant or flower below but makes your glories known; and clouds arise and tempests blow by order from your throne."[21]

While everything that happens in nature is not necessarily "evil," there are circumstantial tragedies from natural disasters that befall mankind. It is not as if God takes no responsibility for these events either. In fact, Amos 3:6 says God causes them to occur: "If a calamity occurs in a city has not the LORD done it?" God does not shirk his responsibility in these events. When the people of Israel were judged, and taken into exile, Jeremiah testifies that it would happen on account of the Lord: "I brought all this great disaster on this people" (Jer. 32:42). That is not to say that all natural disasters are on account of sin (cf. John 9:3). Nevertheless, God ordains them as well.

God also controls disease and pain, which every one of his creatures experience. In Exodus 4:11, God says to Moses, "Who has made man's mouth? Or who makes him mute or deaf, or seeing or blind? Is it not I, the LORD?" A prime example of this is Job. Job likely suffered more than any man prior to Christ in Scripture. While the direct agent responsible for Job's sores and ailments was Satan (Job 2:7), Job nevertheless realized it was only according to God's ultimate plan.

When Job rebuked his wife for tempting him to curse God on account of his ailments, he said, "You speak as one of the foolish women speaks. Shall we indeed accept good from God and not accept adversity?" (Job 2:10). Job understood that God was ultimately in control of the matter and didn't hesitate to say so. The purpose in Satan's intentions were drastically different than God's and their involvement was likewise different, yet both take their share of responsibility in the pain of Job. God's good purpose is accomplished through the agency of Satan in the life of Job.

Many texts speak of God's control over catastrophe in general, stemming from the weather to war. Isaiah 45:7 says about God: "The

---

21   Isaac Watts, "Praise for Creation and Providence," in *The Poetical Works of Isaac Watts*, collected by Thomas Park (London: Stanhope, 1807), 1:173.

one forming light and creating darkness, causing well-being and creating calamity; I am the LORD who does all these." The prophet Isaiah is not saying that God merely fashions an already evil situation for his otherwise good purposes; rather, he uses the word "to create," בָּרָא. On a linguistic level, "The root *bārā'* has the basic meaning 'to create.' It differs from *yāṣar* 'to fashion' in that the latter primarily emphasizes the shaping of an object while *bārā'* emphasizes the initiation of the object."[22] One cannot conclude that God is merely fixing a problem, but in some measure he is causing it to exist. In fact, this is the same term used in Genesis 1:1 to refer to God's creation of the world. It is not merely reshaping old material but creating something that has not existed.

Next, God's control should not be limited to natural events or generic calamity at a national scale. It can also be seen in his control of animals, as well as extending to the extremes—from life to death. God, who is the author of life, is also the sovereign over death. Deuteronomy 32:39 says, "And there is no god besides me; it is I who put to death and give life. I have wounded and it is I who heal, and there is no one who can deliver from my hand." God killed the firstborn of all those in Egypt who did not have the blood of the Passover lamb on their doorposts (Exod. 12:29). He struck dead the child born of adultery between David and Bathsheba (2 Sam. 12:15). According to Scripture, God caused the Israelites to stray from him (Isa. 63:17), caused the pillaging Sabeans and Chaldeans to murder Job's family (Job 1:15–22), caused David to take a census that he had previously forbidden and then judged David for it (1 Chron. 21:1–8; 2 Sam. 24:1), and caused Eli's sons to dishonor him by desecrating the sacrifice (1 Sam. 2:12–17, 25). Climactically, God caused the betrayal and murder of Jesus Christ (Acts 4:27–28). One thing is certain: according to the Bible, God indeed ordains people to sin. Commenting on this fact, Jonathan Edwards writes,

---

22 Thomas E. McComiskey, "בָּרָא," eds. R. Laird Harris, Gleason L. Archer, and Bruce K. Waltke, *Theological Wordbook of the Old Testament* (Chicago: Moody, 2004), 1:127.

> The crucifying of Christ was a great sin; and as man com-
> mitted it, it was exceedingly hateful and highly provoking
> to God. Yet upon many great considerations it was the will
> of God that it should be done. Will any body say that it
> was not the will of God that Christ should be crucified?
> Acts 4:28, "For to do whatsoever thy hand and thy counsel
> determined before to be done."[23]

Once again, this is a prime example of God's relationship to evil. A
similar text concerning God's relationship to evil is found in Genesis
50:20, which states the following with regard to Joseph's betrayal at the
hands of his brothers: "you meant evil against me, but God meant it
for good." These texts demonstrate that God does not need any excuses
for why sin exists. From all these instances, it is unquestionable that
sin exists because God wanted it to and ordained it to be. Therefore,
the real question is: How does one correlate these testimonies with
the fact that God is holy and undefiled by sin (cf. 1 Sam. 2:2; 1 Peter
1:16; James 1:13)? Causality is the answer. Without causality one
cannot abstract God from being the linear cause of sin.

---

23   Jonathan Edwards, "Concerning the Divine Decrees in General, and Election in Par-
     ticular," in *The Works of Jonathan Edwards* (Peabody, MA: Hendrickson, 2005), 2:529.

CHAPTER 14

FIRST AND SECONDARY CAUSES

*E*very biblical theologian affirms that God is perfectly holy and is the source of all goodness and righteousness. In him these attributes are inherent and necessary, and in creation they are derived and contingent (contingent on God for their existence and sustenance).[1] While this is affirmed in Reformed perspectives, such a concept of goodness is not universally held by theologians. Many affirm that God's goodness is contingent on his desire to eliminate evil.[2] This understanding of "good" implies that God is either omnibenevolent or omnipotent, but not both. Their reasoning is that because evil exists, if God is omnibenevolent then he is not omnipotent. Or, if he is omnipotent and allows evil to exist, then by necessity he is not omnibenevolent. These "solutions" to the issue of theodicy often set one of God's attributes against another.[3]

---

1   See Scott MacDonald, *Being and Goodness: The Concept of Good in Metaphysics and Philosophical Theology* (Ithaca, NY: Cornell University Press, 1991), 31–55.

2   J. L. Mackie, "Evil and Omnipotence," in *The Philosophy of Religion*, ed. Basil Mitchell (Oxford: Oxford Press, 1971), 93.

3   The author is using "theodicy" and "problem of evil" as synonyms, which is a common practice. There are some who would recognize a distinction, placing "theodicy" as a subset of the overall "problem of evil." However, this is a more nuanced distinction than is recognized by most systematics nor was this distinction recognized by Gottfried Wilhelm Leibniz, who coined the term "theodicy." In the strictest sense any evil in the world, even social evil, could be labeled as "a problem of evil" which is why some make a distinction between the two. For the sake of the book the two

The reason nondeterminists (and incompatibilists) come to these conclusions is because of their lack of understanding regarding responsibility and causality. They assume that if God is in any way responsible for "causing" evil, then the human agent can be in no way responsible. However, this disregards the detailed explanations and theological precision presented by compatibilists. Ignoring such careful distinctions removes the difference between natural causes and contingent causes, resulting in making human beings intramundane natural causes, removing their volition completely (which compatibilism is careful to safeguard against).[4] The doctrine of causality safeguards the integrity of both agents (God and man), so God ensures a particular outcome without rendering it a robotic necessary cause.

As has been demonstrated, Scripture indicates that sin does not occur outside the ordained plan of God (the ultimate responsibility of God). Since Scripture says both concurrent realities are true (that God ordains sin while remaining holy and unchargeable for sin), the need for theological categories of causation is established. However, before categorizing the secondary causes God uses to bring about reprobation, it is important to discuss and establish divine determinism as it relates to first and secondary causes. Revisiting a basic definition of divine determinism can be helpful. Divine determinism, also called theological determinism, is defined as follows: "(i) The facts about God's will wholly determine every other contingent fact, and (ii) the facts about God's will explain every other contingent fact."[5]

God's meticulous sovereignty demands that he is sovereign over both necessary and contingent causes. This, however, should not be confused

---

concepts will be used interchangeably. There are many different approaches to solving the apparent problem, such as: free will, the soul-making model, the possible worlds/ great design argument, eschatological hope, God's suffering from evil, theology of the cross, among others.

4   Paul Helm, "God Does Not Take Risks," in *Contemporary Debates in Philosophy and Religion*, eds. Michael L. Peterson and Raymond J. VanArragon (Malden, MA: Blackwell, 2004), 228–37. Helm seems to have coined the phrase "Intramundane causation."

5   Heath White, "Theological Determinism and the 'Authoring Sin' Objection," in *Calvinism and the Problem of Evil*, eds. David E. Alexander and Daniel M. Johnson (Eugene, OR: Pickwick Publications, 2016), 79.

with the teaching that God is the only active agent in the universe. Rather, other agents act according to their nature and desires, and in this respect men's wills effectively produce results in this world. However, the effective wills and actions of dependent causes are governed and determined by God's will as the ultimate cause. White explains this concept when he states, "God is not one agent acting in the universe, on par with various other agents, differing only in his degree and power and insight. No—God is the ultimate agent, the one that makes it all happen, including other agents and their exercises of agency."[6]

MODELS OF CAUSALITY

Two key elements are crucial to understand, when it comes to divine determinism and how God interacts in time (horizontal) and over time (vertical). Because God is timeless and eternal, he is not limited or restricted from interacting directly or indirectly in creation.[7] On the contrary, he does both. God's direct influence in creation, and how it relates to causality, can be described by what has been called the domino theory of causality (horizontal). This is not an exhaustive explanation of God's causality in creation, but merely a manner to describe one element of his interaction in creation.

The second category describes primary causation and secondary causation. God's function as the primary cause (ultimate cause) is his determination of and sovereignty over every person, place, or thing that has ever existed (vertical). It applied to humans before they were every created or sinned and it applies after that fact (this is on the basis of the Creator-creature distinction). This applies to Arminian and Calvinist theologians alike.

The problem of theodicy at this point is not alleviated by Arminianism, because even if God determined this world on the basis of

---

6   White, "Theological Determinism," 80.

7   White explains, "The block of space-time has a time dimension, and slices taken across this dimension will differ from one another, so there is alteration *in the creation* over time. Yet there is no alteration *in the creator* over time, as time is simply a dimension of the creation and not something that the creator participates in." White, "Theological Determinism," 81. This is not intended to imply that God cannot interact in time (as Deists claim), but that nothing in time can influence God's will or actions.

prescient foreknowledge, he still chose to create this world (and it cannot be any way other than what he determined). This still makes God the ultimate reason for a world which includes the existence of sin. He could have created a world in which humans never sinned and were immutable, but he instead determined a world in which Adam was mutable and did, in fact, sin. Whether God foresaw this (as Arminians propose) or ordained it unconditionally (as Calvinists propose), he was not obligated to create the world in this fashion and is therefore responsible to some degree for sin's existence.

God's involvement in the decrees and execution of his decrees has been sufficiently defined as follows: "For every event E, God decided that E should happen and that decision was the ultimate sufficient cause of E."[8] God's will is the sufficient cause insofar as the fact that nothing causes God's will to be what it is. There was not a prior influence on God that determined his will in the eternal decrees. To discuss how God interacts with creation, two different explanations show how God can interact with his creation through primary (direct) and secondary (indirect) causes. The first is known as the domino theory (shown in Chart 14.1).

The domino theory depicts God's activity as a person who sets up a row of dominoes and then pushes the first one to cause a chain reaction. The pushing over of the first domino causes the falling of every subsequent domino. This theory alone is not sufficient to describe all of God's casual actions in creation, but only his immediate and direct causes. This sort of causation can be observed in numerous biblical examples, such as: the resurrection of Jesus from the dead, the act of creation, the incarnation, or every act of regeneration. These are all examples of God's direct work. Any supernatural event in Scripture could be described this way, when God overrides necessary causality (or suspends natural law). In those instances, God is the primary and efficient cause, not just the ultimate cause.

---

8   James Anderson, "Calvinism and the First Sin," in *Calvinism and the Problem of Evil,* eds. David E. Alexander and Daniel M. Johnson (Eugene, OR: Pickwick, 2016), 204.

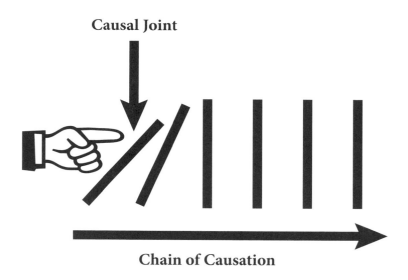

Chart 14.1: Domino Model

The downside of this analogy is that it only works on the horizontal level. When God interacts in time in a horizontal way, it is in a similar (though not identical) capacity as other causal agents in the creaturely realm. Conversely, this analogy fails to explain the vertical elements, and how God is involved in, and presiding over, every subsequent cause in a nontemporal way. It is correct insofar as it depicts God's interacting immediately and directly with his creation in order to instigate a particular event. However, the subsequent events (the following dominos) do not accurately reflect what the biblical accounts describe. The purely "linear" aspect of the domino model is correct if one understands only a single domino in the chain. But when it comes to multiple dominoes, another model is necessary to properly explain this relationship.

The model often employed to describe the interaction of God from a vertical standpoint is known as the "Authorial Model of

Providence."[9] The authorial model presents God's execution of his decrees through the example of an author of a novel. The author is the ultimate cause of everything that happens in his novel. He brings all the characters, situations, and actions in the novel to life (so to speak). The author has an intention in writing the novel—an overall story he intends to tell. In order for him to tell this story, there needs to be behavior in the novel to progress the storyline; some behaviors which he personally would condone, others which he personally would condemn.

When it comes to morally objectionable behavior in a narrative, much of it is carried out by an antagonist; the character in the story who provides difficulty and obstacles for the protagonist (the hero or main character) to overcome. Even the tamest of children's stories contain some form of antagonist. The antagonist often acts in an evil manner, behavior which the author does not personally approve of, but necessary for the drama to unfold according to the author's intention. Despite the fact that the author composed the narrative, the evil actions of the antagonist are his own responsibility, not the author's. Anderson explains, "We might say then that the author of the novel has ordained that sinful actions take place within the world he has created, but the author himself does not thereby commit any sinful actions or imply his approval of them."[10]

For example, it would be illogical to assume that Mary Shelley was responsible on a moral level for the monstrosities of the Frankenstein monster, or that Bram Stoker was morally responsible for the actions of Dracula. This captures the theological concept well, and as A. W. Pink explains, "Remember that God is the Creator of the wicked, not their wickedness; He is the Author of their being, not the Infuser of their sin."[11]

This model best accounts for the different ways in which God operates, and becomes particularly helpful when discussing how

---

9   This model is given exceptional attention (along with the Domino Model) in Anderson, "Calvinism and the First Sin," 207–10. Also, for other versions of this model, see J. A. Crabtree, *The Most Real Being: A Biblical and Philosophical Defense of Divine Determinism* (Eugene, OR: Gutenberg College Press, 2004).

10   Anderson, "Calvinism and the First Sin," 208.

11   Pink, *The Sovereignty of God*, 101.

God is the ultimate cause of sin without being its author or its efficient cause. It can be expressed with the following figure (Chart 14.2):[12]

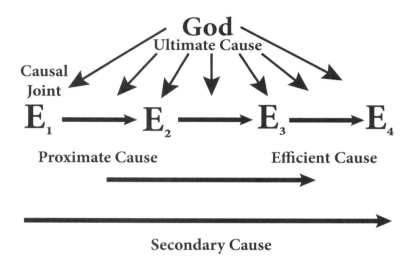

Chart 14.2: Authorial Model

This model demonstrates God's interaction in determining and upholding the chain of causes in creation. In this case, it is God who creates each causal agent (E) and gives them the ability to act.[13] Their actions, although dependent upon God's power for their existence, become causal powers which are distinct from God's causal power. In this scenario, God does not have to directly cause one event in order to bring about another; rather, he gives the intermediate causal agents the ability to be causes themselves.

---

12 A helpful chart explaining this model can be found in Anderson, "Calvinism and the First Sin," 209.

13 It should not be mistaken in Anderson's model that "E" always represents an event but rather an agent with the ability to act, causing an event.

Each of these models reflect two different aspects of God's ability to cause the execution of his decrees: either through an ultimate cause or an efficient cause. God's causation and human causation should not be confused, because God's operations are distinct, unique, and vastly different from human operations.

The horizontal explanation of causality (Domino Model) is not sufficient in and of itself, and cannot account for "sin" without making God responsible on the same plane as other causal agents. The vertical explanation of causality (Authorial Model) accounts for God's determination and ultimate responsibility. It also maintains a distinction between God's actions and responsibility and the creature's actions and responsibility. Nevertheless, the more abstract Authorial Model, operating in a vertical manner within the timeline of history, does not make God's interactions in the world as readily accessible to our finite minds as the Domino Model.

Regardless of the model used to describe the metaphysics of God's causal providence over creation, a question still remains: What is the nature of God's interaction? What is the "causal joint?" As briefly mentioned earlier, the causal joint is the point of contact through which God directly interacts in the creaturely realm (in addition to merely upholding it). It is this causal joint which gives the secondary causes their existence.

The concept of the casual joint has a tradition reaching back to Augustine. It is an attempt to discuss God's relationship to the execution of sin according to his eternal decree. The Augustinian way of explaining this is based on God's withholding of good, which results in evil. By "withholding," it is not to be understood that God is depriving individuals of something that is owed to them, but the opposite. He is withholding grace (often in the form of restraining sin), to which no creature is entitled. A simple explanation can be offered using the analogy of a doughnut. God creates the doughnut, causing its existence. However, the hole in the doughnut is the withholding of God's goodness. He set the boundaries for the shape of the doughnut, and the hole is not due to his direct activity (since a hole is a non-created entity, by definition). In this case, the doughnut's existence, which is good, is directly attributed to God. But the hole (the existence of evil) is due to the fact that God withheld the boundaries of that which is good. While such an analogy is open to legitimate criticism, it helps in briefly explaining a concept which becomes more precise in accounting for how God is the ultimate cause, but not the chargeable cause, of sin. For example, Garrigou-Larange explains,

> If, in fact, the bestowal of efficacious grace is the cause of one's not resisting, which is a good, then its non-bestowal is the cause of one's resisting, which is an evil. . . . Thus it is true to say that man is deprived of efficacious grace because he resisted sufficient grace, whereas it is not true to say that man resists or sins because he is deprived of efficacious grace. He resists by reason of his own defectibility, which God is not bound to remedy.[14]

What is often lacking in the Augustinian explanation is divine intentionality. Although such an explanation is not initially necessary to express the manner in which God causes a doughnut's existence (having a certain size hole), nevertheless, most who present this view ultimately fail to address the real issue of theodicy. In other words, why did God create such a doughnut, knowing it would have a hole? God's intentions are important to consider when discussing the existence of sin. God never intends for sin to exist merely for the sake of evil, but he always has an ultimate intention for ordaining sin. In order for God to display his grace and justice, the existence of sin is a necessary means. There is simply no way to explain justice apart from the existence of sin. Thus, the means are not an end in and of themselves, but always a means to a divinely intended end. This is an essential element of divine determinism: God's will supersedes and determines every cause (whether necessary or dependent).

---

14   Reginald Garrigou-Larange, *Predestination: The Meaning of Predestination in Scripture and the Church*, trans. Dom Bede Rose (1939; repr., Charlotte, NC: TAN, 1998), 332–33.

ESSENTIAL QUALIFICATIONS OF
INTENTIONALITY IN CAUSALITY

For many, the difficulty comes in determining the intentions of causes. Specifically, what are God's intentions with respect to ordaining evil? Looking only at secondary causes would seem to indicate that God is the author of sin, however, this is not the case. For example, Acts 2:23 reads, "This Man, delivered over by the predetermined plan and foreknowledge of God, you nailed to a cross by the hands of godless men and put him to death." This passage indicates three levels of causes (and likewise three levels of responsibility). God is the ultimate cause of Christ's death (he predetermined it), the Jews were the proximate cause of Christ's death (they instigated it), and finally, the Gentiles were the efficient cause of Christ's death (they actually nailed him to the cross until he died).

God intended the death of Jesus as a means to fulfill his glorious ultimate plan. Jesus's death was not merely foreseen or merely a necessary condition to achieve salvation. Yes, Jesus's death was the means of salvation, but also an end in and of itself to pay the penalty of death for sin. Isaiah 53:10 plainly states this: "But the LORD was pleased to crush him, putting him to grief." God's intentions in all the evil acts associated with Jesus's death were all good intentions. The betrayal, false trial, beatings, and crucifixion unto death were all intended for good. This crucifixion event, serving as the heart of Christian theology, demands a responsible appraisal of causation and determinism.

The intentions of the ultimate cause and the secondary (proximate or efficient) causes are oftentimes vastly different. One cannot look at a secondary cause in order to evaluate God's intention as the ultimate cause. For example, the Jews (proximate cause) and the Gentiles (efficient) had vastly different purposes in crucifying Christ than God (the ultimate cause). In the Genesis narrative about Joseph and his brothers, Joseph was sold into slavery for evil purposes by his brothers, yet God superintended the event for a good purpose. Likewise, the intentions of Satan, the Sabeans, and the Chaldeans in afflicting Job were vastly different than God's, yet God purposefully ordained the affliction of Job (Job 1:21). In each of these instances, Augustine's words hold true: "And again it may happen that man wills that with evil will, which God wills with good will. . . . For God fulfils certain of His wills, assuredly good, by means of the evil wills of evil men."[15]

This returns the discussion back to the causal joint. The casual joint is simple to explain when it comes to the elect: God is the ultimate cause of the salvation of the elect. He determined that they would be a people loved in a special way and given to the headship and care of his Son. God is the only efficient agent in the cause of salvation. He is the proximate cause, the efficient cause, and the ultimate cause in the regeneration of the heart of the elect, causing them to be new creations. He works both vertically and horizontally. While he uses the means of the preaching of the Word, it is his involvement which makes it efficacious to the ears, mind, and heart of the elect.

The difficulty when it comes to specifying the causal joint in reprobation is due to the involvement of sin for the execution of this dreadful decree. How can God be the ultimate cause of sin, yet not its author, if a causal joint can be identified? This leaves most theologians to chalk the answer up to mystery. Undoubtedly, there exists a limit to finite human minds discerning the eternal counsel of God (and its execution in time). Nevertheless, deferring to such a generic response does not provide anything meaningful to biblical passages that demand a more robust answer.

James Anderson provides greater insight: "In the case of Adam's first sin, while the external circumstances included a diabolical tempting agent, that outside influence cannot be considered a sufficient explanation for Adam's sin, otherwise he could not be held morally responsible, even on compatibilist grounds."[16] The reason why Adam's sin cannot be merely due to external circumstances is because it does not adequately explain what led to Adam's actions. External circumstances are not the efficient cause of Adam's decisions (although they play a role). Rather, it is his internal decision leading to external

---

15   Augustine, "Concerning Faith, Hope, and Charity," in *Certain Smaller Treaties of St. Augustine*, ed. H. De Romestin (Oxford: Parker, 1885), 235.
16   James Anderson, "Calvinism and the First Sin," 203.

action, which is the efficient cause of his sin. While it is acceptable to appeal to mystery at certain points, it is not always necessary where reasonable conclusions can be drawn from Scripture.

HUMAN RESPONSIBILITY

The key issue concerning God's sovereignty over necessary and dependent causes rests in the volition and ability of human agency as secondary causes. The most important dependent cause in respect to theodicy is human volition. Human volition is not always dependent upon necessary causes (although it may be influenced by it), and in that case it can be said to be nonphysical. What a person thinks, feels, or believes (all of which influence the decisions he makes) are not necessarily contingent on anything physical. Contrary to the assumptions of empirical science, these causes are not all discernable by measuring neurological activity or physical conduct. However, human decisions are unquestionably influenced by external and internal causes.

For example, someone has in front of them two meal choices: a salad or a steak. Which will they choose? Their decision is determined by the strongest inclination of the heart. While one person may choose the salad for a particular reason, another may choose the salad for an entirely different reason. Another may choose the steak for an entirely different set of reasons. No matter the outcome, one is never free to make a totally uninfluenced choice. They may be influenced by their appetite, taste buds, concern for one's health, or concern for protein intake to gain muscle mass. Regardless of the reason, humans will always choose according to the strongest desires of their hearts. Therefore, no human action is ever apart from any influence. This raises an important question: Can God influence or intervene in a person's will without being morally responsible for the outcomes of the actions of that person?

CAN GOD INTERVENE IN THE HUMAN WILL?

Before addressing the issue of God's moral responsibility in influencing the wills of his creatures, we need to consider whether God can truly influence the human will at all. First, can he determine the will of fallen creatures? Second, can it be in a way that he is not morally culpable for their evil actions? Jonathan Edwards provides a helpful clarification to evaluate this by stating, "By 'determining of the will,' if the phrase be used with any meaning, must be intended, causing that the act of the will or choice should be thus, and not otherwise: and the will is said to be determined when, in consequence of some action or influence, its choice is directed to and fixed upon a particular object."[17]

This principle means that for every cause there is an effect, and vice versa. The will is the determiner in the sense that it makes choices, but it is determined in the sense that the will makes choices which are grounded and influenced by the strongest motive in the mind (as well as other factors) at the time of decision. Edwards continues this line of reasoning, explaining, "The will is always determined by the strongest motive, then it must always have an inability, in this later sense, to act otherwise than it does; it not being possible, in any case that the will should, at present, go against the motive which has now, all things considered, the greatest advantage to induce it."[18]

The matter of whether God can intervene, influence, or direct the will is significantly impacted by this distinction.

One of the most puzzling issues in theology is attempting to harmonize the sovereignty of God and the responsibility of man. D. A. Carson rightly identifies that the sovereignty-responsibility tension, "lies at the heart of the questions about the nature of God, and it poses difficult conundra about the meaning of human 'freedom.'"[19]

---

17   Jonathan Edwards, "Freedom of the Will," in *The Works of Jonathan Edwards* (1835; repr., Peabody, MA: Hendrickson Publishers, 2005), 1:11.
18   Edwards, "Freedom of the Will," 1:11.
19   D. A. Carson, *Divine Sovereignty and Human Responsibility: Biblical Perspective in Tension* (Eugene, OR: Wipf & Stock, 1994), 1.

For some, this tension has led to polarization to the point where they deny one doctrine in favor of the other. Still others simply give up on asking the tough questions and are content to live with "dynamic tension."[20] However, in a compatibilist approach, this tension is not irreconcilable.

---

20 Brian McLaren embodies this concept in numerous ways throughout his work. For example, he states, "[G]enerous orthodoxy is aware of the need to keep listening and learning in openness to the Spirit and the world for the sake of the gospel, it seeks to keep conversations going and not to end them." Brian D. McLaren, *A Generous Orthodoxy* (Grand Rapids: Zondervan, 2004), 13. McLaren's advice leads many to ultimately not draw any final conclusions regarding doctrine, to never land on a fixed orthodoxy, but to acknowledge an ability to be uncertain about everything. This was the approach taken by many in the Emergent movement, yet today it is exclusive to many postmodern theologians or simply those who don't want to do the hard labor of studying the positions.

CHAPTER 15

HUMAN VOLITION AND ABILITY

*A*ny discussion on God's sovereignty over first and secondary causes naturally raises the question of human responsibility for sin. Even the first sin (which was angelic, committed by Satan, and not human) falls under the principles of first and secondary causes (2 Peter 2:4; Jude 6). However, before addressing God's sovereignty and human responsibility in regard to the first sin, it is essential to examine three questions. First, what is meant by "responsibility?" Second, can God govern the human will? Third, if he can, how is he not the chargeable agent for sin? Since the first sin was angelic, the first issue is the concept of volition; the ability to make real choices. This is the capacity to say "yes" or "no" in any given situation. It is a Christian axiom that God created Adam and Eve both able to sin and not to. Augustine famously phrased that concept *posse non peccare et posse peccare*. He writes,

> Thus it was fitting that man should be created, in the first place, so that he could will both good and evil—not without reward, if he willed the good; not without punishment, if he willed the evil. But in the future life he will not have the power to will evil; and yet this will not thereby restrict his free will. Indeed, his will will be much freer, because he will then have no power whatever to serve sin. For we

205

surely ought not to find fault with such a will, nor say it is no will, or that it is not rightly called free, when we so desire happiness that we not only are unwilling to be miserable, but have no power whatsoever to will it.[1]

Through the fall of the first man, human will was catapulted into a state of depravity, but it was not destroyed. So first, the responsibility of the will irrespective of sin needs to be defined.

HUMAN RESPONSIBILITY EXPLAINED

The concept of human responsibility means that humans will be held accountable to God for their actions. For example, Romans 14:12 says, "So then each one of us will give an account of himself to God." The Greek word translated "account" conveys the idea of giving a judicial review of oneself.

The fact that everyone is accountable before God for their actions establishes responsibility. Humans answer to God for what they do. Human responsibility is measured by God's expectations as Creator (Eccl. 12:13). Humanity is under the law of God, and God measures human motives as well as their actions. This then becomes the framework for morality (Acts 24:16). Romans 2:15 represents this concept well, describing the Gentiles (who were devoid of the Mosaic law) with the work of the law of God written on their hearts. This passage explains, "they show the work of the law written in their hearts, their conscience bearing witness and their thoughts alternately accusing or else defending them." Humans possess the ethical capacity for good and evil, which distinguishes them from nonmoral creations such as plants and animals (though angels are moral creatures as well). When discussing human responsibility, it is essential to note that humans owe their behavior to God.

Responsibility implies a standard to which one is expected to conform. It demands a response; one must comply or dissent. Yet,

---

1   Augustine, *Handbook on Faith, Hope, and Love*, trans. Albert C. Outler (1955; repr., Radford, VA: Wilder, 2012), 80.

this raises the crucial issue: Human responsibility does not require neutrality of the will in order for a person to be morally accountable. This is where Calvinists and Arminians differ. Arminians argue that moral responsibility necessitates equal opportunity; an unfettered will is the necessary prerequisite to moral culpability. The Calvinist disagrees. John Gerstner explains,

> Your choices as a rational person are always based on various considerations or motives that are before you at the time. Those motives have a certain weight with you, and the motives for and against reading a book, for example, are weighed in the balance of your mind; the motives that outweigh all others are what you, indeed, choose to follow. You, being a rational person, will always choose what seems to you to be the right thing, the wise thing, the most advisable thing to do. If you choose not to do the right thing, the advisable thing, the thing that you are inclined to do, you would, of course, be insane. You would be choosing something that you did not choose. You would find something preferable that you did not prefer. But you, being a rational and sane person choose something because it seems to you the right, proper, good, advantageous thing to do.[2]

The ability to make choices belongs to one's personhood. Two features distinguish the Calvinist position from the Arminian position: First, God can govern the human will without nullifying human responsibility, and second, that the human will is never neutral.

The flawed assumptions that undergird the Arminian concept of a neutral will cannot properly account for human activity. For example, the Arminian believes that Adam had a neutral will prior to his first sin. Such thinking is fallacious, however. It is the operation of the will that moves a person to action, thus, the concept of a neutral will would result in inaction. Action (a product of the will) requires either

---

2   John H. Gerstner, *A Primer on Free Will* (Phillipsburg, NJ: P&R, 1982), 4–5.

an appreciation of something or a rejection of something, neither of which are neutral. Scripture plainly teaches this concept in Matthew 12:30, "He who is not with Me is against Me." Furthermore, Matthew 6:24 says, "No one can serve two masters." Adam was not neutral, nor is anyone at any other time.

The second error associated with the Arminian understanding of the will is autonomy; that the human will is self-determining. Arminians often teach that people condition their wills toward certain things based on previous choices. However, the will is not self-determining on its own. It is governed by the desires, the heart, and human nature. The will always chooses for a reason. It is internally affected by the mind, and the mind is dominated by human nature (Matt. 7:17). This misconception fails to take into account Jesus's words when he said in Matthew 15:18–20, "But the things that proceed out of the mouth come from the heart, and those defile the man. For out of the heart come evil thoughts, murders, adulteries, fornications, thefts, false witness, slanders. These are the things which defile the man; but to eat with unwashed hands does not defile the man." It is out of the heart that we think, act, and do (Luke 6:45). The heart is not neutral; in fact, it is desperately wicked (Jer. 17:9). Consequently, there is no biblical warrant for an autonomous will found anywhere in Scripture.

After the introduction of original sin, humanity is morally unable to produce what it is naturally responsible for: righteousness. God gave humanity the ability to reason, desire, will, and act in such a way as to obey his commands. God never commands us to do what is outside our natural ability. He does not command us to fly or live under water; these are things we are incapable of doing. In contrast, we do have the natural ability to understand God's commands. We have the metaphysical components (such as desires, will, and an ability) to respond to them. Yet, original sin destroyed our moral desire and thereby our moral ability to obey God.

A. W. Pink explains, "By nature [humanity] possesses natural ability but lacks moral and spiritual ability. The fact that he does not possess the latter does not destroy his responsibility, because his responsibility rests upon the fact that he does possess the former."[3] With this distinction, theologians recognize the impact of original sin on human nature: the hearts of people are averted to God's will to such a degree that they willfully disobey him in high-handed rebellion.

GOD'S IMPACT ON THE HUMAN WILL

The distinction between the natural ability and the moral ability of humans to obey God divides Calvinism and Arminianism even further. The issue commonly associated with monergism and synergism is the ability of God to work in the human heart to produce the moral ability (desire) for fallen humans to repent and believe the gospel. The Calvinist asserts that based on humanity's moral inability, it is necessary for God to intervene in the human heart. Yet this does not nullify human responsibility; the faith of humans is still their faith. God's work in regeneration, which precedes (and produces) faith does not diminish responsibility in any way.

However, many versions of theological Arminianism or philosophical libertarianism disagree. A closer examination of the metaphysics undergirding the concept of human free will reveals the error with the Arminian position. The metaphysical explanation of human nature in respect to human actions (also known as action theory) sets the stage for the ethical responsibility of humans in respect to God. The distinction between natural ability and moral ability is chiefly denied by libertarian theologians. They assert that responsible human actions are contingent upon the existence of an autonomous will. They believe that if humans are not autonomous, then they are robots; incapable of creativity, activity, love, morality, and therefore, responsibility.[4]

The assertion of such a prerequisite to free will has wide acceptance in both philosophical libertarianism and theological

---

3 Pink, *The Sovereignty of God*, 154.
4 W. S. Anglin, *Free Will and the Christian Faith* (Oxford: Clarendon, 1990); Robert Kane, *The Significance of Free Will* (Oxford: Oxford University Press, 1998); Laura Waddell Ekstrom, *Free Will: A Philosophical Study* (New York: HarperCollins, 1999); Timothy O'Connor, *Persons and Causes: The Metaphysics of Free Will* (Oxford: Oxford University Press, 2000); Peter Van Inwagen, *An Essay on Free Will* (Oxford: Clarendon, 1983).

Arminianism. But these two perspectives are not in agreement as to the metaphysical makeup of the will. One explanation of the metaphysics of the will is known as the Hierarchical Theory of the will, proposing that the human will has various interacting and competing levels of desires.[5]

This model proposes that a person internally possesses levels of desires that interact with one another, and the manner in which they manifest themselves in life indicates the level of importance they have in a particular person. This view asserts that people have desires but that not all desires are acted upon. The reason why some desires are acted upon and others are not is due to the hierarchy of desires which exist in the will. However, according to this view, a person can "up-level" certain desires to the point where the particular desire becomes primary; the one upon which the will acts. For example, suppose someone wants to become a power lifter (desire level 2). Yet, at the same time, the person in question wants to eat junk food and watch television all day (equally at a desire level 2).

How would such a person decide between these two competing desires? A person can determine to desire one more than another, resulting in an action which then establishes a hierarchy (making this a desire level 1 which is more influential). But the more a person is influenced, the more their desires will be rearranged, and the more their hierarchy can be rearranged.[6] Ultimately, this view proposes a nurture over nature view of the will that allows for outside coercion to influence and shape the will. The influence can remove their responsibility, depending on its invasiveness.[7]

---

5   Harry Frankfurt, "Freedom of the Will and the Concept of a Person," in *Free Will*, ed. Derk Pereboom (1971; repr., Indianapolis: Hackett, 1997), 167–83. See also Thomas McKay and David Johnson, "A Reconsideration of an Argument against Compatibilism," *PT* 24 (1996): 113–22.

6   See Ekstrom, *Free Will: A Philosophical Study*; David Widerker and Michael McKenna, *Moral Responsibility and Alternative Possibilities: Essays on the Importance of Alternative Possibilities* (Farnham: Ashgate, 2003); Peter Strawson, "Freedom and Resentment," in *Free Will*, ed. Derk Pereboom (1963; repr., Indianapolis: Hackett, 1997), 119–42.

7   John Martin Fischer, *The Metaphysics of Free Will* (Oxford: Blackwell, 1994); Derk Pereboom, *Living without Free Will* (Cambridge: Cambridge University Press, 2001).

Another view of the metaphysical makeup of the will is based on the influence of logic or reason. This perspective explains the metaphysics of the will based on its perception of what is reasonable or logical. A person possesses free will if they respond with deliberate intentionality. For example, if someone were going to drive to the store to pick up groceries, their intention is to go to the store. However, if they read the newspaper in the morning and discovers that the grocery store was looted by vandals the night before, they may not go out of fear for safety. In this situation, the volition is influenced by information which then directs the will. Thus, according to this view, it could be said that the person no longer possesses free will because it is being influenced.[8]

Now on the basis of these views of the will, outside agency can inhibit free will and thereby nullify responsibility. This has resulted in the incompatibilist understanding of the will and divine sovereignty: that God cannot intervene in the human will or else he would be removing human responsibility.[9] Those who hold this view maintain a libertarian understanding of the will.[10] What incompatibilists insist is that humans must be the first cause of their actions or their will cannot be truly free nor held responsible.[11] Likewise, according to this view, if someone is influenced then they cannot be held morally responsible because they are not the author of their own actions.

This philosophical construct finds almost universal support among mainstream Arminians. C. S. Lewis famously espoused this view when he stated, "Merely to over-ride a human will (as His felt presence in any

8   See Fischer and Ravizza, *Responsibility and Control.*

9   Some incompatibilists are hyper-Calvinists, believing the two doctrines cannot coexist. Derk Pereboom calls this position "hard determinism" and gives an overview of the position from a philosophical standpoint in *Living without Free Will.*

10   Robert Kane, *A Contemporary Introduction to Free Will* (Oxford: Oxford University Press, 2005), chaps. 3–4. C. D. Broad, "Determinism, Indeterminism, and Libertarianism," in *Ethics and the History of Philosophy* (London: Routledge & Kegan Paul, 1952), 195–217. For further study, see Saul Smilansky, *Free Will and Illusion* (Oxford: Clarendon, 2000); David Lewis, "Are We Free to Break the Laws?" *Theoria* 47 (1981): 113–21; Galen Strawson, "The Impossibility of Moral Responsibility," *PS* 75 (1994): 5–24.

11   See Kane, *The Significance of Free Will.*

but the faintest and most mitigated degree would certainly do) would
be for Him useless. He cannot ravish. He can only woo."[12] Various
other philosophers have offered similar understandings of freedom.[13]

None of these libertarian considerations can account for the
words of Scripture on this matter. Scripture demonstrates that God
not merely operates, controls, and influences the wills of the elect,
but also those of the reprobate. Proverbs 16:1 presents this reality:
"The plans of the heart belong to man, but the answer of the tongue
is from the LORD." The term used to describe human plans is מַעֲרָךְ,
defined as follows: " *ʿārak* is a verb of preparation, arranging (so its
Phoenician cognate), setting in order."[14] In this passage, Solomon is
describing the ability of someone to choose, to arrange plans, and to
make decisions. These determinations are located in human hearts,
which obviously attests to human responsibility. However, God is
sovereign over both the plan and the outcome. Furthermore, Proverbs
16:9 says, "The mind of man plans his way, but the LORD directs his
steps." In terms of the "plans" made by men, one Hebrew scholar
notes, "The basic idea of the word is the employment of the mind
in thinking activity."[15] No one is questioning the ability of people to
make decisions, however, as God's sovereignty is indicated in these
passages, the ability people is subservient to the ability of God.

However, it is not just that God's ability merely looms over men,
but that he has the ability to overrule them. Proverbs 19:21 exclaims,
"Many plans are in a man's heart, but the counsel of the LORD will
stand." Furthermore, Proverbs 21:1 states, "The king's heart is like
channels of water in the hand of the LORD; he turns it wherever he
wishes." In the latter proverb, the human capacity for decisions is
compared to a river. A river does not set its own trajectory but follows

---

12   C. S. Lewis, *The Screwtape Letters* (1942; repr., New York: HarperCollins, 1996), 39.
13   Thomas Hobbes, "Leviathan," in *The Philosophy of Hobbes in Extracts and Notes Collated from His Writings*, ed. Frederick J. E. Woodbridge (Minneapolis: H. W. Wilson, 1903), 168; David Hume, "An Enquiry Concerning Human Understanding," in *The Harvard Classics*, ed. Charles W. Eliot (New York: P. F. Collier & Son, 1914), 37:23 ("Of Liberty and Necessity").
14   Ronald B Allen, "מַעֲרָךְ," *TWOT*, 2:695.
15   Leon J. Wood, "חָשַׁב" *TWOT*, 1:330.

a course carved out in the earth. Likewise, the human will does not set its own course, but is instead subject to outside influence. God works in the hearts of people in such a way as to incline their wills to do whatever he wants. Because the human will is influenced, it therefore becomes a secondary cause. God does not destroy the human will, or render it inoperative. It is simply important to clarify that the human will is never the first cause.

With such a distinction made, it then becomes necessary to explain how God operates on the human heart, for both the elect and the reprobate. God influences the human will both positively and negatively.

God's Positive Influence

Scripture depicts God actively influencing the human heart in a positive fashion—that they do what is good in the eyes of God. Ezra 6:22 provides a dual illustration of God's positive influence in both elect and reprobate individuals: "And they observed the Feast of Unleavened Bread seven days with joy, for the LORD had caused them to rejoice, and had turned the heart of the king of Assyria toward them to encourage them in the work of the house of God, the God of Israel." The first influence is that God caused the people to delight in him and to rejoice in his ways.

The second illustration is found in the fact that God caused the pagan king of Assyria not only to allow the Israelites to follow the Lord, but to encourage them to do so. This provides a fitting illustration of God's positive ability to direct the heart to do what it ought to do. Furthermore, Ezra 7:27 says, "Blessed be the LORD, the God of our fathers, who has put such a thing as this in the king's heart." The text plainly indicates that the king was not overridden like a mindless robot, but actually did what was in his heart to do. God did not destroy the will of the king but positively influenced it to accomplish his plans. In the Old Testament, there is no indication that the Assyrian king became a believer, or that he abandoned paganism. Rather, God operated in his heart in a way that produced something good. This would be an example of God's positive operation to bring about common good, civil good, and temporary good.

This positive influence can be seen in the New Testament a number of times as well. One such example is found in Philippians 2:13, which states, "for it is God who is at work in you, both to will and to work for His good pleasure." In this example, a believer's volition is not removed by God's intervention. Rather, God's willing is still the believer's willing. God simply operates in and through the believer's will for his pleasure. God puts plans in the hearts of people (2 Cor. 8:16) and causes them to willfully do his will (Heb. 13:21), which is why Paul says God "works all things in all persons." God can positively influence the heart in non-salvific ways.

However, the best example of God's ability to work positively in the human heart is found in his direct influence in bringing about an eternal good: regeneration. One of the finest texts that illuminates this concept is John 3, in which Jesus explains God's work in regeneration to Nicodemus. Jesus gives the analogy of a second birth to explain the work of regenerating a human heart; the promised sign of the new covenant described in Ezekiel 36:26. This operation is not influenced by human instigation or will. Rather, it is a divine work. As Jesus explains, "Truly, truly, I say to you, unless one is born of water and the Spirit he cannot enter into the kingdom of God. That which is born of the flesh is flesh, and that which is born of the Spirit is spirit" (John 3:5–6). The fact that God holds people accountable for this work upon their hearts and their subsequent actions is expressed in John 3:18, which explains, "He who believes in Him is not judged; he who does not believe has been judged already." God holds people accountable for their belief (or lack thereof). Nevertheless, in the case of the regenerate, such belief is influenced and ultimately caused by God.

God's Negative Influence

Likewise, God works in the hearts of sinful people (and in a double manner). God influences the hearts of sinners for temporal evil (purposing either a temporal or eternal good), but also influences their hearts for their eternal judgment. However, the nature of God's operation in negative influence is not symmetrical, or of the same manner, as it is in God's positive and direct influence on the elect for salvation.

Temporal evil can be ordained for two reasons: as a judgment from God or to reap judgment from God. In many instances, it is for both. For example, Isaiah 10:5–7 provides an illustration expressing this dual purpose:

> Woe to Assyria, the rod of My anger and the staff in whose hands is My indignation, I send it against a godless nation and commission it against the people of My fury to capture booty and to seize plunder, and to trample them down like mud in the streets. Yet it does not so intend, nor does it plan so in its heart, but rather it is its purpose to destroy and to cut off many nations.

In this text, Assyria is a pagan, godless nation functioning as an instrument of God, yet condemnation is pronounced upon them. This raises the question: How can a people be under God's judgment all the while being an instrument he is using? Assyria is being used by God for judgment upon Israel and yet they are oblivious to this.

Assyria is not seeking to do God's will; on the contrary, they hate him, don't acknowledge him as the one true God, and have no intention of being his agents. Their purpose was to control the land and expand their territory by defeating an enemy. They would have assumed they were acting independently: invaded the nation of Israel, committed heinous sins against them, and then sold them into slavery. Despite acting as agents of God, they are not absolved of moral culpability. On the contrary, God holds them fully responsible, as Isaiah 10:12 says: "So it will be that when the Lord has completed all His work on Mount Zion and on Jerusalem, He will say, 'I will punish the fruit of the arrogant heart of the king of Assyria and the pomp of his haughtiness.'"

It is important to note that there are many specific instances where God is said to control the heart of the wicked, yet no means is explicitly provided. Acts 2:23 and 4:27–28 both show that humans were secondary (proximate and efficient) causes and God was the primary (ultimate) cause of the crucifixion, yet no means is described. However, the fact that Jesus was betrayed at the hands of Judas does indicate the reality that concurrent causes are at work: "For indeed, the Son of Man is going as it has been determined; but woe to that man by whom He is betrayed!" (Luke 22:22). It is the plan of God that Jesus would be betrayed, but Judas is the agent worthy of blame.

If the Arminian presupposition is accepted (that people cannot be held accountable for their actions if they are influenced), then how were Adam and Eve held accountable when they were tempted by Satan? How was Judas blameworthy when Satan entered his heart? How was it that the Jews and Romans were held accountable when they crucified Jesus? The Arminian proposal does not give a satisfactory explanation of these biblical examples, and must therefore be unwaveringly rejected.

God's Relationship to Human Responsibility

The Reformed confessions are consistent in maintaining that God, in his sovereignty, ordains everything that comes to pass, and God's sovereignty itself is what establishes men's responsibility as secondary causes. Yet, this occurs in such a way that God maintains his blamelessness and humans earns their blameworthiness. The confessions maintain that God's work through or upon the human will does not violate their volition. God does not robotically program, force, or manipulate in an unnatural way so as to destroy human volition. The Reformed position does not reject human responsibility nor human volition; it simply denies the existence of a morally neutral will (a will uninfluenced by sin or anything else). For example, when a baseball player hits a ball with a bat, he does not destroy the ball in order to send it into motion. In a similar manner, when God operates upon the heart (either positively or negatively), he uses means, and these means do not destroy human responsibility in any manner.

THEODICY

The issue of the existence of sin in the world and the existence of a sovereign and holy God (who could prevent the existence of sin) appears to present a theological problem known as theodicy. However, this "problem" is improperly called such. This is only a problem insofar as human reason fails to understand concurrent realities presented in God's Word. Students of Scripture should rest assured that the existence of sin in the world does not undermine God's holiness, nor is it a problem for him. Many have called the issue of theodicy a paradox. Speaking of this concept, R. C. Sproul explains, "Paradoxes are difficult for us because at first glance they 'seem' to be contradictions, but under closer scrutiny resolutions can often be found."[16] Sproul's definition is helpful because the issue of theodicy appears to be a paradox at first glance, yet is founded upon assumptions which are invalid. Similarly, the issues of reprobation alongside human culpability appear as a paradox. But they too are reconcilable after common underlying assumptions are addressed. J. I. Packer explains the nature that exists between the tension of such paradoxes when he explains,

> An antinomy exists when a pair of principles stand side by side, seemingly irreconcilable, yet both undeniable. There are cogent reasons for believing both of them; each rests on clear and solid evidence; but it is a mystery to you how they be squared with each other. You see that each must be true on its own, but you do not see how they can both be true together.[17]

Theologians recognize these two concurrent realities. For example, D. A. Carson writes,

---

16 R. C. Sproul, *Essential Truths of the Christian Faith* (Wheaton, IL: Tyndale House, 1992), 8.

17 J. I. Packer, *Evangelism and the Sovereignty of God* (Downers Grove, IL: InterVarsity Press, 1961), 18–19.

God is absolutely sovereign, but His sovereignty never functions in such a way that human responsibility is curtailed,
minimized or mitigated. Human beings are morally responsible creatures—they significantly choose, rebel, obey, believe,
defy, make decisions, and so forth, and they are rightly held
accountable for such actions; but this characteristic never
functions so as to make God absolutely contingent.[18]

The relationship between the two matters is not indistinguishable.
However, it requires careful attention and care. Logically, divine sovereignty precedes human responsibility and is not dependent on it.
Divine sovereignty can (and does) exist on its own. However, human
responsibility cannot exist on its own, because it is derived, created,
and endowed—but not independent of—God's sovereignty. God
made humans in such a way that we would be responsible for our
actions. It is important to see both truths together; sovereignty and
responsibility are concurrent realities.

In speaking to this issue, many have believed there to be a
need to defend God in these twin truths. The German philosopher Gottfried Wilhelm Leibniz, recognizing an apparent paradox
between human responsibility and God's sovereignty, first coined
the term *Theodicy* to explain the relationship between God and
natural evil in the world.[19] Leibniz believed that the evil of the
world was necessary in order to display the good. For example, if
compassion is understood to be a virtue, then suffering exists in

---

18   D. A. Carson, *How Long, O Lord?: Reflections on Suffering and Evil* (Grand Rapids:
     Baker, 1990), 201.
19   Leibniz was a contemporary of Spinoza. While Spinoza recognized the same issues as
     Leibniz, his conclusions were very different. Leibniz saw that Spinoza's conclusions
     were not only unorthodox but also undermined the integrity of Scripture. For more
     on this relationship, see Frederick C. Copleston, *The History of Philosophy, Vol. IV:
     Modern Philosophy: From Descartes to Leibniz* (1958; repr., New York: Doubleday,
     1994); Gottfried Leibniz, *Leibniz: Philosophical Essays*, eds. Roger Ariew and Daniel
     Garber (Indianapolis: Hackett, 1989), 272–84; also, Gottfried Leibniz, *Leibniz: Phil-
     osophical Papers and Letters*, ed. Leroy Loemker (London: Reidel, 1956), 14, 20. For a
     modern compilation of Leibniz's work on theodicy, see Frank Magill, *Masterpieces of
     World Philosophy* (New York: Harper Collins, 1990).

the world in order to display the glory of compassion. From this, he rationalized that natural evil is a necessity (known as the philosophical law of Plenitude).[20] Leibniz argues in his work *Théodicée*, that this is best of all possible worlds, including the natural evil in it, because it was created by an omnipotent and omniscient God who is incapable of creating an imperfect world. His argument, then, is that God cannot stop natural evil because it was necessary to display his goodness.

Leibniz is wrestling with the truths expressed in Scripture regarding God's sovereignty and man's responsibility. These truths are:

(1) God is sovereign, and he ordains all evil.
(2) God is holy. He cannot be blamed for evil.
(3) Humans alone are blameworthy for their sinful desires and actions.
(4) God is just and will punish all evil.

The first principle, that God's power ordains evil in the world, has already been thoroughly addressed (according to Rom. 9; Acts 2:23; 4:27–28). However, the second principle can be expressed with James 1:13–14, which reads, "Let no one say when he is tempted, 'I am being tempted by God'; for God cannot be tempted by evil, and He Himself does not tempt anyone. But each one is tempted when he is carried away and enticed by his own lust." The matter of the sin of temptation is being discussed by James, answering the question, "What is God's involvement in temptation?"

Two statements can be derived from this, which detail God's role in the outworking of sin (in this case, temptation). First, God is not susceptible to sin (he is impeccable; he is not temptable). Second, he is never the direct agent of sin (he does not tempt anyone). God does not tempt anyone directly. He never commands sin, solicits iniquity, nor directs into wickedness. He is holy and cannot do so.

---

20   Arthur Lovejoy, "Plenitude and Sufficient Reason in Leibniz and Spinoza," in *The Great Chain of Being* (Cambridge, MA: Harvard University Press, 1936), 144–82.

This conundrum then leads to a question based on the third principle: How is it that God can ordain sin and yet he is never the chargeable cause? How can it be that humans are blameworthy for what God has ordained? A proper response does not need to retreat to a generic appeal to divine mystery (per Deut. 29:29). The solution is not to deny one doctrine over another, nor claim it to be an unsolvable tension and abandon the discussion. The issue is not a problem to anyone who is willing to accept the plenary meaning of Scripture on the matter and to work hard to see the harmony presented with these twin truths (rather than molding one to fit the shape of a perceived view of the other). God does not need a human defense; the student of Scripture simply needs to take into account all the vital information provided. God does not deny any responsibility for the existence of evil in the world; however, that does not make humans any less responsible for the sins they commit.

CONCURRENCE BETWEEN GOD'S HOLINESS WITH HUMAN EVIL

To understand the essential categories regarding God's responsibility and man's responsibility with respect to evil, numerous examples can be considered. One prime example is illustrated in King David's sin of taking a census of the people. It demonstrates the sovereignty of God over all creatures and how he uses secondary causes to carry out the execution of his decree.

The example of David's sin is presented in two places. The first text, 2 Samuel 24:1, describes, "Now again the anger of the LORD was kindled against Israel, and it incited David against them, saying, 'Go, number Israel and Judah.'" The important phrase וַיָּסֶת is mistranslated by the NASB as "it incited," but the ESV gives the proper rendering: "He incited." The verb סוּת (dictionary form) is a term which "refers to suspicions or charges that someone has enticed or incited another."[21] God is often the subject doing this inciting (Job

---

21   Ronald Youngblood, "סות," *NIDOTTE*, 3:240.

36:16; 2 Chron. 18:31; 1 Sam. 26:19), however, it can also be used of Satan as inciting others—even God (Job 2:3). In fact, a second text (1 Chron. 21:1) says, "Then Satan stood up against Israel and moved David to number Israel." This presents the question: who moved David to number the people? Was it God, was it Satan, or was it David himself? Who is the cause of this sin? The answer is all three. However, not in the same degree, manner, or purpose. Second Samuel 24:1 unmistakably states that God incited David, while Satan is not even mentioned. However, this text does not necessarily tell us how God incited David. The second text, 1 Chronicles 21:1, shows that Satan also incited David, thereby establishing a three-tiered (at least) level of causality.

It would be improper to read these two texts in tandem and ascribe the same responsibility to each party. God is the primary cause in the matter (ultimate cause); Satan (as proximate cause) was employed as the direct influence on David. Nevertheless, it was David who sinned, making him another secondary cause (the efficient cause) in this case. It is not as though God tries to shirk his responsibility in the matter, yet it would be inaccurate to assert that God was more responsible than David or that David was less responsible than Satan. The first degree of blame rests on the most active agent (David) and the second degree of blame rests on the agent directly inciting the sin (Satan). Furthermore, the attribution of blame becomes even more clear when the intentions of the three agents are evaluated.

David recognizes his own sin in the matter after numbering Israel and consequently being punished by God for doing that which was forbidden (yet ordained) by God. David acknowledges his direct responsibility for the sin in 2 Samuel 24:10: "Now David's heart troubled him after he had numbered the people. So David said to the LORD, 'I have sinned greatly in what I have done. But now, O LORD, please take away the iniquity of Your servant, for I have acted very foolishly.'" David's own words establish who the guilty party is, confirming which level of causation is most significantly to blame for the sin.

CONCLUSIONS REGARDING GOD'S RESPONSIBILITY
AND MAN'S RESPONSIBILITY

The aforementioned scenario raises a question about God's integrity when it comes to his inciting someone to sin yet not becoming the chargeable agent for it. The only conclusion that can maintain the concurrent truths regarding God's holiness, God's sovereignty, and human culpability rests in an answer that does not distort nor neglect the biblical data. Causality, then, adequately responds to this tension without violating any of the foundational information provided in Scripture: God is the first cause (ultimate cause) but he uses Satan and the fallen human will as secondary causes (proximate and efficient). As observed in Scripture, God is never the one directly responsible for sin, but secondary causes are. This validates the ultimate cause as being distinct from the proximate and efficient causes.

As expected, some question the legitimacy of this conclusion. Roger Olson objects, "How does this appeal to secondary causes get God off the hook for evil or rescue his reputation?"[22] The answer is simple: it doesn't. God takes ultimate responsibility, as the text unashamedly depicts. Olson's question assumes that explanation of secondary causality is given as a means to "get God off the hook." However, it is not. Helm explains: "God ordains evil but does not intend evil as evil, as the human agent intends it. In God's case, there is some other description of the morally evil action which He intends the evil action to fill. There are other ends or purposes which God has in view."[23] Reformed theologians have always recognized God's responsibility in ordaining all that comes to pass. As A. W. Pink elucidates, "He sovereignly chose to place each of His creatures on that particular footing which seemed good in His sight."[24]

There are many who misunderstand the doctrine of causality as making God the author of sin, despite the fact that it is really intended

---

22   Roger E. Olson, *Against Calvinism* (Grand Rapids: Zondervan, 2011), 183. For all of his claims to logic, his logical integrity will not allow him to let a truism stand or fall on its own merit. It is rather evident that his bias against reprobation/Calvinism will not allow definitions to stand as they are given without great reimagining.

23   Paul Helm, *The Providence of God* (Downers Grove, IL: InterVarsity Press, 1994), 190.

24   Arthur Pink, *The Attributes of God* (1975; repr., Grand Rapids: Baker Books, 2006), 33.

to explain concurrent realities found in Scripture. Objecting charges rest on a faulty understanding of the true doctrine of causality. They fail to recognize that there is a chasm of difference between mediate and immediate causes; ultimate and secondary causes (also described as direct and indirect by some).

A simple analogy clarifies the concept. Suppose a pitcher in a baseball game throws a curve ball with the intention of getting the batter out. The batter swings the bat as hard as he can, making contact with the ball and driving it deep into center field, where the center fielder catches the ball, resulting in an out for the batting team. One might ask, "What caused the batter to get out?"

It could be said that the pitcher caused it, or that the manner in which the batter swung the bat caused it. It might be explained that the flight trajectory of the ball off the bat caused it. Or, perhaps even the speed and placement of the center fielder could be attributed with causing it. Each of these would be true in terms of causality. However, they all have a different relationship to one another—different intentions and outcomes, which ought not to be blurred together. Therefore, distinctions are needed to understand the actual cause of the out.

In this scenario, the pitcher had a different intention than the batter. The pitcher was trying to get the batter out, and the batter was trying to not make an out. The batter acted willingly to hit the ball but did not intend to hit it to the center fielder. The immediate cause of the ball going to the center fielder was the batter striking the ball with the bat, but the preceding cause or ultimate cause was the pitcher's pitch. Had the pitcher thrown a different pitch, or thrown to a different location, or simply refused to throw the ball at all, the outcome would have been drastically different. Thus, the pitcher is the ultimate cause because it was his action and intention which produced the desired result. However, there were various relationships of cause and effect among the intention of the pitcher, the efficient cause of the batter, and the final cause of the out.[25]

---

25   This is what compatibilists have always believed. Anthony Flew states, "God is the First Cause in a procession which is not temporally sequential." Antony Flew, "Compatibilism,

Such an analogy illustrates the principles of causality and helps to associate the proper responsibility to the proper agents. Based on this understanding, God can be the ultimate cause of something (even evil) and not be the efficient cause. This is possible for two reasons, as previously stated: first, because God does not cause evil directly, and second, because he always ordains evil for an ultimate good. Jonathan Edwards explains this well when he declares,

> God has decreed every action of men, yea, every action that is sinful, and every circumstance of those actions; that he predetermines that they shall be in every respect as they afterwards are; that he determines that there shall be such actions, and just so sinful as they are; and yet that God does not decree the actions that are sinful, as sin, but decrees them as good, is really consistent. For we do not mean by decreeing an action as sinful, the same as decreeing an action so that it shall be sinful; but by decreeing an action as sinful, I mean decreeing it for the sake of the sinfulness of the action. God decrees that they shall be sinful, for the sake of the good that he causes to arise from the sinfulness thereof; whereas man decrees them for the sake of the evil that is in them.[26]

The distinction between the actions and intentions of primary and secondary causes has been maintained thoughout the Reformed tradition. Joel Beeke explains, stating, "What He decreed infallibly comes to pass. But the voluntary acts of the creature are in no way coerced or compelled by God's secret decree. God works through means as secondary causes. He does not handle men as if they were

---

Free Will, and God," *Philosophy* 48, no. 185 (1973): 236. It is helpful to see more of Flew's discussion on God being the first cause and yet not the author of sin in the section "The Creator and First Cause," in *An Introduction to Western Philosophy: Ideas and Argument from Plato to Popper* (New York: Thames & Hudson, 1989).

26 Jonathan Edwards, "Concerning the Divine Decrees," in *The Works of Jonathan Edwards*, 2 vols. (1835; repr., Peabody, MA: Hendrickson, 2005), 2:527.

mindless stones but moves their wills by working through their understanding."[27]

Instead of being mindless stones, humans have natural responsibility, while also being constrained within God's sovereignty.

---

27   Joel R. Beeke and Mark Jones, *A Puritan Theology: Doctrine for Life* (Grand Rapids: Reformation Heritage, 2012), 122. Beeke was summarizing William Perkins, *Manner and Order of Predestination*, in *The Workes of That Famous and Worthy Minister of Christ in the Universitie of Cambridge, Mr. William Perkins,* ed. John Legat (London: John Legatt, 1626), 2:619.

CHAPTER 16

CATEGORIZING CAUSES AND THE CAUSALITY OF DIVINE ABANDONMENT

A correct understanding of threefold causation and God's ability to use secondary causes to execute reprobation is one of the most misunderstood elements of preterition. God brings about this decree of reprobation in numerous ways without being directly involved (without being a proximate or efficient secondary cause). Some are described in vague ways and others are more thoroughly defined in Scripture. These means are scattered throughout Scripture, and, when coupled together, help form a cohesive and systematic understanding of God's responsibility as the ultimate cause of all and man's culpability for sin. This relationship is best understood when the various means of reprobation are assembled, catalogued, and studied together as a group.

Various theologians in the past have alluded to the process of categorizing the means of reprobation. But modern systematics provides little to no categorization of secondary causality in reprobation.[1] The

---

1   Robert Duncan Culver is skeptical the doctrine even exists; see Robert Duncan Culver, *Systematic Theology: Biblical & Historical* (Bercker, Germany: Mentor, 2005), 678, 680. Michael Horton has no mention of any means in reprobation, although he describes it in the order of the decrees well. See Michael Horton, *A Christian Faith: A Systematic Theology for Pilgrims on the Way* (Grand Rapids: Zondervan, 2011), 314, 316. Wayne Grudem has a great section where he affirms and defines reprobation, but no attention is given to means whatsoever. See Wayne Grudem, *Systematic Theology*

most expansive detailing of categories by a modern scholar is Curt Daniel. He presents the following: blinding, hardening, giving them up, withholding grace, turning their hearts, and evil spirits.[2] Consequently, the majority of the discussion on categorizing God's means to fulfill his decree of reprobation is found in literature from the past. However, much of this literature is also very brief in its discussion of causality. One of the most thorough is Herman Bavinck, but while his list of means is exhaustive, it is not categorized in any way.[3] In the past many categories have been recognized. Indirect hardening and some form of abandonment are the most popular means listed by systematic theologies. However, while surveying the Scriptures it is evident that these categories need to be updated and worked out.

Four scriptural categories stand out in systematizing the means of reprobation. These categories of means are: (1) the causality of divine abandonment, (2) the causality of hardening, (3) the causality of personal agency, and (4) the causality of nonpersonal agency. Assembling Scripture into these categories helps one study and analyze the execution of reprobation, in view of the fact that, as Bavinck notes, "There is a distinction, after all, between the decree of reprobation and reprobation itself. The former, namely, the decree, has its ultimate ground in the will of God alone, but the act of reprobation itself takes account of sin. The decree of reprobation is realized through human culpability."[4] Thus, a study of the means of reprobation considers not the decree of reprobation, but the diverse ways that God brings about that decree. This still simultaneously maintains God's holiness and human responsibility.

(Grand Rapids: Zondervan, 1994), 684–87; John Frame, *Systematic Theology: An Introduction to Christian Belief* (Phillipsburg, NJ: P&R, 2013), 221–24. John MacArthur and Richard Mayhue, eds., *Biblical Doctrine: A Systematic Summary of Biblical Truth* (Wheaton, IL: Crossway, 2017), 504–11.

2   Curt Daniel's material is from lecture notes from a class he taught in the 1980s titled "The History and Theology of Calvinism." This was subsequently self-published: Curt Daniels, *The History and Theology of Calvinism* (Springfield, IL: Scholarly Reprints, 1993), 356–60.

3   Bavinck, *Reformed Dogmatics*, 2:393–94.

4   Bavinck, *Reformed Dogmatics*, 2:396.

God can also use one, two, three, or more various means to execute and accomplish his decree. Thus, the order in which the means are examined is not intended to give any indication that there is a predictable pattern of the means God chooses to use. He may use any number of them in any order.

Most important, a systematic analysis of the means of reprobation will establish that the execution of God's decree of reprobation does not require him to implant sin into people to bring about his eternal decree. Rather, God preserves both the volition of the creature and his own holiness by the secondary causes within these categories. The categorization of these secondary causes helps elucidate a vast number of Scripture passages while simultaneously preserving God's holy sovereignty and human accountability in regard to theodicy.

Based on a comprehensive view of Scripture, at least eight secondary means can be identified as implemented for accomplishing God's decree of reprobation (two in each category). Each category (divine abandonment, hardening, personal agency, and nonpersonal agency) will be treated in its own separate section. For a chart presenting many of the pertinent texts relating to each category and subcategory, see Appendix One.

THE CAUSALITY OF DIVINE ABANDONMENT

The causality of divine abandonment is an important category to consider first. While it cannot be said with certainty, it could be deduced that this category is the causal joint philosophers have been in search of to explain divine action in respect to evil. The link in the chain—the direct manner in which God himself acts to execute the decree of reprobation—could very well be the causality of abandonment. This would represent the way God directly knocks over the first domino (per the Domino Theory illustration presented earlier, describing God's horizontal interactions in executing reprobation).

This means of reprobation (divine abandonment) is likely the first means God employed in executing the fall (which could be said of either Adam or Satan). How did humanity fall? Adam was created good, so how exactly was his heart enticed to sin under temptation?

The simple answer is that God withheld grace that would sustain Adam. To a certain degree, he abandoned Adam.

Man was created mutable and unable to sustain righteousness in himself, because righteousness in Adam was merely derived, not inherent. At the same time, God cannot be blamed for not upholding Adam, because Adam had within his natural faculties the ability to sin or not sin. Thus, it was according to God's good pleasure to leave Adam to his own abilities, which, left unaided by God's preserving grace, would eventually result in Adam's volitional downfall. Adam's nature, unsupported by God's grace, is comparable to an object that is subjected to the pull of gravity. Suppose, for example, that a person is holding an apple in the air. The apple cannot hold itself in the air; it does not possess the natural abilities to uphold itself. Consequently, as soon as the support is removed, the apple falls under its own weight.

This means is the most direct way in which God works in executing his decree of reprobation, making it appear to be a primary cause. Yet, it can more accurately be classified as a secondary cause because its execution requires his choice to abandon either by letting alone, or by withholding grace (which if otherwise supplied would result in a different outcome). Therefore, this category can be divided into two subcategories: Removing Restraints and Withholding Grace. Although the two would, at first glance, seem to be indistinguishable, subtle nuances provide a way to differentiate them.

William Perkins recognized the impact of abandonment and describes it in a similar fashion to a causal joint. He writes,

> [God] doth all together order every event, partially by inclining and gently bending the will in all things that are good, and partly by forsaking it in things that are evil: yet the will of the creature, left unto itself, is carried headlong of [its] own accord, not of necessity in itself, but contingently that way which the decree of God determined from eternity.[5]

---

5   Perkins, "Manner and Order of Predestination," in *Works*, 2:621.

By this statement, Perkins not only recognizes the relationship of God's abandonment to the outcome of sin in humanity, but also properly explains how it is in accordance with human volition. As previously explained, human volition is not a necessary cause but a dependent cause; nevertheless, it is a cause under the ultimate sovereignty of God.

REMOVING RESTRAINTS/GIVING PEOPLE OVER

The first means within divine abandonment occurs when God removes moral restraints and gives people over to their sinful desires. Scripture indicates that God can restrain sin. Genesis 20:6 reads, "I also kept you from sinning against Me." Another text describing this same expression is found in 1 Samuel 25:39, which reads, "Blessed be the LORD, who has pleaded the cause of my reproach from the hand of Nabal and has kept back His servant from evil." The Hebrew term translated "kept" in both Genesis 20:6 and 1 Samuel 25:39 is חָשַׂךְ, of which it is said, "God may restrain man's sinfulness. Thus he keeps Abimelech from taking Sarah (Gen. 20:6), and David from killing Nabal (1 Sam. 25:39). So the Psalmist beseeches God to keep him from presumptuous sin (Ps. 19:13 [v. 14 in Hebrew])."[6]

First Samuel 25:26 presents a different expression of this same truth: "since the LORD has restrained you from shedding blood, and from avenging yourself by your own hand." Likewise, 1 Samuel 25:34 reads, "Nevertheless, as the LORD God of Israel lives, who has restrained me from harming you." In both of these texts a different Hebrew word is used to express the concept of "restraint": the Hebrew word is מָנַע, which means "the right or power to withhold something belongs ultimately to God or his representative."[7]

What can be deduced from these texts is that the moral ability to resist sin does not originate in fallen man. It comes from perfect holiness of heart; a characteristic inherent only in God, and derived in creatures. In humanity, the attributes which are endowed upon them are derived and nonessential. Therefore, if God purposes for

---

6   L. J. Coppes, "חָשַׂךְ," *TWOT*, 1:329.
7   G. L. Carr, "מָנַע," *TWOT*, 2:515.

humanity to fall, all God needs to do is remove restraints that give opportunity for humanity to sin. Thomas Watson stated it well: "God does not infuse evil into men, He withdraws the influence of His graces, and then the heart hardens itself; even as the light being withdrawn, darkness presently follows in the air; but it was absurd to say that therefore the light darkens the air."[8]

God is under no obligation to keep people from sinning. He was not obligated to uphold Adam in a state of righteousness and he is under no obligation to prevent sinful people from acting upon the sinful desires of their hearts at any time (apart from his sovereign plan). God's ordaining of sin and executing it in this manner is also described not just in restraint language, but also in permissive language. This should not be misunderstood, as clarified previously, that God is passive or does not ordain what comes to pass. Rather, the term often translated as "permit" in English carries the concept of God's abandonment when it appears in Scripture. For example, Acts 14:16 says, "In the generations gone by He permitted all the nations to go their own ways." The term translated "permit" (ἐάω) means, "To allow someone to do something, to refrain from disturbing, detaining, or restraining."[9]

The execution of reprobation by the means of abandonment, giving over, does not require God's direct involvement. Perkins aptly asserted that God "planted nothing in Adam, whereby he should fall into sin, but left him to his own liberty, not hindering his fall when it might."[10] This manner of executing the decree of reprobation involves God lowering his restraints, removing his restraining (common) grace, and abandoning sinful people to their own appetites. In removing his restraints from the wicked he allows the wicked to act on wicked desires.

The account of Job provides a primary example. Although Job himself was not reprobate, two reprobate groups of individuals were allowed to act in a depraved manner upon Job. Satan is told to consider

---

8   Thomas Watson, *A Body of Divinity* (1692; repr., Carlisle, PA: Banner of Truth, 1992), 122.
9   "ἐάω," *BDAG*, 269. See also M. E. Glasswell, "ἐάω," *EDNT*, 368; "ἐάω," A-S, 126.
10   Perkins, "Manner and Order of Predestination," in *Works*, 2:619.

Job, not by his own observation while walking upon the earth, which he was previously doing (Job 1:7), but by God's design (Job 1:8). However, Satan recognizes that there is "a hedge of protection" around Job (Job 1:10). While Satan was roaming the earth, God's hedge protected Job; but even when God gave Satan permission to act out evil desires, the hedge of protection was not totally lifted (Job 1:12), for Satan was not permitted to harm Job.

The second group was the Sabeans, who appear and attack Job's possessions and servants (Job 1:15). Where did the Sabeans come from? Did they not know about Job previously? The Sabeans always coveted and desired Job's possessions, yet there was a hedge which kept them from harming Job. This restraint held them at bay, kept them from acting upon their wicked desires. It was only when God removed his restraints upon their wicked desires that they were allowed to attack Job, pursuing their sinful desires to a greater degree. Therefore, it can be said that when God lets someone go, he lets them fall according to their own desires. God lets go of the proverbial leash in order for the reprobate to act out the wickedness that is incubating in their hearts.

WITHHOLDING GRACE

A second means God uses to execute divine abandonment occurs when God chooses not to grant grace to the reprobate.[11] An example of this is found in Matthew 15:14, which states, "Let them alone; they are blind guides of the blind. And if a blind man guides a blind man, both will fall into a pit." God's common grace restrains people from being as evil as they could be, so when people act more and more wicked, it is due to God's abandonment of them. By not granting them the

---

11 Dave Hunt questions Calvinism by objecting to the notion that God is able to not give grace to all people equally. He sees this as vilifying God, since he would therefore be withholding something everyone was due. James White explains the error in this when he states, "A pardon cannot be 'withheld' because it is not owed to anyone in the first place. Grace cannot be 'withheld' because by nature it must be free to be grace," Dave Hunt and James R. White, *Debating Calvinism: Five Points, Two Views* (Sisters, OR: Multnomah, 2004), 323–24. The term "withhold" as a category is used to merely explain God's choice to not give something that he is not obligated to give to anyone.

common grace of moral restraint, God lets them go to act upon their diabolical desires. James White explains, "God sent Isaiah to preach a message of judgment even though He said that the people would not believe, and in fact, that He would not allow them to (Isaiah 6:8–13)? Was this a 'blasphemous and senseless' thing for God to do, or does He have a purpose in proclaiming His truth even when it results in judgment?"[12]

In discussing this means, it is of utmost importance to remember that grace is, by definition, not owed to any man. God is not obligated to grant grace to anyone. A few texts express this point rather obviously, such as Deuteronomy 29:4, which reads, "Yet to this day the LORD has not given you a heart to know, nor eyes to see, nor ears to hear." The moral ability to hear, follow, and love the Lord comes from the Lord. It is a gift of grace which he is not obligated to grant to anyone and, in many cases, it is withheld according to God's purposes.

This principle is expressly described in the New Testament throughout Jesus's ministry. The regeneration of the heart is the only way we are made morally able to respond to spiritual truths. Jesus continually spoke the truth in front of the Pharisees and Sadducees and yet they could never respond.

Jesus was even thankful that they were not granted the ability to perceive the truth, praying in Matthew 11:25, "I praise You, Father, Lord of heaven and earth, that You have hidden these things from the wise and intelligent and have revealed them to infants." For this reason, Jesus's earthly ministry recorded in Scripture portrays a recognizable shift in methodology; turning from teaching clear truth to teaching in parables in order to hinder the ability of his hearers to naturally perceive what they had already morally rejected. Jesus explains this in Mark 4:10–12:

> As soon as He was alone, His followers, along with the twelve, began asking Him about the parables. And He was saying to them, "To you has been given the mystery

---

12   Hunt and White, *Debating Calvinism*, 323.

of the kingdom of God, but those who are outside get everything in parables, so that *while seeing, they may see and not perceive, and while hearing, they may hear and not understand, otherwise they might return and be forgiven.*" (emphasis added)

Jesus did not grant understanding to the reprobate and instead concealed his teachings in parables. It takes a supernatural work of the Spirit to enlighten the mind to understand and to regenerate the heart to accept what Jesus spoke (John 10:6). This is why in the New Testament both Jesus and Paul recite Isaiah 6:9 to explain the fact that God gave them "eyes to see not and ears to hear not" (Matt. 13:13–17; Rom. 11:8).

We may further distinguish the two subcategories. Firstly, removing restraints is when God takes away something already present. He removes the obstacles which stop people from acting on their sinful desires so that they are uninhibited and will act upon their sinful desires. The second subcategory—withholding grace—is when God chooses not to supply what is lacking in the individual, which if provided would divert them from sinning.

The doctrine of divine abandonment is crucial to understand God's role in the wicked acts that take place according to his ordained plan. While this may be the causal joint (how God acts directly), it is also not always the first cause. God can remove restraints or withhold grace upon individuals who have rejected him, and this could result in a doubly hardened heart or seared conscience. Where it falls on the horizontal plane of causality (based on the Domino Theory) varies. It is often found at the beginning of the causal chain, but it can also be a cause that occurs anywhere in the line of causes that results in the judgment of the reprobate. Sproul explains, "All that God has to do to harden people's hearts is to remove restraints. He gives them a longer leash. . . . In a sense he gives them enough rope to hang themselves."[13]

---

13   Sproul, *Chosen by God*, 145.

CHAPTER 17

THE CAUSALITY OF HARDENING

*H*ardening would be the next category of causes God utilizes to execute his decree of reprobation upon the non-elect. The doctrine of hardening is one of the most misunderstood categories of causality. Some in modern movements would like to excuse the perceived harshness of it by attempting to soften its implications. This was even a common practice in Calvin's day. He reprimands his opponents for such a compromise, writing, "The word 'hardens,' when applied to God in Scripture, means not only permission, (as some washy moderators would have it) but also the operation of the wrath of God: for all those external things, which lead to the blinding of the reprobate, are the instruments of His wrath."[1] This category, like the others, can be subdivided into specific secondary means: unstated hardening and self-hardening. Many commentators prefer to combine the two and regard all hardening as self-hardening (as the Arminian position prefers). Nevertheless, God can use other means to harden a person.

In many cases, God chooses not to reveal how he hardens the non-elect. Such occurrences should be a distinct category, as accuracy is essential when examining such an important matter. Finally, it is

---

1   John Calvin, "Commentaries on the Epistle to the Romans," in *Calvin's Commentaries* 19 (Grand Rapids: Baker Books, 2005), 362.

important to avoid the hyper-Calvinistic tendency to try to imply equal ultimacy in texts where God's implementation of hardening is unstated. Horton reminds us that, "God is not active in hardening hearts in the same way that he is active in softening hearts."[2] The key phrase Horton uses here is, "in the same way." It is not that God is never involved, but he is not involved in the same manner or degree (unequal ultimacy).

Perhaps the most significant example of hardening provided in Scripture, is that of Pharaoh. The Exodus narrative discusses the hardening of Pharaoh nineteen times. Three times it is apparent that Pharaoh was the subject of his own hardening (Exod. 8:15, 32; 9:34). Six times the subject is absent from the immediate context, leaving the subject of Pharaoh's hardening unclear (Exod. 7:13, 14, 22; 8:19; 9:7, 35). However, ten times God is the agent responsible for Pharaoh's hardening (Exod. 4:12; 7:3; 9:12; 10:1, 20, 27; 11:10; 14:4, 8, 17). In light of these detectible differences, it is necessary to not treat them generically but to allow for the uniqueness inherent in these texts. For this reason the category of hardening can be broken into two subcategories: unstated hardening and self-hardening.

UNSTATED HARDENING

The category of *unstated hardening* is one of the most used expressions in Scripture to describe God's execution of reprobation. God has revealed in Scripture that he hardens the hearts of the non-elect, in many instances without stating anything other than that he himself will cause it to happen. God states that he will harden Pharaoh's heart and he does so in many examples, such as Exodus 7:3, which states, "I will harden Pharaoh's heart that I may multiply My signs," and in Exodus 9:12; 10:20, 27; 11:10; 14:4, all of which read, "The Lord hardened Pharaoh's heart." Despite the common refrain throughout the account, God does not state how he will bring about this hardening of Pharaoh. The texts merely state that it is something he will do.

While the hardening of Pharaoh is the most well-known example, God is said to harden the hearts of reprobates throughout Scripture.

---

2   Michael Horton, *For Calvinism* (Grand Rapids: Zondervan, 2011), 57.

Deuteronomy 2:30, revealing why king Sihon of Heshbon did not allow Israel to pass through his land, says, "for the LORD your God hardened his spirit and made his heart obstinate." Again, Joshua 11:20 explains, "For it was of the LORD to harden their hearts, to meet Israel in battle in order that he might utterly destroy them, that they might receive no mercy, but that he might destroy them." God brings about his own wrath upon the enemies of Israel by turning their hearts to hate Israel. In fact, Psalm 105:25 explicitly states this: "He turned their heart to hate His people, To deal craftily with His servants." Not only did God do this in the Old Testament to his enemies, he also did it in the New Testament to the Pharisees (John 12:40), and ultimately whomever he pleases (Rom. 9:18).

To properly understand the hardening of the heart, it is important to return to the passage on the hardening of Pharaoh, since this account represents the first time hardening is mentioned in Scripture. Exodus 4:21 says, "The LORD said to Moses, 'When you go back to Egypt see that you perform before Pharaoh all the wonders which I have put in your power; but I will harden his heart so that he will not let the people go.'" The phrase, "I will harden his heart" is critical to examine in order to fully develop this category.

Interestingly, the syntax of the phrase is very important for establishing this category. The Hebrew phrase translated "I will harden his heart" is וַאֲנִי אֲחַזֵּק אֶת-לִבּוֹ, including the *waw* conjunction, which functions as an adversative that, as Arnold and Choi note, "often introduces contrasting or antithetical ideas."[3]

In this case, the contrast is between the signs that Moses will perform and what God had ordained to take place with Pharaoh's heart. This is followed by a verb in the *Piel* imperfect. "Traditionally the Piel has been considered intensive in meaning. . . . The Piel frequently expresses the bringing about of a state."[4] In this context the Piel is factitive because it is a "cause producing a state."[5] Therefore, when

---

3   Bill T. Arnold and John H. Choi, *A Guide to Biblical Hebrew Syntax* (Cambridge: Cambridge University Press, 2003), 146.

4   Arnold and Choi, *Guide*, 42.

5   Arnold and Choi, *Guide*, 44.

God instructs Moses to do miracles before Pharaoh, even though God will harden his heart, Pharaoh's heart is the direct object of the action.[6] The Lord reveals to Moses his plans for Pharaoh, in spite of the miracles which are to be performed.

Not only does the syntax exhibit that God is the one performing the action of hardening Pharaoh's heart, but the syntax of the two key words is crucial to understanding this category as well as that of self-hardening. Both of these terms require brief examination in order to help clarify this category.

The term חזק ("harden") is a dynamic word, used 289 times in the Old Testament alone.[7] This word is one which also has a vast spectrum of ways in which it has been translated, and can only be defined according to its context. The word appears sixty-four times in the *Piel* form with twenty-one occurrences having the heart (לֵב) as the direct object. This word can also be used in a positive sense when associated with the heart. Therefore, context is greatly important in order to see how the word should be translated. In the ESV, for example, its most frequent translations vary across over twenty different renderings.

The word used for "harden" in reference to the hardening of Pharaoh in Exodus 4:21 is אֲחַזֵּק from the root חזק. This word can be used to talk about physical strength, internal strength in the resolve of one's character; to be courageous, to tie, gird, support, seize, and many others.[8] Despite the number of possible meanings, the translation of this word based on the context of Exodus 4 is virtually undeniable in meaning "to strengthen, to make hard or stubborn."[9]

Lexical scholars have agreed on the basic meaning of the term.[10] The word is used to speak of physical strength of individuals (Judg.

---

6   This is pointed out by the direct object marker and the anarthrous noun, which is masculine singular with a third masculine singular suffix.

7   All concordance information found using Logos Bible software.

8   Ludwig Koehler, Walter Baumgartner and Johann Jakob Stamm, "חזק," *The Hebrew and Aramaic Lexicon of the Old Testament* (Leiden: Brill, 2001), 303.

9   William L. Holladay, *A Concise Hebrew and Aramaic Lexicon of the Old Testament* (Leiden: Brill, 1971), 99. Hereafter referred to as *Holladay*.

10 Ernst Jenni and Claus Westermann, "חזק," *Theological Lexicon of the Old Testament* (Peabody, MA: Hendrickson, 1997), 403–6.

1:28), of the intensity of a battle (2 Kings 3:26), of courage when in conjunction with the word "hand" (2 Sam. 2:7), of the fortification of non-living objects (2 Chron. 26:9), and many others.

To understand the hardening of Pharaoh, it is also necessary to examine the synonymous words used in other passages concerning this issue, כָּבֵד and קָשָׁה. The word כָּבֵד seems to convey an understanding of Pharaoh being hardened to the point of being unable to respond. Regarding כָּבֵד, Wilson explains that it means, "To be heavy. This word is also applied to the hardness of the heart of Pharaoh, and seems to point to his insensibility and want of conviction, as the same word is applied to the ear when not duly impressed with sounds, or the eyes when it becomes dim."[11] Holladay also confirms this to be the case by defining כָּבֵד as "dull, hard (heart) Ex 7:14."[12]

The other synonymous word קָשָׁה means, "To be hard, harsh, severe; to be obstinate, intractable, perverse; applied to that which is very difficult and distressing."[13] This word carries with it the idea of unreasonableness and grotesqueness that comes with ignoring the demands of God.

These two words (כָּבֵד and קָשָׁה) seem to be speaking to two aspects of the same cause: Pharaoh's hardening results in his inability to respond and his perverse action taken against God. However, according to many, the two words seem to be combined when the word חזק is used. Wilson explains, "To brace up or tighten, in opposition to a state of relaxation. . . . This is the word used of the hardness of Pharaoh's heart. . . . It is in the Piel that this word is used of God's hardening his heart, when He left him to his own obstinacy and rebellion, and withdrew that favor or benevolence by which he might have been brought to relent."[14]

The theological understanding of this word is of vast importance. Many instances in Scripture do not reveal the means by which God

---

11   William Wilson, *Old Testament Word Studies: An English Hebrew and Chaldee Lexicon and Concordance* (Grand Rapids: Kregel, 1978), 207.

12   "כָּבֵד," *Holladay*, 150.

13   William Wilson, *Old Testament Word Studies: An English Hebrew and Chaldee Lexicon and Concordance* (Grand Rapids: Kregel, 1978), 207.

14   Wilson, *Old Testament Word Studies*, 207.

brings this reprobation to pass. In some instances, the means God uses to harden Pharaoh's heart is shown to be Pharaoh himself, while at other times it is simply said that God causes this hardening. Whether the hardening takes place directly or indirectly is left to speculation, based on the context. However, the important point to note is that the hardening takes place while Moses is being commissioned, before he ever returns to the land of Egypt.

To fully understand this causal means, remember that God ordains the hardening of hearts for the purpose of displaying his glory (cf. Rom. 9:22–23). This is a critical aspect because it reminds us that God's glory is the precursory cause to all forms of hardening—it is not a reaction to the hard hearts of fallen men. Grammatical scholar Hesse explains the nuanced meaning of "hardening the heart," which helps to establish this critical theological aspect.[15]

Therefore, it would be inaccurate to assert that Pharaoh's unresponsiveness is what resulted in the initial hardening. This would require imposing a theology of foreknowledge or another eisegetical explanation to bypass what is exegetically present. While rejection may be true of subsequent hardenings, it is not true when God speaks to Moses about his plans before Moses ever goes to Pharaoh. In at least the very first instance, Pharaoh's unresponsiveness and stubbornness are a result of external hardening already taken place.

God ordains Pharaoh's external hardening to show his sovereignty through the miraculous plagues that resulted from Pharaoh's internal hardening. In a broader sense, God also shows his sovereignty over the destinies of men; from the kings of nations down to their children. Commentator Durham explains,

> Moses is then told, in a marvelous summary of both the purpose and the range of these signs and the mighty acts, that Yahweh will be working through both him and the Pharaoh to establish irrevocably the powerful reality of His presence. . . . Through Pharaoh He will multiply the

---

15   F. Hesse, "חזק," *TDOT*, 4:303.

number of deeds, prolonging their sequence, and heighten their impact by postponing the movement of Pharaoh's unqualified belief. This statement anticipates what had frequently been called the "hardening of the heart" motif.[16]

Calvin likewise affirms that hardening is for the purpose of God displaying his glory to Moses and the rest of God's people:

> [T]hat he did not immediately obtain the victory, or might consider it strange that the miracles should be evaded with impunity by a mere mortal, as if he stood before God unchanged, in his boldness, God Himself foretells that He would be the moderator of all this contest, nay, that whatsoever should seem to oppose the deliverance of His people would arise from His own secret will.[17]

The Hebrew term for "heart" is also vital to understand in this discussion. This is key because, as previously explained, the heart is the driving factor of the will and the choices that people make. The word לֵב ("heart," also לֵבָב) is a fairly common and straightforward word, appearing 591 times in the Old Testament (or 596 times depending on which source is referenced). This word has seven basic ways in which it can be translated, the two most common being "heart" and "mind." This word, appearing forty-five times in the book of Exodus, is of particular importance within the context of Exodus 4:21 and its relation to חזק ("harden").

The word appears in Exodus 4:21 as אֶת-לִבּוֹ, a very common word in all Semitic languages.[18] While the word does not have a variety of meanings, one specific definition is of great importance to understand. The word is defined as simply the "heart . . . inner self, seat of feelings and impulses . . . mind, character, disposition, inclination, loyalty,

---

16   John I. Durham, *Exodus*, WBC 3 (Waco, TX: Word, 1933), 56.
17   John Calvin, "Commentaries on The Last Four Books of Moses," in *Calvin's Commentaries*, trans. Charles William Bingham (Grand Rapids: Baker Books, 2005), 2:101.
18   Heinz-Josef Fabry, "לֵב," *TDOT*, 7:400.

concern: thoughts or schemes of one's mind,"[19] or more importantly, "inclination, disposition."[20]

Contrary to what might be mistakenly concluded, the heart is not a term referring to a vital human organ, but rather to one's disposition or inclination. The heart is used to describe the entirety of a person; character, will, nature, and desires. Wilson states it plainly, "The heart is the seat of feelings and the affections, and takes those verbs which designate the affections themselves. But the Hebrews regard it more generally as likewise the seat of intellect; hence, (1) mind, purpose, intention; (2) understanding, knowledge, insight; (3) courage, spirit."[21]

Thus, in Exodus 4:21 the "heart" functions as the embodiment of Pharaoh's attitude, actions, and volition. The results of this hardening on Pharaoh's heart occur due to the active decree of God.

There are other instances in which the combination of "heart" and "harden" are used together but it is not in an active tense. This is the very first time it is used that way (along with other occurrences). God sets out at the beginning to let Moses know, before he even went to Egypt, what he was going to do to Pharaoh's heart. The result of one's heart being hardened is explained as being due to the fact that, "It finds expression in his inability, in the face of all the evidence, to recognize the meaning of the plagues and act accordingly. This clear purpose of Pharaoh's obduracy makes it . . . more likely correct in identifying the context as 'judgment in the prophetic tradition.'"[22] It is important to note about the use of "heart" with "harden" that this occurs through God's agency.[23] In this case, the use of heart then,

> encompasses all dimensions of human existence . . . the content of the motif of hardening the heart in the exodus pericope is the fact that Yahweh deprives the pharaoh of

---

19   "לֵב," *Holladay*, 171.
20   "לֵב," *HALOT*, 514.
21   Wilson, *Old Testament Word Studies*, 212.
22   Wilson, *Old Testament Word Studies*, 212.
23   "לֵב," *TLOT*, 403–6.

the intellectual and psychological capacities to understand
the significance of the plagues and to act accordingly. Its
goal is to demonstrate Yahweh's historical power in its total
compass: this power reaches even to his enemy's capacities
for thought and perception.[24]

People of all levels of power, from peasants to the mightiest people
on earth, are under the power of God. All the volitional facilities of
Pharaoh rest in the hands of God Almighty. The heart of Pharaoh is
what God holds in the power of his might. As Calvin explains,

> He declares that the king of Egypt would not be thus ob-
> stinate contrary to His will; as if He could not reduce him
> to order in a moment; but rather that He would harden
> his heart in order that He might violently overwhelm his
> madness. . . . Since undoubtedly God would make it ap-
> parent that He would be the President (as it were) of all
> the contests in which Moses was to engage, so as even to
> control the heart of his adversary, and to harden it into
> obstinacy.[25]

This understanding of the passage seems to do the greatest justice to
the grammar of the verb and its relationship to "heart." Recognizing
that the heart is the object of the verb, not the cause, leaves other
interpretations much weaker conclusions (such as Arminian foresight).

Some commentators assert that such a grammatical interpretation
is but one of many possible alternatives. Commentator Walter Kaiser
states, "By way of summary the Lord revealed the key features . . .
Pharaoh will harden his heart and not release the people."[26] However,
this does not do justice to the *Piel* of the verb in the context with the

---

24   "חָזַק," *TLOT*, 638–42.

25   Calvin, "Commentaries on The Last Four Books of Moses," in *Calvin's Commentaries*,
     2:102.

26   Kaiser, "Exodus," in *Expositor's Bible Commentary*, ed. Franks E. Gaebelein (Grand
     Rapids: Zondervan Publishing, 1992), 2:331.

"heart." Keil and Delitzsch more accurately account for the exegetical information: "The hardening of Pharaoh is ascribed to God, not only in the passage just quoted, but also in Ch 9:12; 10:20; 11:10; 14:8 and that not merely as foreknown or foretold by Jehovah, but as caused and effected by Him."[27] It is simple to see how vital such grammatical nuances are in providing a proper interpretation of the text. However, it is important to remember one significant aspect regarding the hardening of Pharaoh, as stated by Prokopenko:

> In this connection, it seems apparent that the hardening did not necessarily involve making the pharaoh's heart worse than it was initially. It only involved not letting him believe or have regard for the miracles and thus give up his foolish opposition. Therefore, it seems that the hardening was not so much ontological as it was epistemological—i.e., it had to do with a change in his understanding or cognition, not in his nature.[28]

SELF-HARDENING

The second subcategory of the causality of hardening is *self-hardening*. Self-hardening does not imply that hardening is first the idea of wicked people and that God responds by taking their advice and granting their request. But it accurately identifies the agent responsible for the hardening. When it comes to self-hardening, God ordains for the wicked to harden their own hearts.

Yet again, Pharaoh is presented in Scripture as a prime example of this. In addition to the times in Scripture when the manner of Pharaoh's hardening is unstated, there are also occurrences when Scripture reveals the manner; namely, that Pharaoh hardened his own heart. Exodus 8:15 says, "When Pharaoh saw that there was relief, he hardened his heart and did not listen to them, as the LORD had said."

---

27 Kiel and Delitzsch, *The Pentateuch*, vol. 1, *Keil and Delitzsch Commentary on the Old Testament* (Peabody, MA: Hendrickson, 2001), 294.
28 Alex Prokopenko, "The Relationship between the Divine Decree and the Human Will in Exodus 1–14" (ThM thesis, The Master's Seminary), 2007, 124.

However, Pharaoh is not the only one said to harden his own heart; others do as well. In fact, Proverbs 28:14 declares, "He who hardens his heart will fall into calamity."[29]

Another example of self-hardening is found in Nebuchadnezzar, whom Scripture describes as "stiffening his own neck" and hardening his own heart so as not to turn to the Lord (2 Chron. 36:13). Hardening not only occurs in the Old Testament, but New Testament audiences are warned about the dangers of self-hardening as well. Hebrews 3:7–8, speaking to a new covenant community, says, "TODAY IF YOU HEAR HIS VOICE, DO NOT HARDEN YOUR HEARTS, AS WHEN THEY PROVOKED ME" (see also Heb. 4:7).[30] The result of self-hardening is a calloused conscience which lends itself to a degradation of both the will and actions of men, going from bad to worse (Rom. 1:27, 32).

It is important to remember that evil is already present in the reprobate—God simply gives the person more allowance to act upon his evil nature. It could be said that the self-hardened reprobate falls by his own weight. God does not push him or trip him; God simply places him in slippery places.

Three things must be observed about this meaning of hardening. First, God claims hardening is a result of something he does. Second, God's holiness requires that he not force, cause, or create sin, so there is an intermediary means he uses (which is not always explicitly stated). Third, the actions which God hardens the reprobate to perform are already in their nature, and are simply directed or heightened by

---

29 Jamieson, et al. explain the phrase "hardens his heart" as, "makes himself insensible to sin, and so will not repent (Pr 14:16; 29:1)." R. Jamieson, A. R. Fausset, and D. Brown, *Commentary Critical and Explanatory on the Whole Bible* (1802; repr., Oak Harbor, WA: S. S. Scranton, 1997), 1:401. See also Keil and Delitzsch, *Commentary on the Old Testament*, 6:418.

30 Commentators seem to universally agree with Kistemaker when he states, "The phrase *harden not your hearts* is Semitic in origin, but no one has difficulty understanding its meaning." Simon J. Kistemaker and William Hendriksen, *Exposition of Hebrews*, NTC 15 (Grand Rapids: Baker Book House, 1953–2001), 91–92. See also John Peter Lange, et al., *A Commentary on the Holy Scriptures: Hebrews* (New York: Scribner, 1869), 76–77; William L. Lane, *Hebrews 1–8*, WBC 47A (Dallas: Word, 1998), 85–86; David L. Allen, *Hebrews*, NAC (Nashville: B&H, 2010), 257–58; J. Harold Greenlee, *An Exegetical Summary of Hebrews*, 2nd ed. (Dallas: SIL International, 2008), 97–99.

God's purposes. So, even self-hardening is still under God's control. As God draws the proverbial waters of grace out of the clay heart of Pharaoh, he becomes harder. As a result of this supernatural hardening, Pharaoh determines not to let God's people go. This results in the plagues, which in turn brings about a call to repentance by Moses, which causes Pharaoh to become harder and harder.

CHAPTER 18

THE CAUSALITY OF PERSONAL AND NONPERSONAL AGENCY

*T*he third category of causality, regarding personal agency, is likely the easiest to observe. Personal agency not only speaks of people committing personal acts of sin, but includes the influence which encourages or tempts them to sin; coming from outside themselves through other created persons. As with the others, this category can also be subdivided into two categories: evil people and evil spirits.

EVIL PEOPLE

The causality of personal agency by evil humanity is one to which every person can relate. It is certainly the most common and observable in the natural world. In Scripture, this appears in two broader instances—first when God uses the wicked to perform temporal evil, resulting in their eternal ruin. These temporal acts become the wood for the fire, so to speak, that kindle God's wrath in their judgment in hell. The second is God's use of the wicked to influence and further corrupt other reprobate individuals. This often stems into a broader influence often on a social level, where morality becomes a social anomaly, rather than a social norm.

First, God oftentimes will ordain evil people to perform evil acts to accomplish his holy purposes, resulting in their judgment but intended for God's glorious ends. Genesis 50:20 reads, "you meant evil against me, but God meant it for good." The term translated "evil" is the Hebrew word רָעָה.[1] In the clause, "God meant it for good," the pronoun "it" is a feminine singular suffix in Hebrew that agrees with the preceding singular noun, which is "evil." The agreement of the verb "meant" in both instances demonstrates that God intended the past actions of evil at the hands of Joseph's brothers for his ultimate good purpose. The parallel text further describing God's role in the matter is Psalm 105:17 which reads, "He [God] sent a man before them, Joseph, who was sold as a slave." While Joseph was sold into slavery at the hands of his brothers (Gen. 45:5), nevertheless God holds a decisive degree of responsibility for their actions.

Another example in the Old Testament is found in the life of Moses. Moses, being an Israelite, is born to a people in slavery to Egypt. During the time of his infancy, Pharaoh orders all the male Israelite children to be killed, which results in Moses ending up in Pharaoh's own household. The command of Pharaoh serves as the causal personal agency found in Exodus 1:22, which states, "Then Pharaoh commanded all his people, saying, 'Every son who is born you are to cast into the Nile, and every daughter you are to keep alive.'" This was purposed by God in order to place Moses into Pharaoh's household. However, it would also be a means by which God would judge the cruel actions of Pharaoh.

The New Testament also gives ample evidence of God's sovereignty over the causal acts of wicked people to establish his purposes, which in turn result in divine judgment. One of the greatest examples in the New Testament is Judas, who is described in John 17:12 as "the son of perdition." A son of perdition is someone born to be lost; implying that destruction is the ultimate purpose for decreeing and executing reprobation (in this case, specific to Judas). In other words, the ultimate purpose of Judas's life was destruction.[2] Judas's betrayal of Christ was always part of God's plan—it was ordained before the

---

1   G. Herbert Livingston, "רָעָה," *TWOT*, 2:856.
2   "ἀπώλεια," L&N, 1:231.

foundation of the world. This is why Jesus says in John 6:70, "Did I Myself not choose you, the twelve, and yet one of you is a devil?"

The crucifixion of Jesus at the hands of wicked people stands as a chief example of the means of personal agency. Acts 2:23 states, "this Man, delivered over by the predetermined plan and foreknowledge of God, you nailed to a cross by the hands of godless men and put Him to death." This is reiterated in Acts 4:27–28, which says, "For truly in this city there were gathered together against Your holy servant Jesus, whom You anointed, both Herod and Pontius Pilate, along with the Gentiles and the peoples of Israel, to do whatever Your hand and Your purpose predestined to occur." These texts illustrate the causality of human agency in God's ordained plan. However, they further illustrate how people can influence each other, specifically how the leaders of Israel swayed the opinions of the majority of Israel to desire Jesus's death over Barabbas (for example, "And all the people said, "His blood shall be on us and on our children!").

These sinful actions, particularly as wicked people are seen to be influencing one another to go from bad to worse, are a means God uses to seal people in their ordained reprobation. Romans 1:32 further confirms this, by explicitly stating how people have a common negative influence upon each other: "although they know the ordinance of God, that those who practice such things are worthy of death, they not only do the same, but also give hearty approval to those who practice them."

In regard to the agency of wicked people, God can use them to perform moral evil on the earth, resulting in their eternal judgment, and he may use them as a means to influence and further corrupt other reprobate individuals. By way of contrast, just as believers are ordained by God as a means to bring about sanctification in one another through encouragement, exhortation, prayer, and God's Word, so too are reprobates ordained by God to provoke one another to greater and greater evil.

EVIL SPIRITS

The previous subcategory of evil people is easy to accept and understand because of the basic common experience everyone has had at the hands of other evil people. However, another personal agency

God uses—one which is less observable—is the agency of evil spirits (including all demons and Satan himself). In Scripture, this appears in two broader instances: first when God uses evil spirits to perform evil which adds to their eternal judgment; and secondly, when God uses them to lead reprobate people into judgment.

To illustrate the first form of God's work, the work of Satan toward Job illustrates God's method in both moral evil and natural evil. The first two chapters of Job teach that God was testing Job through Satan, indicating that Satan was the means used by God. God did not tempt Job, nor did he sin against Job. Instead, God permitted Satan to do the tempting and sinning. Satan was a secondary cause which God employed.

While Satan is the most vile, deceitful, despicable, and deplorable creature in all of God's creation, he is still God's devil. He is on God's leash, so to speak, and does God's bidding. David S. Clark notes, "Satan could go no farther with Job than God permitted; but it is certain that he would go as far as God allowed."[3]

Job recognized that the evil tragedies that befell him, and even his wife's temptations, were also from the hand of God (Job 2:10). This example demonstrates that God can use evil spirits as well as evil people for their own judgment. Indeed, Satan will pay for his sins against Job.

First Samuel 16:14 describes how God uses evil spirits as a means to execute his decree of reprobation of people: "Now the Spirit of the Lord departed from Saul, and an evil spirit from the Lord terrorized him." It is important to note that this evil spirit which terrorized Saul came from the Lord. In fact, God does this on numerous occasions in order to accomplish his plan. For example, a similar statement is made in Judges 9:23, speaking of the mistreatment of Abimelech: "Then God sent an evil spirit between Abimelech and the men of Shechem; and the men of Shechem dealt treacherously with Abimelech."

Another example of this in the Old Testament is found in 1 Kings 22:19–23, which reads,

---

3   David S. Clark, *A Syllabus of Systematic Theology* (Philadelphia: P&R, 1887), 47.

Micaiah said, "Therefore, hear the word of the LORD. I saw the LORD sitting on His throne, and all the host of heaven standing by Him on His right and on His left. The LORD said, 'Who will entice Ahab to go up and fall at Ramoth-gilead?' And one said this while another said that. Then a spirit came forward and stood before the LORD and said, 'I will entice him.' The LORD said to him, 'How?' And he said, 'I will go out and be a deceiving spirit in the mouth of all his prophets.' Then he said, 'You are to entice him and also prevail. Go and do so.' Now therefore, behold, the LORD has put a deceiving spirit in the mouth of all these your prophets; and the LORD has proclaimed disaster against you.'"

By taking the reader into the very throne room of God, this text explains in remarkable detail how the secondary means of evil spirits functions within God's plan of causality. In this passage, the evil spirit was ordained by God and even claimed to be sent by God. The final description of Micaiah even explains that God is the one who is ultimately responsible for the actions of the evil spirit. As the reader gets a glimpse into the heavenly situation, the evil spirit is shown to be eagerly willing and anxious to perform this vile deed. In other words, God did not have to violate the volition of the demon in order for it to do his bidding. Instead, this account perfectly illustrates that compatibilism holds true even when it comes to evil spirits.

These passages demonstrate that God is not just in control of the restraints of people, but also of demons. God also uses demons to harden reprobate people, by deluding, lying to, blinding, deafening, and obscuring the reprobate. This tempting into sin is all according to God's decree of reprobation. Second Thessalonians 2:11 states this: "For this reason God will send upon them a deluding influence so that they will believe what is false." Once again, the delusion is in accordance with the desires of the evil spirit. God does not work evil into the hearts of the reprobate demons, but uses their already demonic tendencies to bring about his decree of reprobation.

This concept is likewise found in Romans 11:8, which states, "GOD GAVE THEM A SPIRIT OF STUPOR, EYES TO SEE NOT AND EARS TO HEAR NOT, DOWN TO THIS VERY DAY." God's execution of his decree to bring about the damnation of the reprobate and drag them further into the mire of their own baseless depravity is shown, at times, to occur not only through evil people but also through the agency of evil spirits. In either case, one must, as Arthur Pink notes, "remember that God is the Creator of the wicked, not of their wickedness; he is the Author of their being, but not the Infuser of their sin."[4]

THE CAUSALITY OF NONPERSONAL AGENCY

The fourth and final category of secondary causes is the category of nonpersonal agency, divided into two subcategories: general and the Word of God. The first subcategory encompasses the multifaceted ways in which Scripture depicts the execution of reprobation without ascribing to it a direct relationship between God's decree and the means used to carry it out. In other words, this subcategory represents a means without a revealed direct agent. The second subcategory, also nonpersonal, is perhaps the most surprising—the truth of the Word of God.

General Means of Nonpersonal Agency

This general means of nonpersonal agency can simply be defined as any time God speaks about the execution of the decree of reprobation without stating a direct agent involved. This is seen when God rejects Cain and has no regard for his offspring (Gen. 4:5),[5] curses Canaan (Gen. 9:25),[6] dismisses Ishmael (Gen. 21:12; Rom. 9:7; Gal. 4:30), hates Esau (Gen. 25:23–26; Mal. 1:2–3; Rom. 9:13; Heb. 12:17),[7] and allows the Gentiles to go their own way, without special revelation or special grace (Acts 14:16).

God chooses to reject many individuals, which is demonstrated in two ways. The first is God's active choice to not choose certain

---

4   Pink, *The Sovereignty of God*, 101.
5   Hermann J. Austel, "שָׁעָה," *TWOT*, 2:944.
6   Victor P. Hamilton, "אָרַר," *TWOT*, 1:75.
7   This particular element of reprobation, God's "hatred," was dealt with in part 2 .

individuals (1 Sam. 15:23, 26; 16:1; 2 Kings 17:20; 23:27; Ps. 53:5; 89:38; Jer. 6:30; 14:19; 31:37; Hos. 4:6; 9:17). As Psalm 78:67 explicitly states, "He also rejected the tent of Joseph, and did not choose the tribe of Ephraim." The second is when God is said to create calamity. Isaiah 45:7 reads, "The One forming light and creating darkness, causing well-being and creating calamity; I am the LORD who does all these." Further, Amos 3:6 reads, "If a calamity occurs in a city has not the LORD done it?" God creates the wicked for the day of evil (Prov. 16:4), inclines the hearts of all people to do his will (Prov. 16:9; 21:1), and orders their steps (Prov. 20:24; Jer. 10:23). God's sovereignty over the hearts, plans, and steps of people extends to the evil as well as the good; these texts make no distinction between the two.

This category would also include all the times Scripture says God blinds (Matt. 13:13; Deut. 29:4), deafens (Isa. 6:9), and makes people incapable of understanding (Luke 1:20), among others (Jude 4). From these passages, the secondary causes employed in executing reprobation can be described in diverse ways. Sometimes God does not directly reveal the process of reprobation except by general language.

The Truth

The truth of God's Word stands as perhaps the most controversial means God uses in executing his degree of reprobation. Pascal exposes why this may be the case, stating, "The prophecies quoted in the Gospels were put there . . . to discourage you from believing."[8] He also declared, "God therefore gives the reprobate enough obscurity to manifest their evil hearts, which refuse to believe, but enough light to condemn them in their unbelief."[9] Pascal's claims are based on the fact that obscurity comes to all those who reject the gospel (Mark 4:10–12). They have enough revelation that God exists but they do

---

8   Blaise Pascal, *Pensées*, trans. A. J. Krailsheimer (New York: Penguin, 1976), 736. He elsewhere states, "there is enough light for those who desire to see, and enough darkness for those of a contrary disposition" (140).

9   Gregory A. Boyd, "The Divine Wisdom of Obscurity: Pascal on the Positive Value of Scriptural Difficulties," *JETS* 28, no. 2 (1985): 200.

not possess the heart to believe in the special revelation of Scripture and believe unto salvation (Rom. 1:21).

It is through the furnace of the truth that the clay pots of reprobate hearts are hardened. Although the truth is a fragrance of life for the elect, it is a fragrance of death for the reprobate (2 Cor. 2:16). God explicitly stated throughout the ministry of Isaiah that the truth would be a means of people's blinding, deafening, and hardening. "Go, and tell this people: 'Keep on listening, but do not perceive; Keep on looking, but do not understand'" (Isa. 6:9).

Likewise, the New Testament parables were not to make things easier to understand, but for the hardening of the reprobate. In fact, Jesus's earthly ministry exhibits a shift in which he began speaking plainly in the beginning, but then changed to speaking in parables as the time of the crucifixion neared. To the elect it was granted to know the way to eternal life, but to the reprobate it was hidden in parables. Luke 8:10 says, "To you it has been granted to know the mysteries of the kingdom of God, but to the rest it is in parables, so that SEEING THEY MAY NOT SEE, AND HEARING THEY MAY NOT UNDERSTAND" (see also Matt. 13:13; Mark 4:12; Luke 8:10; 9:39; John 12:40). The reason why wicked people do not believe the saving news of the gospel is so that they might serve as instruments of God's wrath according to his decree of reprobation (Acts 28:26).

First Peter 2:8 provides a helpful statement explaining the relationship between the truth and the reprobate's preordination to condemnation: "'A STONE OF STUMBLING AND A ROCK OF OFFENSE'; for they stumble because they are disobedient to the word, and to this doom they were also appointed." A more literal Greek translation reads, "and the stone of stumbling and a rock of offense for they stumble because they disobey the word as they were appointed to do."[10] Commentators have very divided opinions as to the nature of the "appointment." The question commentators try to resolve is, "What is the antecedent of ὅ in the phrase εἰς ὅ καὶ ἐτέθησαν?" Some take it to be ἀπειθοῦντες ("disobedience"), while others take it to be

---

10 Translation mine.

προσκόπτουσιν ("stumbling"). Those who appeal to προσκόπτουσιν ("stumbling") do so on the basis of various proofs. Some propose that disobedience is not preordained, yet stumbling is. Their proposal results in making "stumbling" a mere consequence or penalty for disobedience.[11] According to such an interpretation, God ordains punishment (stumbling) but not the crime (disobedience).[12] Beyond the fact that it would be illogical for God to ordain the effect (the punishment of stumbling) without ordaining the cause (the crime of disobedience), it is difficult to see what difference such a view makes. After all, stumbling is a form of disobedience. These proposals do not alleviate the involvement of God in anyway.

One simply cannot ignore the reality that this text presents God as ordaining people to disobedience. With the pronoun being nearer to the relative clause, it makes little sense to jump over the clause and connect the pronoun with stumbling to the exclusion of disobedience. Further, stumbling is a form of disobedience. The fact that God ordains people to punishment is indicated by the word ἐτέθησαν because God has ordained people unto a rejection of his Word resulting in their damnation.[13] The stone of stumbling is none other than Jesus Christ and the truth that he is Savior. They were appointed to stumble upon him, to reject salvation by faith in him. Condemnation was their appointment and Christ was the means of sealing their fate.

The fact that the truth provokes in the non-elect a response of rejection, by divine appointment, unmistakably indicates that it is a means of reprobation. Theologians have recognized this for a long time.

---

11 Archibald Thomas Robertson, "The First Epistle General of Peter," in *Word Pictures in the New Testament* (Nashville: Broadman, 1933), 6:98.

12 R. Jamieson, A. R. Fausset, and D. Brown, *A Commentary, Critical, Experimental and Practical on the Old and New Testaments* (1871; repr., Grand Rapids: Eerdmans, 1967), 6:605; Albert Barnes, "1 Peter," *Notes on the New Testament* (Grand Rapids: Baker, 1971), 10:141.

13 Francis W. Beare, *The Epistle of St. Peter* (Oxford: Basil Blaskwell, 1958), 100; "τίθημι," *BDAG*, 824; William E. Vine, *Expository Dictionary of New Testament Words* (Old Tappan, NJ: Fleming H. Revell, 1966), 68; Karen H. Jobes, *1 Peter*, BECNT (Grand Rapids: Baker Books, 2005), 155–56.

Charles Spurgeon illustrates, "The same sun which melts wax hardens clay; and the same Gospel which melts some persons to repentance hardens others in their sins."[14] Michael Horton states, "The same word that is faith-producing and life-generating for some is for others an occasion to become more resolute in unbelief."[15] Ultimately, Peter explains that the Gospel is inherently scandalous for an additional reason often overlooked: the same message has drastically different outcomes on the elect and the non-elect, based on God's foreordained intention.

The means of the execution of reprobation are very important for a proper understanding of God's eternal decree. The charge that reprobation makes God morally responsible for sin simply ignores the vital nuances provided by Calvinists. An adequate understanding of reprobation relies upon a knowledge of first and secondary causes, the difference between God as the ultimate causal agent and the secondary agents, and the level of involvement (direct or indirect), intention, and responsibility of each. Scripture teaches that God can, and does, govern the human heart, both for good and for ill. It is simply up to the responsible exegete to determine how this occurs.

A proper understanding of means directly influences how one understands God's responsibility for the actions of people and his involvement in bringing about the sins that he has ordained. While this naturally provokes a negative response from many, it is important to return to Paul's words on this very matter: "Oh, the depth of the riches both of the wisdom and knowledge of God! How unsearchable are His judgments and unfathomable His ways! For who has known the mind of the lord, or who became his counselor? Or who has first given to him that it might be paid back to him again? For from Him and through Him and to Him are all things. To Him be the glory forever. Amen" (Rom. 11:33–36).

Descartes in his *Principles of Philosophy* rightly states, "His power is so immense that we would sin in thinking ourselves capable of ever

---

14   Charles Spurgeon, "The Lesson of the Almond Tree," in *C. H. Spurgeon's Sermons Metropolitan Tabernacle Pulpit* (1900; repr., Pasadena, TX: Pilgrim Publications, 1977), 46:271.
15   Horton, *For Calvinism*, 69.

doing anything which He had not ordained beforehand."[16] In many ways, human reason is disappointed because it is insufficient to attain a knowledge of God's decretive work. It is rendered powerless by the stone of stumbling and the rock of offense—God's sovereignty. The human mind is bewildered by the fact that God can execute his decree of reprobation through the aforementioned means (abandonment, hardening, personal agency, and nonpersonal agency) so as to leave the creature the only blamable agent of sin.

When human reason tries to subject God to its own arbitrary standards, it comes up short. God is sovereign even over the mind and will of people. The so-called problem of evil is a human problem, not a divine problem. The creator does not need creaturely excuses to alleviate him of creaturely standards of justice and equity; the potter need not give an account to the clay. Calvin said, "Monstrous indeed is the madness of men, who desire thus to subject the immeasurable to the puny measure of their own reason!"[17] Undoubtedly, this doctrine does not find acceptance with everyone. Nevertheless, it is the obligation of every man, and especially every Christian, to submit to God's Word. In the end, it can simply be said that, "The unrepentant will of the reprobate, in contrast [to the elect], does not love and seek God's truth but rather seeks to avoid it. Their minds are therefore deflected from honestly considering it by their prejudiced will and turned toward that aspect of revelation that their will prefers."[18]

Quite simply, the doctrine of reprobation (in both its decree and execution) humbles humanity and exalts God.[19] This doctrine stresses the great gulf between God's majesty and human frailty.

---

16 René Descartes, "Principles of Philosophy (1644)," trans. John Veitch, in *The Method, Meditations and Philosophy of Descartes* (New York: M. Walter Dunne, 1901), 316.

17 John Calvin, *The Institutes of the Christian Religion*, ed. John T. McNeill, trans. Ford Lewis Battles, LCC 2 (Louisville: Westminster John Knox, 1940), 952.

18 Such prejudice is often cloaked under the guise of "obscurities" or "mysteries" of Scripture, according to Boyd, "The Divine Wisdom of Obscurity," 201.

19 Joel R. Beeke and Mark Jones, *A Puritan Theology: Doctrine for Life* (Grand Rapids: Reformation Heritage, 2012), 121.

CONCLUSION

In the previous chapters, we set out to test the claim that God's eternal decree of reprobation does not require him to implant sin into people to guarantee his intended outcome. This assertion is predicated on the basis that, by using secondary causes, God is able to preserve both his own holiness and the volition of his creatures in theodicy.

First, we explored Romans 9, seeing that Romans 9:6–23 affirms the historical definition of reprobation. Romans 9:6–23 demonstrated that reprobation is God's unconditional decree, according to his will, to pass by individuals who are non-elect (preterition). Then, he holds each one accountable to his justice to display the glory of his justice (predamnation).

After looking at reprobation in Romans 9, we highlighted how it expresses preterition (God's choice to pass by and reject the non-elect). Esau was shown to be not merely a representative of a national entity, but rejected on the basis of God's unconditional choice before his birth or deeds were ever considered.

Other New Testament passages indicate, more specifically, that God's electing choice was made even "before the foundation of the world" (Eph. 1:4).

Further, Romans 9 explains that the motivating cause in God's distinction between the elect and non-elect is his will, not man's ancestry or works. This passage displayed that God's choice in both election and reprobation was not conditioned on prescient foreknowledge regarding any actions performed by Jacob or Esau. This matter establishes God's unconditional choice—not influenced by the order of their birth, their faithfulness or rejection, nor any of their deeds. Ultimately, God's choice in reprobation is not a matter of indifference. Esau was rejected by God and, in time, brought to punishment. Ultimately, this passage provides invaluable insight into God's ability (and prerogative) to harden whomever he wishes and to have mercy on whomever he wishes.

God's freedom in the choice of the non-elect as vessels of destruction is solely grounded in God's intention to demonstrate his attributes of justice and wrath. The example of Pharaoh and the vessels prepared for destruction depict God's decree an active decree, even if he is not the active agent in its execution.

We then explored the fact that a clear definition of reprobation is important for any meaningful discussion concerning its legitimacy. The doctrine of reprobation has been plagued with a negative reputation primarily because of prevailing misunderstandings and misrepresentations. Many misunderstandings either fail to understand the doctrine correctly or have purposefully suppressed the clarifications offered by those who affirm it. Often, this suppression portrays the doctrine as devious or repulsive, contrary to how Scripture describes it.

Those who object to reprobation often confuse compatibilism with immediate agency, thereby making God the author of sin. Oftentimes, they generally do not allow for the distinction between primary and secondary causes, which leads to even more confusion.

God's choice to not elect certain individuals for salvation is not merely non-election. The decree of reprobation historically contains two elements and its execution also contains two elements. Within the decree there is preterition and predamnation (also known as precondemnation), and within the execution there is causality and condemnation.

We defined preterition as God's choice to pass by and to reject (or exclude) every non-elect individual from the eternal benefits of salvation (see Rom. 9:6–23). Therefore, every time election is mentioned, preterition is assumed for those not elected.

Next, predamnation was defined as God's affirmative decision to hold the non-elect to the standards of his justice. Predamnation is predicated on biblical passages in which sinners are said to be appointed to "doom" (1 Peter 2:8) and "long beforehand marked out for this condemnation" (Jude 4). Paul's statements found in Romans 9:22 exegetically confirm this when he says sinners are "vessels of wrath prepared for destruction."

God's execution of the decree of reprobation in time is divisible into two elements: causality and condemnation. Condemnation was defined as the judicial act of God, in which he chooses to cause the penalty for the sin of unbelievers to visit them (cf. Heb. 9:27; 2 Tim. 4:1; 1 Peter 4:5; Ps. 9:7; Mark 9:44). In this sphere, causality was defined as the means God employs to bring about all that he has ordained. Most importantly, causality related to sin is always done via secondary agency (cf. Acts 2:23; 4:27).

The means of the execution of reprobation are vastly important for a proper understanding of God's eternal decree. Ignoring these elements not only leads to the unfounded charge that reprobation makes God morally responsible for sin, but also renders the exegete incapable of rightly interpreting texts which substantiate the doctrine in the first place (i.e., Acts 2:22–23).

We then looked at the serious question raised concerning the relationship between reprobation, sin, and damnation. It is important that this relationship can be adequately defined, so that God is not the chargeable cause of the sin he has ordained his creatures to commit. A working knowledge of primary and secondary causes is crucial—understanding the difference between God as the ultimate causal agent and secondary agents, and the level of involvement (direct or indirect), intention, and responsibility of each.

The final portion of our survey demonstrated that to categorize secondary causes is the only acceptable way to exegetically explain a vast number of passages of Scripture which, at first glance without an understanding of causation, might seem to incriminate God in sin. A proper knowledge of causality and secondary means competently maintains God's sovereignty and man's accountability related to theodicy.

FURTHER STUDY

One additional area of study would be lapsarian positions in their historical context. Many today are ill-informed regarding the historical origins and definitions of the various lapsarian positions in relation to the decree. An exploration of these would greatly benefit this study.

A second area of further study can be centered on further testing, expanding, and perhaps adding categories of causality to those presented in this book. This could include further dissection of the "general" means of causality, examining Scripture examples and other distinct categories.

Another area of study could be the relationship between the secondary causes God employs. Is there a discernable order to the execution of the decree? Does one generally, or always, precede or follow another? Further exploration into the order of the execution would be beneficial.

GREATER IMPLICATIONS

Believers are responsible for searching out and teaching the whole council of God's Word, which includes a meaningful examination of the doctrine of reprobation. It is unwise and unsafe to speculate about matters with eternal ramifications, like this one. With the clarity of its teaching in Scripture, the doctrine of reprobation is best taught in contrast to election. Just as the Reformed have regarded the means of God's decree in the execution of election as "the golden chain of salvation,"[1] reprobation could be considered the "black chain of damnation."

Like the golden chain, the black chain extends to eternity past, as God decreed the ends of the non-elect to display the glory of his justice. The middle links of the chain—the execution of the decree—are the various means God employs in secondary causality: abandonment, hardening, personal agency, and nonpersonal agency. After death, the reprobate meets their eternal destiny of condemnation, in the wrath

---

1   R. C. Sproul, *What Is Reformed Theology? Understanding the Basics* (Grand Rapids: Baker Books, 1997), 9.

The Black Chain of Damnation

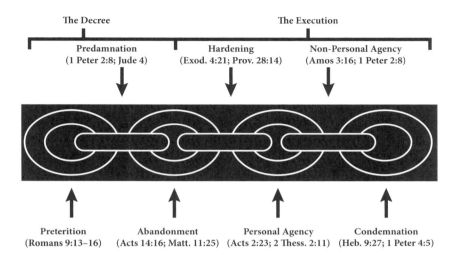

of God's justice, as God holds each person accountable to the sin they have committed on earth.

It is important for the Christian to keep election and reprobation held in balance. It explains how God's holiness is not impugned despite the existence of sin. No one can know who is among the reprobate as long as they are alive in the world. From a human vantage point, as long as anyone remains on the earth, they may simply be among the unconverted elect. It is only in death that confirmation can be made as to those who are reprobate.

This doctrine of reprobation calls all people to keep their life and faith under surveillance so as not to assume that someone is elect. Paul warns the elect to constantly examine themselves so they do not enter into damnation assuming they were elect: "Examine yourselves, whether ye be in the faith; prove your own selves. Know ye not your own selves, how that Jesus Christ is in you, except ye be reprobates?" (2 Cor. 13:5, KJV).

Most important, those who affirm the biblical basis of reprobation are committed to compatibilism and causality. In Reformed theology, heavy emphasis is placed on the fact that God not only determines the ends but also the means. While the means of reprobation are varied, the means of salvation are fixed. Salvation comes exclusively by grace through faith in Christ. God uses the means of the preaching of the Gospel to execute his decree of election (Rom. 10:17). Because believers, from their human vantage point, cannot differentiate the elect from the reprobate, they are compelled to preach the gospel to everyone without exception! Neither election nor reprobation will truly stifle the evangelistic spirit of faithful believers, as they seek to fulfill their gospel mandate.

WHAT MAKES THESE DOCTRINES NECESSARY?

So why are reprobation, causality, and predestination so important? Because without it, people would lack the ability to properly explain key verses in Scripture.

For example, in the third major section of Ezekiel (chapters 12–14), the prophet began what can only be described as a polemic against the false hopes of the exiles in Babylon. At this point in time, Ezekiel had already been given two visions of God (cf. Ezek. 1:1, 8:3). In the second, God's glory had departed from the temple in Jerusalem, leaving the people defenseless against the encroaching Babylonian forces. Having sinned against God repeatedly, the nation of Judah had forfeited not only their fellowship with Him, but also his protective hand. Jerusalem would not survive another attack. The captured exiles would remain there much longer than they thought. There would be no quick return to Jerusalem.

Unfortunately, Ezekiel wasn't the only one preaching to the exiles in Babylon. Self-appointed prophets—*false* prophets—were peddling their false teaching as vigorously as Ezekiel was spreading his true teaching. Just as Hananiah opposed Jeremiah over in Jerusalem, lying to the people and telling them that Babylon's dominance would last a mere two years (cf. Jer. 28:11), bad actors in Babylon were undermining Ezekiel's ministry. They were promising the exiles that there would soon be "peace" in Jerusalem (cf. Ezek. 13:10). Naturally, many Israelites in Babylon welcomed the hopeful words of these false prophets, preferring pleasant lies to unpleasant truths. Failing to recognize that the exile had come as the result of God's punishment for their sin, these exiles had itching ears. They wanted to be told all would be well. Thus, Ezekiel's ministry, like that of pastors today, not only involved teaching the truth, but exposing lies—and *liars* (cf. Titus 1:9).

TRUE AND FALSE PROPHETS

To that end, God explained an important truth to Ezekiel concerning true prophets:

> Son of man, these men have set up their idols in their hearts and have put right before their faces the stumbling block of their iniquity. Should I be consulted by them at all? Therefore, speak to them and tell them, "Thus says the Lord GOD, 'Any man of the house of Israel who sets up his idols in his heart, puts right before his face the stumbling block of his iniquity, and then comes to the prophet, I the LORD will be brought to give him an answer in the matter in view of the multitude of his idols, in order to lay hold of the hearts of the house of Israel who are estranged from Me through all their idols.'" Therefore say to the house of Israel, "Thus says the Lord GOD, 'Repent and turn away from your idols and turn your faces away from all your abominations.'" (Ezek. 14:3–6)

In other words, if an Israelite asked a prophet for spiritual insight concerning Jerusalem's future, all the while secretly harboring sin in his heart, he would not cooperate by providing a positive word for them—that is, if he were a true prophet. After all, no true prophet would ever coddle an idolater's feigned devotion to God. Instead, he would rebuke the inquirer for his hypocrisy, and call him to repentance. People like Ezekiel would expose the inquirer's sin and *not* give them the lie they wanted.

On the other hand, God explained how false prophets would respond to these inquirers:

But if the prophet is persuaded so that he speaks a word, it is I, the LORD, who have persuaded that prophet; and I will stretch out My hand against him and eliminate him from among My people Israel. And they will bear the punishment for their wrongdoing; as the wrongdoing of the inquirer is, so the wrongdoing of the prophet will be, in order that the house of Israel may no longer stray from Me and no longer defile themselves with all their offenses. So they will be My people, and I shall be their God," declares the Lord GOD. (Ezek. 14:9–11)

Here, God explained that if an Israelite approached a prophet in feigned devotion, and the prophet was convinced or persuaded to give him the soothing lie that he wanted, both the false prophet and the one who inquired of him would suffer judgment. Nevertheless, don't miss this vital detail in the passage: "If the prophet is persuaded so that he speaks a word, *it is I, the LORD, who have persuaded that prophet*" (Ezek. 14:9, emphasis mine).

In other words, God said he would *persuade* false prophets to lie to those who sought prophetic counsel while treasuring idols in their hearts. God would give the false prophet a ministry opportunity that would bring about both the prophet's and the hearer's own condemnation. *He* would be the one enticing false prophets to give the people what they wanted. To those who wished to fake holiness, pretending to genuinely seek God's interests while actually seeking their own, God would give them the deception they desired. And then they would suffer the consequences for their high-handed rebellion.

This undoubtedly raises a whole host of questions from the careful student of Scripture. Does God really persuade a false prophet to lie? Doesn't the Bible say that God cannot tempt anyone? Is this really what the passage teaches? How involved is God when it comes to deception?

THE PREDICAMENT

Scripture insists that God is in control of all human affairs, including, in this instance, the giving of false prophecy. Sadly, however, rather than grappling with the statement made in Ezekiel 14:9, many treat it the way they treat other seemingly difficult passages (such as Rom. 9:22, 1 Peter 2:8, or Ps. 5:5)—they doubt, distort, downplay, or outright deny what it plainly says. Frankly, such responses to Scripture are shameful and unbecoming of any serious Christian. We must instead give God's Word the serious consideration it deserves. In this case, the apparent predicament is obvious: How can God be said to "persuade" a false prophet to lie to someone, when passages like James 1:13 say that God cannot tempt anyone, and passages like Numbers 23:19 say that God cannot lie? In light of God's holiness, to what extent is his involvement with sin?

Some might try to resolve this by saying that the Hebrew word for "persuade" doesn't actually mean what we understand it to mean in English. However, underlying the verb "persuade" is the Hebrew word *pathah,* which means "to allure or deceive." In passages like Job 31:9 and Judges 16:5, it is rendered "entice," in reference to a woman seducing a man. In Deuteronomy 11:16, it is rendered "deceive," in reference to the Israelites being led astray to worship false gods. And in Proverbs 25:15, it is rendered "persuade," used to refer to convincing a national ruler to make a particular decision. Lexically, then, the semantic range and use of the word *enforces*, rather than refutes, a straightforward understanding of the word. "Persuade" means "persuade."

Others might argue that God merely "allows" the false prophet to lie. They would say, "God *permitted* these enticements to test the people's loyalty." Nevertheless, to take this position is to portray God as a spectator to the events that occur in his world, contrary to Ephesians 1:11. Rather than actively governing, this idea suggests that God passively consents—at least when it comes to sin. But again, the text does not allow for this. On the contrary, the text expressly establishes just the opposite: when Ezekiel 14:9 uses the phrase "I, the LORD," it is like using a reflexive pronoun to say "I, myself" in order to make an emphatic point. God doesn't tell Ezekiel, "It is I who have persuaded," nor does God say, "It is the Lord who has persuaded," but instead he says, "It is I, the Lord, who have persuaded." This double reference to himself shows that God is actively presiding over the lie that false prophets speak. God has no problem with taking credit for this situation; and if he doesn't, neither should we hesitate to give it to him.

How then do we reconcile all of this? We need to understand categories of causation.

CATEGORIES OF CAUSATION

So what exactly are categories of causation? Whether you realize it or not, you likely already have a subconscious understanding of various categories of causation. If I were to ask you, "When a carpenter is building something, who, or what, pounds the nails into the lumber that he uses?" what would your response be? Some might answer, "The hammer." Others might answer, "The carpenter." Which would be correct? The answer is obvious: *both are correct*, simply in different ways. The carpenter is the cause of the nail being pounded in, in the sense that he determined that it would happen, using his skill and strength to make it so. On the other hand, the hammer could also be labeled a cause of the nail being pounded in, in that the hammer's weight directly applied the force to drive the nail in. In this example, then, the former cause governs the action, while the latter cause interacts directly with it. Once you recognize this kind of distinction, you recognize categories of causation.

When it comes to theological categories of causation, academic theologians note the following categories:

1. *Ultimate cause.* The ultimate cause of every action that occurs in the world is God, who providentially governs all actions for his purposes (cf. Eph. 1:11; Rom. 11:36).
2. *Proximate cause.* The proximate cause of an action is the agent, human or otherwise, who influences, directs, or enables an action.
3. *Efficient cause.* The efficient cause of an action is the agent, human or otherwise, who directly carries out the action.

Of course, this kind of thinking is nothing new. Not only do most people inherently understand it (even if they don't realize it), but even naturalistic philosophers going all the way back to Aristotle have been describing it for centuries. And lest you dismiss this as nothing more than extrabiblical philosophical mumbo-jumbo, it should be noted that this framework of understanding causality is vital to understand many passages of Scripture.

Scripture indicates that sin does not occur outside of the ordained plan of God, who is the ultimate cause and responsibility of all things. But since Scripture says that both concurrent realities are true—that God ordains sin while remaining holy and unchangeable for sin—the need for theological categories of causation is established.

GIVING THE PEOPLE WHAT THEY WANT

Returning to Ezekiel 14:9 with an understanding of the various categories of causation gives us the proper framework we need to rightly interpret it. In this case, when an unbelieving exile inquired of a prophet, the prophet—serving as the *efficient cause*—would commit the sinful act of prophesying falsely. God, serving as the *ultimate cause*, would take full credit for enticing the false prophet to do it. But there is a third component, the *proximate cause*—that is unstated in this passage, though implied, based on a similar scenario found in 1 Kings 22:19–23.

In 1 Kings 22:19–23, we see God using false prophets to lie to King Ahab in order to bring about his demise. Ahab was another case of someone who preferred a smooth lie to a rough truth, and wanted to try to leverage God for his own personal gain. After patiently enduring years of Ahab's evil, God was determined to bring about his downfall. Thus, the passage states that when Ahab sought prophetic counsel to determine whether or not he should go into battle, his four hundred false prophets assured him of victory. What Ahab didn't know at the time, however, was that God had enticed these false prophets to lie to him.

And how did God do it? By enlisting the help of demons: "And the LORD said, 'Who will entice Ahab to go up and fall at Ramoth-gilead?' And one spirit said this, while another said that. Then a spirit came forward and stood before the Lord, and said, 'I will entice him.' And the LORD said to him, 'How?' And he said, 'I will go out and be a deceiving spirit in the mouths of all his prophets.' Then He said, 'You shall entice him, and you will also prevail. Go and do so'" (vv. 20–22). Using the same Hebrew word for "entice" as is found in Ezekiel 14:9, as God determined in this passage to provide a lie to one of his false devotees in order to bring about his demise, he didn't do it *directly*; instead, he commissioned an eager and willing demon to carry out the task. And so it is that demons serve as the *proximate cause* in the lies that false prophets tell (cf. 1 Tim. 4:1, 2 Thess. 2:10–11). God is the ultimate cause of the lie, a fallen angel is the proximate cause of the lie, and a false prophet is the efficient cause of the lie.

FINAL REMARKS

How should the church as a whole and especially the Christian minister respond to these truths? Preach the gospel with fervency. Since we understand God uses causes to execute his decree, we should be invigorated to preach the gospel even more. Preach the gospel without compromise, compassionately, openly, passionately, consistently.

People may wonder "Why evangelize if reprobation is true?" Hopefully, this book helps explain why. Because the God of the decree is also the God of its execution, and he ordained the foolishness of preaching as its solitary means. Not through visions, miracles, dreams, direct conversations with God; no, simple preaching.

Another thing to consider, those reformed people who understood the doctrine of reprobation and cherished the doctrine of predestination without compromise were the greatest evangelists the world has ever known. Both John Knox and John Bunyan wrote great books on reprobation, and yet turned the world on its head through their preaching.

Don Green, a great preacher, once told me, "Hard preaching produces soft people, soft preaching produces hard people." This has stuck with me through the years, and has time and time again proven to be true. Preachers who shy away from hard issues, such as predestination, who never make strong stances, who don't have deep seeded convictions drawn in concrete, are never used by the Lord to advance his kingdom.

Spurgeon once said:

> Oh! dear brethren, what a mercy it is that there are such things as the grand old truths which men nickname Calvinism, but which are the very marrow of the Gospel. I find when the heart aches and the spirit is heavy, there is nothing like reading the eighth and ninth chapters of the Romans, and when things go amiss with me, and everything is perversely disappointing my hopes, it is very delightful to throw oneself back upon the soft couch of God's eternal purpose, to pillow one's head upon the certainty that what He said He will perform, and that what He has commanded shall stand fast. Here are royal dainties! Costly cheer for fainting pilgrims! If you want the wings of eagles, study these doctrines, and they shall bear you up aloft; if you would creep along the ground, and be full of doubts, fears, and miseries, and distractions, live on baser food; but if you would walk in the strength of a giant, and fight with the valor of a David, live on these loaves of heaven's best bread, and your youth shall be renewed. Yet, these things are strong meat, and are not for babes, but for strong men.[2]

This sound advice should be the refrain of anyone who reads this book. Preach the gospel, tenderly, persuasively, with conviction, and let God determine the results.

Although the doctrine of reprobation has been hampered by an unnecessary stigma, it is clear there is a necessity for clarity and affirmation regarding such a critical doctrine. Ultimately, to deny God's eternal plan for sin simply does not do justice to the text of Scripture. Therefore, the essential harmony of texts proves that reprobation is a vital cog in the believer's understanding of predestination. It must be handled with precision and care, but it must not be neglected.

---

2   Charles Spurgeon, "Strong Meat," in The Metropolitan Tabernacle Pulpit (1863; repr., Pasadena, TX: Pilgrim Publications 1998), 9:232.

In response to such a vital doctrine, believers should praise God for his remarkable—though mysterious—wisdom. It is a marvel that any of us should be saved, so the doctrines of election and reprobation are two sides of the same coin. They both uniquely reveal the majesty of God's sovereign decree.

Because of the steadfastness of God's character and purpose, we know he works all these decrees and means for the splendor of his glory and the good of his people. All aspects of his divine decree—even complex doctrines like reprobation—reflect the grandeur of our great God. Studying out difficult truths such as reprobation draws Christians to pursue and know the Holy One yet more. And that alone is the worthiest pursuit any of us will endeavor toward—even through eternity.

APPENDIX

THE CAUSALITY OF DIVINE ABANDONMENT

Removing Restraints/Giving People Over

Definition: This is the process whereby God removes moral restraints and gives people over to their sinful desires.

Romans 1:24	Therefore God gave them over in the lusts of their hearts to impurity, so that their bodies would be dishonored among them.
Genesis 20:6	Then God said to him in the dream, "Yes, I know that in the integrity of your heart you have done this, and I also kept you from sinning against Me; therefore I did not let you touch her."
1 Samuel 25:34	"Nevertheless, as the Lord God of Israel lives, who has restrained me from harming you, unless you had come quickly to meet me, surely there would not have been left to Nabal until the morning light as much as one male."
1 Samuel 25:39	When David heard that Nabal was dead, he said, "Blessed be the Lord, who has pleaded the cause of my reproach from the hand of Nabal and has kept back His servant from evil. The Lord has also returned the evildoing of Nabal on his own head." Then David sent a proposal to Abigail, to take her as his wife.

Acts 14:16	In the generations gone by He permitted all the nations to go their own way.

THE CAUSALITY OF DIVINE ABANDONMENT

Withholding Grace

Definition: This occurs when God chooses not to grant grace to the reprobate.

Deuteronomy 29:4	Yet to this day the LORD has not given you a heart to know, nor eyes to see, nor ears to hear.
Joshua 11:20	For it was of the LORD to harden their hearts, to meet Israel in battle in order that he might utterly destroy them, that they might receive no mercy, but that he might destroy them, just as the LORD had commanded Moses.
Matthew 11:25	At that time Jesus said, "I praise You, Father, Lord of heaven and earth, that You have hidden these things from the wise and intelligent and have revealed them to infants."
Matthew 15:14	Let them alone; they are blind guides of the blind. And if a blind man guides a blind man, both will fall into a pit.
John 10:6	This figure of speech Jesus spoke to them, but they did not understand what those things were which He had been saying to them.

THE CAUSALITY OF HARDENING

Unstated Hardening

Definition: This is the process whereby God hardens the hearts of people, in many instances without stating anything other than he Himself will cause it to happen.

Exodus 10:27	But the LORD hardened Pharaoh's heart, and he was not willing to let them go.
Exodus 14:17	As for Me, behold, I will harden the hearts of the Egyptians so that they will go in after them; and I will be honored through Pharaoh and all his army, through his chariots and his horsemen.
Deuteronomy 2:30	But Sihon king of Heshbon was not willing for us to pass through his land; for the LORD your God hardened his spirit and made his heart obstinate, in order to deliver him into your hand, as he is today.
Psalm 105:25	He turned their heart to hate His people, to deal craftily with His servants.
Romans 9:18	So then He has mercy on whom He desires, and He hardens whom He desires.

THE CAUSALITY OF HARDENING

Self-hardening

Definition: Self-hardening is when the object of hardening was the one responsible for its coming to pass. This does not imply that hardening is first the idea of wicked people and God responds by taking their advice and granting their request. When it comes to self-hardening God ordains the wicked to be the agent to harden their own hearts.

Exodus 8:15	But when Pharaoh saw that there was relief, he hardened his heart and did not listen to them, as the LORD had said.
Exodus 9:34	But when Pharaoh saw that the rain and the hail and the thunder had ceased, he sinned again and hardened his heart, he and his servants.
Proverbs 28:14	How blessed is the man who fears always, but he who hardens his heart will fall into calamity.

| 2 Chron. 36:13 | He also rebelled against King Nebuchadnezzar who had made him swear allegiance by God. But he stiffened his neck and hardened his heart against turning to the LORD God of Israel. |
| Hebrews 3:8 | Do not harden your hearts as when they provoked me, as in the day of trial in the wilderness. |

THE CAUSALITY OF PERSONAL AGENCY

Evil People

Definition: In Scripture this appears in two broader instances, first when God uses the wicked to perform temporal evil which results in their eternal ruin. The second, is God's use of the wicked to influence and further corrupt other reprobate individuals. This often stems into a sociological influence on the culture.

Genesis 50:20	As for you, you meant evil against me, but God meant it for good in order to bring about this present result, to preserve many people alive.
Job 1:15	The Sabeans attacked and took them. They also slew the servants with the edge of the sword, and I alone have escaped to tell you.
John 6:70–71	Jesus answered them, "Did I Myself not choose you, the twelve, and yet one of you is a devil?" Now He meant Judas the son of Simon Iscariot, for he, one of the twelve, was going to betray Him.
Acts 4:27–28	For truly in this city there were gathered together against Your holy servant Jesus, whom You anointed, both Herod and Pontius Pilate, along with the Gentiles and the peoples of Israel, to do whatever Your hand and Your purpose predestined to occur.
2 Timothy 3:13	But evil men and impostors will proceed from bad to worse, deceiving and being deceived.

THE CAUSALITY OF PERSONAL AGENCY

Evil Spirits

Definition: In Scripture this appears in two broader instances, like the previous subcategory, first when God uses evil spirits to perform evil which adds to their eternal judgment. Then secondly, God uses them to lead reprobate people into judgment.

Judges 9:23	Then God sent an evil spirit between Abimelech and the men of Shechem; and the men of Shechem dealt treacherously with Abimelech.
1 Samuel 16:14	Now the Spirit of the LORD departed from Saul, and an evil spirit from the LORD terrorized him.
Job 1:7–12	The LORD said to Satan, "From where do you come?" Then Satan answered the LORD and said, "From roaming about on the earth and walking around on it." The LORD said to Satan, "Have you considered My servant Job? For there is no one like him on the earth, a blameless and upright man, fearing God and turning away from evil." Then Satan answered the LORD, "Does Job fear God for nothing? Have You not made a hedge about him and his house and all that he has, on every side? You have blessed the work of his hands, and his possessions have increased in the land. But put forth Your hand now and touch all that he has; he will surely curse You to Your face." Then the LORD said to Satan, "Behold, all that he has is in your power, only do not put forth your hand on him." So Satan departed from the presence of the LORD.
2 Thessalonians 2:11	For this reason God will send upon them a deluding influence so that they will believe what is false.
John 13:27	After the morsel, Satan then entered into him. Therefore Jesus said to him, "What you do, do quickly."

THE CAUSALITY OF NONPERSONAL AGENCY

General Means

Definition: When Scripture states a general means or it can simply be defined as any time God speaks about the execution of the decree of reprobation upon the non-elect without stating a direct agent involved.

Genesis 4:5;	But for Cain and for his offering He had no regard.
Genesis 9:25	. . . So he said, "Cursed be Canaan; A servant of servants He shall be to his brothers."
Deuteronomy 29:4	Yet to this day the LORD has not given you a heart to know, nor eyes to see, nor ears to hear.
Matthew 13:13	Therefore I speak to them in parables; because while seeing they do not see, and while hearing they do not hear, nor do they understand.
Hebrews 12:17	For you know that even afterwards, when he desired to inherit the blessing, he was rejected, for he found no place for repentance, though he sought for it with tears.
Jude 4	For certain persons have crept in unnoticed, those who were long beforehand marked out for this condemnation, ungodly persons who turn the grace of our God into licentiousness and deny our only Master and Lord, Jesus Christ.

THE CAUSALITY OF NONPERSONAL AGENCY

The Truth

Definition: When Scripture speaks of the truth being used as a dual means—for the elect salvation, and for the reprobate it elicits an obstinate or rebellious response toward God.

Isaiah 6:9	Go, and tell this people: "Keep on listening, but do not perceive; Keep on looking, but do not understand."
Mark 4:10–12	As soon as He was alone, His followers, along with the twelve, began asking Him about the parables. And He was saying to them, "To you has been given the mystery of the kingdom of God, but those who are outside get everything in parables, so that while seeing, they may see and not perceive, and while hearing, they may hear and not understand, otherwise they might return and be forgiven."
Luke 8:10	And He said, "To you it has been granted to know the mysteries of the kingdom of God, but to the rest it is in parables, so that seeing they may not see, and hearing they may not understand."
2 Corinthians 2:15–16	For we are a fragrance of Christ to God among those who are being saved and among those who are perishing; to the one an aroma from death to death, to the other an aroma from life to life. And who is adequate for these things?
1 Peter 2:7–8	This precious value, then, is for you who believe; but for those who disbelieve, "the stone which the builders rejected, this became the very corner stone," and, "a stone of stumbling and a rock of offense"; for they stumble because they are disobedient to the word, and to this doom they were also appointed.

SCRIPTURE INDEX

INDEX OF TERMS

INDEX OF PERSONS